The poetry of Carol Ann Duffy

MANCHESTER
1824

Manchester University Press

# THE POETRY OF
# CAROL ANN DUFFY

*'Choosing tough words'*

EDITED BY ANGELICA MICHELIS
AND ANTONY ROWLAND

Manchester University Press
Manchester and New York

distributed exclusively in the USA by Palgrave

*Published by* Manchester University Press
Oxford Road, Manchester MI3 9NR, UK
*and* Room 400, 175 Fifth Avenue, New York, NY 10010, USA
www.manchesteruniversitypress.co.uk

*Distributed exclusively in the USA by* Palgrave,
175 Fifth Avenue, New York, NY 10010, USA

*Distributed exclusively in Canada by* UBC Press
University of British Columbia, 2029 West Mall, Vancouver, BC,
Canada V6T 1Z2

*British Library Cataloguing-in-Publication Data*
A catalogue record for this book is available from the British Library

*Library of Congress Cataloging-in-Publication Data applied for*

ISBN 0 7190 6300 0 *hardback*
0 7190 6301 9 *paperback*

First published 2003

11 10 09 08 07 06    10 9 8 7 6 5 4 3 2

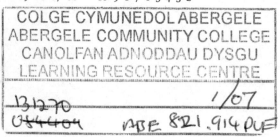
Typeset in Charter
by Northern Phototypesetting Co. Ltd, Bolton, Lancs.
Printed in Great Britain
by Bell & Bain Ltd, Glasgow

# Contents

Notes on the contributors                                   *page* vii
Acknowledgements                                                    ix
List of abbreviations                                               x

Introduction                                                        I
ANGELICA MICHELIS AND ANTONY ROWLAND

1 Duffy, Eliot and impersonality
NEIL ROBERTS                                                       33

2 Female metamorphoses: Carol Ann Duffy's Ovid
JEFFREY WAINWRIGHT                                                 47

3 Love and masculinity in the poetry of Carol Ann Duffy
ANTONY ROWLAND                                                     56

4 'Me not know what these people mean': gender and national
identity in Carol Ann Duffy's poetry
ANGELICA MICHELIS                                                  77

5 'Small Female Skull': patriarchy and philosophy in the poetry
of Carol Ann Duffy
AVRIL HORNER                                                       99

6 'The chant of magic words repeatedly': gender as linguistic
act in the poetry of Carol Ann Duffy
JANE THOMAS                                                       121

7 'What like is it?': Duffy's *différance*
STAN SMITH                                                        143

8 'What it is like in words': translation, reflection and refraction
  in the poetry of Carol Ann Duffy
  MICHAEL WOODS                                                          169

9 'Skeleton, Moon, Poet': Carol Ann Duffy's postmodern poetry
  for children
  EVA MÜLLER-ZETTELMANN                                                  186

  Select bibliography                                                    202
  Index of works by Carol Ann Duffy                                      205
  General index                                                         209

# Notes on the contributors

**Avril Horner** is a Professor of English at Kingston University, Kingston upon Thames. She is the co-author, with Sue Zlosnik, of *Landscapes of Desire: Metaphors in Modern Women's Fiction* (Harvester Wheatsheaf, 1990) and *Daphne du Maurier: Writing, Identity and the Gothic Imagination* (Macmillan, 1998). She has also published articles and reviews on modern and contemporary poetry. She has just published an edited book, *European Gothic: A Spirited Exchange 1760–1960* (Manchester University Press, 2002) and is currently working on *Gothic and the Comic Turn* (with Sue Zlosnik), due to be published by Palgrave.

**Angelica Michelis** is a Senior Lecturer at Manchester Metropolitan University. Her major publications include: *Frauen, Dichter und andere Rätsel: Eine Untersuchung feministischer Aspekte in zeitgenössischer Lyrik englischsprachiger Dichterinnen* (Röhrig Universitätsverlag: Saarbrücken, 1997) (trans.: Women, Poets and Other Mysteries: Feminist Theory and Twentieth Century British and American Women's Poetry); 'Stop Making Sense: Heiner Müller, Germany and Intellectuals', in *Angelaki*; and 'The Pleasure of Saying It: Erotic Speech in Contemporary's Women Poetry', in Detlev Gohrband et al. (ed.) *Saying and Seeing* (Peter lang, 1998). She is also Contributing Editor to *The Year's Work in Critical and Cultural Theory* (History of Art and Visual Culture).

**Eva Müller-Zettelmann** is a Professor at the University of Vienna. She has written a book on the theory of poetry and metapoetry and has co-edited a collection of Delariviere Manley's and Eliza Haywood's plays (Pickering and Chatto, 2001). Her articles focus on genre theory, narratology, twentieth-century British poetry, and children's literature. She is currently preparing two international collections on the theory of poetry to be published by Rodopi.

**Neil Roberts** is a Professor of English Literature at Sheffield University, where he has taught since 1970. His main publications are *George Eliot: Her Beliefs and Her Art* (Elek, 1975), *Ted Hughes: A Critical Study* (with Terry Gifford, Faber, 1981), *The Lover, the Dreamer and the World: The Poetry of Peter Redgrove* (Sheffield Academic Press, 1994), *Meredith and the Novel* (Macmillan, 1997), *Narrative and Voice in Postwar Poetry* (Longman, 1999) and *A Companion to Twentieth-century Poetry* (ed., Blackwell, 2001). He is currently working on a study of D.H. Lawrence, travel and cultural difference.

**Antony Rowland** is a Senior Lecturer in English at the University of Salford. His main publications are *Tony Harrison and the Holocaust* (Liverpool University Press, 2001), *Signs of Masculinity* (ed. with Emma Liggins and Eriks Uskalis) (Rodopi, 1998), a special edition of *Critical Survey* (ed. with Stan Smith) entitled *Linguistic Turns: Performing Postmodern Poetries* (2002) and a special edition of *New Formations* (ed. with Scott McCracken) entitled *Hating Tradition Properly* (1999). He won a Gregory Award for his own poetry in 2000, and is published in *New Poetries III* (Carcanet, 2002).

**Stan Smith** is Research Professor in Literary Studies at Nottingham Trent University. He is currently completing studies on Auden, Eliot (and company) and the Descent of Modernism, and on contemporary poetry, and preparing a critical edition of Auden's *The Orators*. Recent books include: *W.H. Auden* (British Council Writers and their Works series, 1997), and (co-edited with Jennifer Birkett) *Special Issue on Modernism, Miscelanea: A Journal of British and American Studies* (Zaragoza, 2000). He is also editing the Cambridge Companion to W.H. Auden.

**Jane Thomas** is a Lecturer in English at the University of Hull. Her main publications include: *Thomas Hardy, Femininity and Dissent: Reassessing the 'Minor' Novels* (Macmillan, 2000) and new editions of Hardy's *The Well-beloved, Life's Little Ironies* and *A Changed Man*. She edited the *Bloomsbury Guide to Victorian Literature* (1994). She has published articles on a number of contemporary women writers including Michèle Roberts and Caryl Churchill, and her first essay on Carol Ann Duffy, 'The Intolerable Wrestle with Words' appeared in the magazine *Bête Noire* in 1988. She is currently working on a critical survey of Victorian women novelists.

**Jeffrey Wainwright** is Professor of English at Manchester Metropolitan University. His most recent book of poems is *Out of Air* (Carcanet, 1999); previously *The Red-Headed Pupil* (Carcanet, 1994) and *Selected Poems* (Carcanet, 1985). His most recent translation work is Bernard-Marie Kolte's' *In the Solitude of Cotton Fields* (Methuen).

**Michael Woods** is Head of English and Director of Sixth Form at the Chase, Malvern, Worcestershire. He is also a senior A-level examiner for English Literature, and the editor, and publisher, of *Tandem*, an international poetry magazine. His publications include an edition of York Notes Advanced entitled *Carol Ann Duffy: Selected Poems* (Longman, 2000).

# Acknowledgements

We would like to thank all the staff at Manchester University Press and our colleagues and friends at Salford University and Manchester Metropolitan University who helped with this book. Thanks also to the fabulous Manchester gastronomy which kept us going and in good humour. We are grateful to Emily and her cheerful nature and to Emma for her risottos. Special thanks to Nick Austin for the figs and food for thought. Thanks also to Carol Ann Duffy for permission to quote from her various books, as well as Macmillan and Faber and Faber Ltd. Every effort has been made to obtain permission to reproduce copyright material in this book. If any proper acknowledgement has not been made, copyright-holders are invited to contact the publisher.

# Abbreviations

BATB   *Beauty and the Beast*

F   *Fleshweathercock*

FG   *Feminine Gospels*

FLS   *Fifth Last Song*

MT   *Mean Time*

P   *The Pamphlet*

SFN   *Standing Female Nude*

SM   *Selling Manhattan*

TOC   *The Other Country*

TWW   *The World's Wife*

# Introduction

ANGELICA MICHELIS AND
ANTONY ROWLAND

CAROL ANN DUFFY is a naughty poet. Which other contemporary, non-performative poet (apart, perhaps, from Wendy Cope) would rhyme hillock with pillock, as she does in 'Mrs Icarus'? Such cheekiness might derive from the influences of performance poetry and the Liverpool Poets. It might also be due to the confidence of a poet who is now a mainstay of several GCSE and A-level syllabuses. The popularity of Duffy can be vouchsafed, as sales of her volumes in Waterstones attests.[1] Her demotic, and conversational, poetics are key aspects of her populism: Sean O'Brien notes that the accessibility of poems such as 'Warming Her Pearls' means that it 'is as open to the reader of Catherine Cookson as to the educated student of the Brontës'.[2] What might be more open for debate are issues of value, and canonicity. On the subject of cheeky rhyme, Sheenagh Pugh argues that 'Mrs Icarus' 'isn't even vaguely funny'; hillock / pillock 'is so extraneous to the poem that it is obvious it's been introduced purely for the rhyme'.[3] She contends that Eric Morecambe used a hillock far more credibly and inventively in his ode to a cow. Other detractors from Duffy's poetry may argue that the jokiness of the verse offers teachers an opportunity to interest pupils in a genre that might otherwise appear opaque, or that she writes children's poetry for adults.

Simon Brittan, perhaps Duffy's most scathing critic to date, attacks this 'democratic' tendency as resulting in 'simplistic language and overstated imagery', journalistic poetics, the writing of prose 'as though it were poetry', 'empty rhetorical effect[s]', and a preponderance of slang, flippancy and 'slapdash writing'.[4] Brittan's complaint about 'simplistic language' centres on 'The Captain of the 1964 *Top of the Form* Team', but it mistakes the dramatic monologue for lyric poetry with its insistence that the 'clever' satchel must belong to a younger Duffy.[5] Naturalistic monologues require verbal tics in order to initiate characterisation: if the phrases 'Hang on', 'No snags', '*Bzz*', and 'The keeny' from the poem in question are to be dismissed as unsophisticated, then Robert Browning's famous deployment of 'Gr-r-r – you swine!', 'Hy, zy, Hine' and 'Oh, those melons' in 'Soliloquy of the Spanish Cloister' must equally be written off as fatuous (*MT*, pp. 7–8).[6] '[O]verstated imagery' is explained by Brittan in relation to 'Miles Away', in which 'imagine you' is accused of repeating the previous declaration 'I make you up'.[7] This may be the case, but then 'I make you up' in the sense of 'I invent you' (or even 'put makeup on you') might also evoke a different image to 'imagine you'; in the context of the love poem as a whole, the lover is *necessarily* fictionalised precisely because the object of affection remains 'miles away'. 'Poet for Our Times' is singled out as an example of 'slapdash writing', and yet this is due to an expectation of regular iambic pentameter which the poem never promises.[8] Overall, despite the contention that 'Duffy is perfect for those no longer accustomed nor inclined to close reading', Brittan's close readings tend to evade genre and disingenuously berate her work for not being more like that of Philip Larkin or W.H. Auden.

Despite our defence of Duffy's poetry above, Brittan's forcible critique has wider repercussions for her position in, and effect on, contemporary poetry as a whole. Is Duffy's anecdotal style symptomatic of a wider trend for – to paraphrase Thom Gunn on the work of Larkin – aiming so low?[9] Mark Reid certainly believes so in his review of *Mean Time*: 'Duffy typifies the seductive dangers of so much contemporary poetry . . . The deleterious effect of public reading can be heard in the imperative to go for the punchline, the easy pay off, to write poems that can be gulped in one go, sugared with a wisecrack and quickly forgotten.'[10] The latter comments may be true of the pithier poems from *The World's Wife*, such as 'Mrs Icarus' and 'Mrs Darwin', but they also fail to appreciate performance, or performa*tive*, poetry as separate genres.[11] They also risk ignoring the complex engagement with myth that is complemented by humour in poems such as '*from* Mrs Tiresias'. As Jeffrey Wainwright records in this book, that '*from*' arose in response to a pedant who contended at a reading that there was, of course, much more to the story of Tiresias than Duffy's poem could cover. Wainwright retorts that there is indeed more to the myth, and much of it is *in 'from* Mrs Tiresias'. Another way of defending *The World's Wife* would be to argue that it forms an adjunct to the more mainstream poetics in *Mean Time*; however, this reading has been negated by the recent publication of *Feminine Gospels*.[12] Reid's criticisms are aimed at *Mean Time*, not *The World's Wife*, in particular, but it is to hard to see how poems such as 'Small Female Skull' (the origins of which are discussed by Avril Horner in this book), 'The Grammar of Light', 'Adultery' and 'Prayer' can be charged with an 'easy pay off'. Nevertheless, critics and poets as different as Geoffrey Hill and Robert Sheppard have commented, along with Reid, on a trend in recent poetry towards a popular style in a roughly post-Movement tradition, epitomised for some by the 1993 anthology *The New Poetry*.[13] During a reading in Manchester in 1996, Hill bemoaned the reduction of poetry to a branch of stand-up comedy. Sheppard comments, in a review of *The Penguin Book of Poetry from Britain and Ireland since 1945*, that the anthology's plurality of voices 'does not mean plurality of [innovative] techniques'.[14]

Does Duffy's poetry contain a plethora of voices; and, if so, does it result in a plurality of innovative writing? The influence of Philip Larkin – sometimes simplistically reviled as merely a conservative mentor for contemporary writers – on Duffy's work is prevalent, as several of the contributors in this volume note. One example not commented upon is the echo of the famous end of 'This Be the Verse' ('don't have any kids yourself') in the closure of 'Ash Wednesday 1984' ('For Christ's sake, do not send your kids to Mass').[15] To the editors of this volume, an argument which espoused Larkin's and Duffy's betrayal of the modernist tradition of verse would be a simplistic one. As both Neil Roberts and Antony Rowland discuss in this volume, T. S. Eliot has been a clear influence on Duffy's writing, both in her dramatic monologues, and in her re-workings of myth. Adrian Henri – Duffy's partner and poetic mentor for many years – also lists Eliot as *the* influence on his work, contending that Eliot made taxis and other urban paraphernalia relevant to poetry.[16] Just as Sheppard argues in relation to Larkin, however, perhaps a reclamation of Duffy as a postmodernist is 'not very convincing'. John Osborne proposes in *New Larkins for Old: Critical Essays* that Larkin assimilates modernism, and demonstrates his thesis with an ingenious reading of 'The Whitsun Weddings' as a 'post the modern' (but not postmodernist) re-writing of

*The Waste Land*.[17] Duffy, like Larkin, might equally be termed 'post-modern' ideologically, but not aesthetically. On the other hand, perhaps, as Sheppard contends in relation to Larkin, 'those who hear modernism . . . catch the echo of an echo, it seems to me, and amplify that into an inheritance'.

As Antony Rowland argues in this volume, the influence of first-wave surrealism on Duffy, and the depiction of alienated lovers amongst modern cityscapes, does suggest strong modernist influences on her work. Equally, to contest that Duffy is simply a late-modernist or postmodernist poet would clearly be misleading. Two anthologies that Duffy has produced for Penguin in the 1990s demonstrate that her poetic tastes are catholic, but certainly not avant-garde: in *I Wouldn't Thank You for a Valentine*, Carol Rumens, Wendy Cope, Fleur Adcock, U.A. Fanthorpe and Liz Lochhead rub shoulders with Maya Angelou, Carole Satyamerti, Jackie Kay and Jean Binta Breeze; in *Stopping For Death*, Simon Armitage, W.H. Auden, Gavin Ewart and Seamus Heaney complement John Agard, Paul Durcan, Roger McGough and Henry Normal.[18] The form of her work, for the most part – apart from the banal fact that much of it is *vers libre* – could be said to be unmistakably conservative if compared to that of the British Poetry Revival, or recent 'linguistically innovative' writing. Her deployment of dramatic monologues, sonnets and (sometimes) an adherence to the ghost of metrical form are symptomatic of techniques clearly not as sensitive to the legacy of the modernist project as are those the work of other practitioners, such as J.H. Prynne, Lee Harwood, Roy Fisher, Tom Raworth, bob cobbing and Maggie O'Sullivan. Nevertheless, as Linda Kinnahan has argued, the subject matter of much of the poetry may be termed 'postmodern', from the identity politics of the early poetry to the feminist ideologues of the later work, and the blurring of the division between high art and popular culture.[19] Tension thus ensues between the conservative form and politicised content. These tensions can be analysed as productive in their very contradictoriness. Voices and influences clash and contest the poetic ground in Duffy's *oeuvre*: Sylvia Plath vies with Robert Browning; Eliot grates with the Liverpool Poets; Larkin takes fright in the face of André Breton.[20]

Modern subject matter does not automatically grant canonicity, of course. Yet the vast variety of accomplished verse in Duffy's canon to date suggests that this is a poet whose fame is not just a repercussion of a supposedly democratic voice. *Standing Female Nude* and *Selling*

*Manhattan* mark Duffy as a modern exponent of the dramatic monologue, particularly in one of her most successful poems, 'Psychopath',
discussed here by Neil Roberts.[21] *The Other Country* both registers an
interest in post-structuralist linguistics and challenges simplistic
notions of origins, as Angelica Michelis contends in her chapter.[22]
*Mean Time* proves to be Duffy's most thought-provoking volume to
date, mixing elegies for a decaying relationship with *fin de siècle* ennui.
*The World's Wife* and *Feminine Gospels* are high points of satire in
Duffy's *oeuvre*; in *The World's Wife*, no man from Freud to Shakespeare
can escape the scathing tongue of the Wife-of-Bath-like characters. In
this introduction, we provide a chronological survey of the juvenilia
and main collections in order to point out the changing, and continuing, concerns of Duffy's poetry, many of which are covered by the various contributors to this volume. Feminism, myth-making,
postmodernism, post-structuralism, masculinity, children's verse, love
poetry, identity politics, poetic form, philosophy, translation and fairy
tales are among these diverse interests.

## Juvenilia: *Fleshweathercock,*
## *Beauty and the Beast* and *Fifth Last Song*

Duffy's first collection, *Fleshweathercock*, is a notable absence in the list
of collections above. Published when she was a teenager by Outposts,
it is mainly of interest to the critic as a marker of her early influences
(Sylvia Plath, John Donne, Shakespeare and the Liverpool Poets
appear to be among them).[23] Duffy is embarrassed of the volume now:
in an interview in 1999, she refers to it as an 'excruciating pamphlet',
'a mixture of Keats and Sylvia Plath and Dylan Thomas and the Bible.
A sort of teenage mix.'[24] She refuses to give the interviewer the name
of the volume, and laments: 'I was at a signing last year and someone
came up to me with it. I actually screamed. There was this anorak in
front of me who'd paid £30 for it. I offered him £50, I wanted to
destroy it. But he refused.' To be fair to Duffy, most of the verse in
*Fleshweathercock* is undoubtedly unaccomplished compared to her
later work, as in this example from the title poem: 'Oh bird / I shall follow you / Into the burning colours of flawless time'. '[F]lawless time'
registers the main problem in these adolescent poetics: abstractions
attempt to articulate too much emotional slither. '[S]till of time', 'life's
cube', 'whole universe', 'nothingness', 'deep love' appear in the last

poem alone ('Epitaph') (*F*, p. 20). Dylan Thomas's penchant for allit-eration predominates in poems such as 'From' ('fingered fleshy trees'), along with his nonce collocations ('kiss feathers') (*F*, pp. 12, 5). Plath seems to have influenced the anti-men poems 'Century', 'Army' and 'Pollution' (the latter contains the unfortunate line 'Oh has man changed you mud') (*F*, pp. 16, 15, 8–9), as well as metaphors in 'As I Quench' such as the flirting trees which are 'wombing into valleys' (*F*, p. 7). (The former poems function as palinodes in relation to 'Turn to Me Now', in which men are beyond criticism when in the form of pas-sionate lovers: 'Eternity promises that the warmth of man / will always bear like a rock / the day to gentleness' *F*, pp. 9–10.) Donne predomi-nates in the love lyrics, as in the command to 'Cast off your thighs' (what?), 'irrigate the desert of my body's europe' and 'throw your soul's pillow beneath my flesh' in 'Turn to Me Now' (*F*, pp. 9–10). Perhaps the critic should endorse Duffy's dismissal of the volume, and regard it as juvenilia not worthy of critical study. Some poems do offer portents of the work ahead, however. One such example is the 'lemon kisses' buried in the midst of a mixed metaphor ('heaped applecarts of . . .') in 'Turn to Me Now'. Whilst the image also evokes Dylan Thomas, it also looks forward to the collocations in later collections. The influence of the first surrealist manifesto is also anticipated in 'As I Quench' ('There's my world / in this teacup / take a long white sip / from the sea of my eye') (*F*, p. 7). Concerns with the 'curious room' of childhood, as Angela Carter has termed it, arise in 'From' ('I have lost that music / which I once held in the wooden lock / of my nine year self'); this registers an interest in youth and origins which will resur-face in *The Other Country*.

Whereas *Fleshweathercock* is self-consciously poetic, sometimes excruciatingly so, Duffy's next volume, *Beauty and the Beast*, displays the beginnings of a more demotic style influenced by the Liverpool Poets. This was made easier since the pamphlet was co-authored with Adrian Henri, whom Duffy was living with at the time. Published around 1977, it is a thinly veiled celebration of their relationship. Instead of the soul pillows of *Fleshweathercock*, a more playful style subverts poetic moments: 'I am the beholder / you are in my eye' . . . 'I am the lover / you are in my mouth'.[25] In an early indication of Duffy's interest in the dramatic monologue, the Beast forms the initial 'beholder'. Humour and identity politics merge, as they will in *The World's Wife*, with the assertion that 'beauticians refuse to do business with me / they put up large signs / NO BEASTS / NO UNORTHODOX FACES'.[26] *Beauty and the Beast* has attracted little critical interest, perhaps because of the difficulty in obtaining copies of the limited-edition pamphlet, or owing to the difficulty in separating the Duffy voice from Henri's.[27] As a collaborative project, however, this is precisely its strength: the stichomythian structure allows a re-interpretation of traditional folk tales in terms of contemporaneous gender politics. As such, it fits into a tradition of feminist re-writings of nursery rhymes and tales, which includes figures such as Sylvia Plath and Angela Carter. Its cross-referencing of various tales within the overall 'beast' narrative also places it as an early example of a trend to fuse popular tales with 'high' art forms such as poetry. References to roses and a rose garden are prised directly from the original tale: Beauty's father is caught picking a rose for her from the Beast's garden; the Beast threatens to kill him for stealing, so the father promises to give him the first thing he sees on his arrival home. Naturally, this happens to be the affectionate Beauty. An erotic (and Electran) triangle then takes over the narrative: when she is finally allowed home to tend her deteriorating father, she simultaneously senses that the Beast is dying of a broken heart in the selfsame garden.

In Duffy's and Henri's re-write, there is no magical transformation of the Beast into a handsome prince at the end in order to illustrate the potential falsity of a beauty/beast split. At the beginning of the poem the Beast's speech appears to be indicated with roman type, and Beauty's with italics, but the binary nature of this speaker/muse dialogue is then subverted. Soon '*he* [our italics] turns on the light', indicating that she is sometimes represented with roman type. This confusion is explained by the suggestion that she is a tad beastly too, since he stands 'back angry / shouting angry / shouting / you're supposed to turn into a princess'. Beauty is uncovered as an impossible ideal irrelevant to the 1970s lovers, and as potentially monstrous. It remains unclear at one point whether Beauty or the Beast is squirming into high heels (which were attacked by some feminists as confining women physically and preventing their movement at the time); the Beast does appear later to be '*wiping the damp / frog taste*' of Beauty from his lips.[28] This latter example forms one of the instances in which tales are mixed: Beauty becomes the frog prince; in another moment the Beast metamorphoses into Rumpelstiltskin, and later the fox in Little Red Riding Hood. The deliberate resistance of the poem to fall into a masculinity (Beast) and femininity (Beauty) paradigm is registered most markedly in a stanza reminiscent of concrete poetry in which 'BEAUTY / BEASTY' becomes, underneath, 'BEA TY / BEA TY' and finally 'US'. Ultimately, these confusions add up to little more than a suggestion that gender is confusing (a radical enough statement in 1977, perhaps). The poem also has the appearance of an occasional piece or a loose journal – a date is included at one point – as if each poet wrote a verse and then challenged the other to respond with another when they could (an early version of the 'fridge' poem?).[29]

In contrast with this collaborative effort, Adrian Henri was only to supply artwork (along with illustrations by Maurice Cockerill, Henry Graham, Don McKinley, Jeff Nuttall and Sam Walsh) for Duffy's next volume, *Fifth Last Song*.[30] As Deryn Rees-Jones reveals, Duffy 'considers it juvenilia' (even though she was 27 when it was published in 1982), but 'some of the better poems act as an interesting backdrop to her later work'.[31] What is most apparent in this pamphlet is the new influence of surrealism: this finds its apex in 'Dream', based on the 1938 Penrose painting *Winged Domino: Portrait of a Valentine* (*FLS*, p. 15). In the 'better poems', the surrealist love poetry of *Standing Female Nude* is anticipated, as in 'Waves' ('Tides of my body / follow yours like / waves the moon'), and sections of 'Wet' ('Legs spread leaking pearls') (*FLS*, pp. 21, 24). Elsewhere, the surrealist axiom of juxtaposing opposites to create new, exciting relationships founders in Dalíesque silliness; for example, in 'Never Forever', when 'An ape with an erection plays golf / on a barren moon' (*F*, p. 20). Rees-Jones contends that the subtitle of the collection ('*twenty-one love poems*') refers to Adrienne Rich's 'sequence of lesbian love poems "Twenty-One Love Poems", which appeared in her *A Dream of A Common Language: Poems 1974–1977*.[32] At first glance, Rich's groundbreaking sequence appears to have little in common with Duffy's juvenilia. Whereas Rich's work forms one of the most sustained poetic engagements with a lesbian relationship in the 1970s, Duffy's poems still appear to represent mainly heterosexual couplings, since 'Hidden from light, buried watermelons cool / even now was you fuck me' (*FLS*, p. 24). Rich's sequence also investigates the significance of one lesbian affair in terms of personal history and wider historical changes, whereas Duffy's pamphlet charts the ups and downs of several different relationships. Both writers do engage with dialectics of love in the city, however, and this is possibly where Duffy's interest in the pastoral originates; this is then sustained across the future collections, particularly in *The Other Country*. At the beginning of 'Twenty-one Love Poems', the narrator despairs that 'Wherever in this city, screens flicker / with pornography, with science-fiction vampires . . . we also have to walk', but 'We need to grasp our lives inseparable / from these rancid dreams'.[33] Hence the lovers are in the city, but also antithetical to it. To compound this dichotomy, Rich introduces the pastoral image of the lovers as 'sycamores blazing through the sulphuric air, / dappled with scars, still exuberantly budding'; later in the sequence, the partner is 'like the half-curled frond / of the fiddlehead fern in forests' (pp. 77, 83). Similarly, the heterosexual relationships flourish in pastoral contexts in *Fifth Last Song*: in 'Dream', the 'city is grey waiting' for the arrival of a woman with 'butterflies drift[ing] out of her'; in 'Starwords', tongues are linked with grass, spring and stars (*FLS*, p. 15). Equally, Duffy's recourse to the pastoral may arise from her reading of surrealist poetry and paintings in general rather than Rich in particular. It may also be extracted from the vision of Philip Larkin, who contrasts the terrors of motorway cafés and tacky shops with the disappearing England of church spires, crumpets and regular tea. Any association between love and the country that Duffy takes forward from *Fifth Last Song* must also be contrasted with the work of other modern poets: for example, a binary between the amorous and the city would be anathema to a poet such as Frank O'Hara, with his celebrations of gay relationships which flourish in the urban landscape.

### 'Well. Really': Engendering the dramatic monologue in *Standing Female Nude* and *Selling Manhattan*

Whereas *Fifth Last Song* appears to contain few 'speaker' poems ('Doll', a precursor of 'The Dummy', forms an exception), one of the most striking features of Duffy's first two 'mature' collections is the way in which they negotiate the tradition of the dramatic monologue, re-interpreting the genre to make way for 'other' voices. Others come in all shapes and sizes in *Standing Female Nude* and *Selling Manhattan*. Empathy is expected for the following characters in the first collection: an abused child ('Lizzie, Six'), a potential murderer on the dole ('Education for Leisure'), a woman who secretly has an abortion ('Free Will'), a French woman who despairs of her bloated, xenophobic husband ('Alliance'), an Irish woman who loathes her 'devil' of a husband,

and a wife who regrets having children ('A Clear Note'), a man fearing the call of bailiffs ('Debt'), a woman watching her first pornographic film ('A Provincial Party, 1956'), a poor violinist ('Back Desk'), a pregnant woman ('Woman Seated in the Underground, 1941'), three men playing cards during a military conflict ('Poker in the Falklands with Henry & Jim'), a Holocaust victim ('Shooting Stars'), trapped cetaceous mammals ('The Dolphins') and male corpses ('Letters from Deadmen'). In *Selling Manhattan* the reader is forced, to a certain extent, to identify with a ventriloquist's doll ('The Dummy'), a woman whose lover walks strangely ('The Brink of Shrieks'), a woman on the verge of a breakdown ('Recognition'), a patient who shouts 'BAS-TARDS' at doctors ('And How Are We Today?'), a mugged pianist ('Every Good Boy'), a child murderer ('Psychopath'), a man framed by the police ('Yes, Officer'), a child whose father is killed during the Troubles ('Statement'), an Indian ('Selling Manhattan'), a one-eyed flautist ('Three Paintings'), an immigrant struggling with another language ('Foreign'), an adulteress ('Correspondents'), a servant ('Warming Her Pearls'), and a man about to be deported ('Deportation'). Other dramatic monologues in these two collections are narrated by more culpable voices, such as the man in 'Human Interest' who murders his wife, the Nazi who sells another's diaries in 'What Price?', articulate dollar bills ('Money Talks'), and a thief who makes off with a snowman ('Stealing'). *Thrown Voices*, a pamphlet published in 1986, also contains monologues by a devious politician ('2. The Tory Candidate, On the Eve of the General Election, Gets Down on His Knees'), who will 'put the money up to mend' the church roof if the pastor will help him to win, and a misanthrope ('3. The Bitter and Twisted Poet Considers Spring'), who mocks Hopkins and Eliot ('I keep my dappled thing inside a cage. / April is the corniest month').[34] Inevitably, the two lists blur: 'Education for Leisure', 'You Jane', 'Psychopath' and 'Stealing', for example, could fall into either category, so that sometimes it is unclear who exactly constitutes these 'others'. As Deryn Rees-Jones asks, does the 'throb' in the neck of the ape man in 'You Jane' denote the vulnerability of the male figure, or simply emphasise somatic differences between men and women?[35] And when the narrator of 'Stealing' denies the conventional identification expected in the dramatic monologue with an unsettling question ('You don't understand a word I'm saying, do you?'), is the reader meant to sympathise with the unreadable nature of the thief's actions? Despite these examples, the lists are separated mainly along gender lines: the experience of women is clearly of particular concern in the first list above. This is reflected in the first word of the title of the first poem in Duffy's first mature collection ('Girl'). The two initial poems in *Standing Female Nude* ('Girl Talking', 'Comprehensive') are dramatic monologues which challenge the predominance of male voices in the genre. 'Girl Talking' implicitly denigrates the bunkum of the patriarchal in the form of a priest: after having sex with a miller, the girl in question dies; the priest covers up male promiscuity in the village by paradoxically calling for the further suppression of young women, who are henceforth not allowed out at noon.

Duffy's engagement with patriarchal cultures in the East might be compromised by the conservatism of the aesthetic form she inherits from the tradition of the dramatic monologue. Antony Rowland has argued elsewhere that Duffy utilises the genre in the tradition of Browning rather than Eliot, as one might expect, given that the former banker was her favourite poet in 1988.[36] This partial adherence to tradition, and the achievements of the exoteric verse in terms of its naturalistic monologues, can be illustrated in relation to 'Head of English' and the title poem from *Standing Female Nude*. 'Head of English' fulfils the criteria for the dramatic monologue outlined (and then critiqued) by Alan Sinfield.[37] It has a distinct setting (a girl's school), and a reasonably discernible timescale (postmodernism). The characterisation of the head is naturalistic, and fits with the irascible, but lovable, figures of many traditional monologues; as Sinfield notes, the genre expects a certain amount of complicity with the speaker's point of view.[38] Generic expectations of 'revelation' are fulfilled: the teacher presents herself as a balanced commentator on modern poetry, but unwittingly reveals her conservatism; she laments that 'not all poems, / sadly, rhyme these days', and cannot stomach verse after Keats (she quotes the opening words of 'To Autumn') and Kipling (whose work she is teaching to the Lower Fourth).[39] Despite this, she is clearly in awe of the invited writer, as well as threatened by him (or her): hence the alacrity with which she mentions her knowledge of literary tradition, and the fact that she has written some poetry herself. This last gesture might incite the reader's sympathy, since a subtext of failure is suggested: the poem constructs a binary between creativity and teaching. Irony then enters the frame if the poem is considered as potential teaching matter for schools: teachers performing the text must expose their own 'failure' (following Duffy's logic) whilst teaching pupils how to read the monologue correctly. In this sense, it fits into a tradition of 'scholastic' poems which has augmented over recent years.[40] Practitioners as diverse as Seamus Heaney, Tony Harrison and Peter Didsbury have written anti-school pieces which are then ironically institutionalised (in the case of the first two poets) by being set on GCSE syllabuses. The head in Duffy's poem is perplexed by the kind of writing which now provides set texts: she garbles that the reading gave 'an insight to an outside view' (*SFN*, p. 12). What the main audience thinks of the performance is uncertain: as in many monologues, the narrator has potential interlocutors (the pupils) who actually keep silent. The actual poet (as the other addressee) remains passive too: perhaps the reading which takes place in the gap between stanzas four and five is meant to be by Duffy herself, who shocks the teacher with her daring use of assonance.[41]

This possibility highlights Sinfield's critique of the supposed structural keys of the dramatic monologue, and the fact that the reader is coerced into accepting a double bluff in 'Head of English'. The gap in which the radical reading takes place is dependent upon the extremely conservative views of the teacher. Her traditional outlook permeates the text to the extent that even the passing reference to 'winds of change' uncovers her conservatism: the phrase originates from a speech by Harold Macmillan in 1960, in which he referred to the 'wind of change' blowing through the African continent. This engagement with African nationalism is rendered ironic in 'Head of English' since the teacher does not want 'winds' in the room (politicised or stylistically innovative poems?), and asks a pupil to open the window. This denial of change is undercut by the post-colonial classroom: she implies that she will explain the poems to the pupils who have English as a second language after the break. Hence the conventional split between the poet's and narrator's views in the dramatic monologue is upheld. There is no 'feigning' in this text, in which the poet pretends that the speaker is not a ventriloquist's dummy for their own ideas. Unless a poet such as Tom Raworth is meant to be speaking (which is possible), the text invites the reader to construct a writer *such as Duffy* as daringly modern, but only in relation to Keats and Kipling. This obscures the fact that the form of the poem might be regarded as, ironically, conservative itself: it is loosely iambic, admittedly without any set number of feet. Naturalistic character sketches also grate against

the monologues of Pound and Eliot, in which often disparate and incoherent voices speak in sometimes obscure locations. Hence Sinfield
argues that the main tenets of the dramatic form actually arise from a
specialised context: the work of Robert Browning. Our reading of the
poem above in terms of time, setting, character, revelation and ironic
discrepancy thus positions the text in the premodernist tradition of the
monologue. Indeed, Sinfield argues that the genre might become out-
dated after the attempts of Pound and Eliot to mix third-person and
first-person voices to the extent that who is speaking in a given text
becomes unclear. In such a literary scenario, the genre, which relies in
its most basic form on a distinction between the narrator and poet,
might be obsolete. And yet the dramatic monologue has proved tena-
cious in the postmodernist era, particularly, as Deryn Rees-Jones
notes, in women's writing. Perhaps this is due to the fact that politics
sits uneasily with texts in which voices are blurred to the point at
which any viewpoint is interchangeable. Without entering into a
debate between autonomous and committed art, the poetics of Duffy's
poems seem to be cognizant with the view that 'democratic' form is
more likely to make its 'message' clear. Detractors from Duffy's work
might argue that these are the main stylistic and thematic problems
with her work: it pretends to be 'modern', but can do so only in relation to the false stalking horse of premodernist verse; it champions
multiplicity, but is often didactic.

We would argue that the first dichotomy is highlighted here owing
to the relatively unselfconscious nature of 'Head of English'. As an
early poem in *Standing Female Nude* it appears slightly staid in comparison with the self-referential monologues in later collections. In
contrast, some of Duffy's later monologues, such as 'Psychopath' from
*Selling Manhattan*, could be said to be postmodern re-writings of the
genre in that they parade an awareness of their own artificiality. Naturalistic character sketches are abandoned with the focus on the throb
of the neck in 'You Jane', or the shoes scudding sparks against the
night in 'Psychopath'. These form examples of when the 'semi-invisibility' of the poet turns into poetic visibility. Both Deryn Rees-Jones
and Ian Gregson note that at these moments in the monologues the
speaking voice fractures to reveal the 'true' voice of the third-person
poet (which is itself an artificial construction).[42] However, one of
the monologues in the first 'mature' collection does begin to display
these characteristics. 'Standing Female Nude' remains aware of its own

artifice, at the same time as it refuses to reject an implicit gender politics. An artist's model complains at the end of the piece that 'It [the painting] does not look like me': respect for the object has been abandoned in favour of a 'higher' aesthetic. Deryn Rees-Jones suggests that the culprit here is Georges Braque (the first name is mentioned in line 16) (*SFN*, p. 46).[43] Her interpretation can be supported with reference to the last stanza: when the model asks why he paints, the artist replies 'Because / I have to. There's no choice', which chimes with Braque's statement that 'I did not decide to become a painter, any more than I decided to breathe'.[44] The model's complaint would suggest that the painting is from his Cubist phase, but 'Standing' features in only a few of Braque's titles – none of them from this stage in his career – such as *Standing Woman With Basket* (1929) and the *Standing Woman* sculpture (1920). Duffy may not be referring, of course, to a distinct art work; if she is, the post-Cubist *Canephora* series based on sketches of 'standing' nudes in the 1920s become prime suspects. The model's appeal to a gap between the subject and object is registered in the split between the original sketches, with notes for the colours and frame, and the semi-naked women in the final pictures who appear as caryatids or fertility goddesses. Braque openly admitted the lack of referentiality in his paintings of women: 'I couldn't portray a woman in all her natural loveliness. I haven't the skill. No one has. I must, therefore, create a new sort of beauty, the beauty that appears to me in terms of volume, of line, of mass, of weight.'[45] Duffy equates this search for autonomous art with masculinity: the model is concerned with her next meal; the artist, with 'volume, space'. If 'Standing Female Nude' is read as a direct rejoinder to Braque, art critics who comply with his vision must be included in her critique: Jean Leymarie contends that 'whether a painted image bears the "right" relation to its model in nature becomes moot; what matters is the "rightness" of the picture in itself'. Rather than a conservative appeal for a return to naturalism, Duffy's poem can be interpreted as an investigation into the ensuing gap between the model and work of autonomous art.

In 'Standing Female Nude' the main addressee appears to be the reader rather than a more conventional third party; more specifically, one with a basic knowledge of feminist theory and Freudianism, who will immediately recognise the artist's exploitation of the speaker, and endorse the supposition that men long for their mothers. 'Standing' might seem to be an innocuous present participle, and yet the 'Six hours' which open the piece indicate that modelling becomes a kind of paid torture to the detriment of the aesthetic. '[P]ossesses' forms the key word in this text: the artist's fantasies of sexual contact with the model are transposed on to canvas: transference results in his 'possession' of her body through the medium of art; instead of inserting his penis into her he 'dips his brush / repeatedly into the paint'. Any ensuing gap between the subject and object is ironically underlined by the subsequent reference to him as a 'Little man': he metamorphoses into the Titch Thomas character in Larkin's 'Sunny Prestatyn', whose scrawling of a 'tuberous cock and balls' is subverted by the inference in his name that the referent is small.[46] This metaphorical 'dipping' also covers the incestuous impetus behind the artistic creation: he thinks of his mother, the model implies, as his erection thickens; the resulting 'river-whore' is thus a projection of his mother as well as a 'representation' of the model. Despite her pat Freudianism, men in general are not the main targets of her ire. She observes wryly that the poor painter cannot afford her body: the bourgeoisie are derided as they 'coo' when she is 'framed' as a river-whore, unaware of the six hours and paltry 'Twelve francs' prostituted in order to tease out the future audience's sense of aesthetic pleasure. This process connects with the wider examination of the relationship between aesthetics and exploitation in *Standing Female Nude* as a whole, as in 'War Photographer' and 'What Price?' One question remains, however: is it possible that the poet's 'possession' of the model in terms of the overall poem forms an example of artistic exploitation, even if it is done in order to make a political point?

This attack on the artist and bourgeoisie must assume a relatively stable notion of identity politics, an assumption that might be mirrored by the seemingly naturalistic depiction of character. However, 'Standing Female Nude' forms an acutely self-conscious, and potentially anachronistic, representation of a *fin de siècle* prostitute. The semi-invisibility of the feminist author is paralleled by the confusion of identities initiated by the clash between line and syntax sense in the third and fourth lines of the first stanza. 'Further to the right' might appear to be spoken by the model, but the 'Madame' of the next line suggests that this is the artist 'speaking'. A reading of the text as a naturalistic monologue would suppose that the model articulates while she is being painted, and yet his intervention could be indirect speech. If so, the reader would be constructed as the addressee at all times, or she would be speaking into a void. 'Standing Female Nude' might also be read as a translation of an imaginary journal of an early feminist, who, of course, would not recognise herself as such. Without repeating Deryn Rees-Jones's engagement with Freud, Lacan and Irigaray, it can thus be reasonably asked whether 'Standing Female Nude' works 'as a successful strategy to countermand as well as articulate some of the difficulties which arise when [Duffy] seeks to adopt a subject position as both a woman and a poet'.[47] In other words, the 'lack' of Duffys in literary tradition leads to the identification with the 'lack' of the woman in the final picture. Or is this moment naturalistic, as in the moment in Tony Harrison's 'V' in which the pun is at the expense of the skinhead, and for the pleasure of the literate audience, when the skin accuses the elegist of speaking Greek when the poet has just spoken French?[48] Just as the skinhead has not attained the education to discern between different foreign languages, so the model has not learned enough about modern art to realise that a Cubist painting (if it is one) questions traditional theories of representation. The irony is that, in a sense, she already has, since the last sentence leads back to the second line, in which she immediately registers that she will be reduced to the fragmented 'Belly nipple arse'; the woman is paradoxically both present and absent in the picture as a reified object. This presence masks, to a certain extent, the 'lack' of women in the canon of poetry. By pretending to be a French model, attention is taken away from the possibility that Duffy might be attempting to write as a 'woman poet', and all the difficulties that might ensue by situating herself in a male-orientated tradition.

Duffy's work can thus be usefully compared further with the work of Adrienne Rich, who pioneered an anti-patriarchal mode of poetry from the late 1960s onwards. In 1975 Kathleen Gough listed eight aspects of male power; number seven was 'to cramp [women's] creativeness'.[49] Quoting this headline in her 1980 essay 'Compulsory Heterosexuality and Lesbian Existence', Adrienne Rich defines one of the results as 'sexual exploitation of women by male artists and teachers'.[50] The emphasis on all women is instructive. Duffy shares with Rich a concern with female existence which sometimes blurs the distinctions between straight women and lesbians. 'Standing Female Nude' explores Gough's definition number seven in intense detail, but from a *woman's*, rather than strictly lesbian, perspective. This applies to most of Duffy's work: it adheres to Rich's definition of feminism as that which 'means finally . . . we renounce our obedience to the fathers and recognize that the world they have described is not the whole world'. Hence the need for the world's wife, and yet at the same time 'wife' denotes a heterosexist paradigm in which the female remains entangled. Rather than focus on lesbian difference in formulations such as female masculinity as many recent queer theorists do – such as Judith Halberstam with her examination of boilerplate diesels, daggers and drag kings – Duffy and Rich are examples of women artists who explore the 'lesbian continuum' (as Rich refers to it), encompassing both straight feminists and outright lesbians.[51] The critic must still be careful not to blur the feminisms of Rich and Duffy into a singular project. Duffy regards herself as a second-generation feminist: in the 1988 interview, she admits to distrusting the label, at the same time as conceding that she owes a lot to 1970s activists and writers such as Rich.[52] Nevertheless, the parallels between the two authors in terms of their 'feminisms' are instructive: for all the irony and satire of *The World's Wife*, Duffy has yet to appoint a boilerplate bulldagger as a speaker in her dramatic monologues.

### Cultural identities and 'regulatory structures' in *The Other Country* and *Mean Time*

> Within Duffy's poetry, the meaning of art is also a construction and is shown to be produced in relationship to economics, the discourse of the body, and the regulatory structures of gender, race, and class.[53]

*The Other Country*, Duffy's third (major) volume of poetry, published in 1990, is one of her most overtly political collections of poems. In it she explores a wide range of issues of identity, encompassing questions of gender, race, class and national identity. Writing poetry with a political message can be a haphazard enterprise: in the hands of a less talented poet the subject area can take over and eclipse the poetic genre and its formal aspects; the poems gathered in *The Other Country* are never in danger of falling into that particular trap. As David Kennedy points out so aptly, her poetry emerges as an interrogation of the state of contemporary culture by raising questions such as 'how and to whom is it supposed to be sustaining? If this is the surface then what lies beneath? Who owns it? What is the glue that holds all these items together?'[54] Thus, it could be argued that Duffy's poetry is first of all a poetry interested in questions rather than one which advocates definite answers and empirical truths.

*The Other Country* establishes its interrogative tone by opening with the poem 'Originally' which is discussed in several chapters in this volume. It also introduces the themes of otherness, displacement and foreignness which so many poems collected here are concerned with. Unlike some of the poems in its predecessor *Selling Manhattan* - which are similarly interested in the relationship between centre and margin – in *The Other Country* Duffy focuses on life in Britain itself. 'Originally' traces the move from one part of the country to another, perceived from the perspective of a child. This journey involves more than just a geographical change when the poem insists that this is a move to another country, emphasising the cultural diversity of contemporary Britain and its effect on how identity is experienced. For the child this is predominantly the experience of displacement and loss as the last two lines of the second stanza point out: 'My parents' anxiety stirred like a loose tooth / in my head. *I want our own country*, I said' (*TOC*, p. 7). But where and what is our own country? How can we lay claim to a cultural and national identity that can be securely known? This seems to be the most pressing issue here, since the poem concludes with a succession of questions: ' . . . Do I only think / I lost a river, culture speech, sense of first space and the right place? Now, *Where do you come from?* / strangers ask. *Originally?* And I hesitate.' As Angelica Michelis points out in this book, this tone of hesitancy and pausing becomes a pertinacious feature of this volume, and recurs in poems such as 'Hometown', 'Too Bad', 'We Remember Your Childhood Well', 'Away From Home', 'River', 'The Way My Mother Speaks' and 'In Your Mind', which link the concept of national identity to a more general interrogation of identity as such. In these poems Duffy plays on the theme of displacement, the experience of being an outsider in your own country and culture, presenting alienation as an integral part of lived subjectivity. As Neil Roberts argues when discussing the general trajectory of Duffy's poetic *ouevre*:

> Outsidedness in Duffy's poetry extends far beyond the conventional notion of the outsider as a person set against the norm. Outsidedness *is* the norm. It is an aesthetic principle in her representation of subjectivity, especially in the dramatic monologue, and radically influences her dealings with language, explicit and implicit.[55]

But it is not only in relation to the question of national identity that Duffy interrogates notions of subjectivity and the experience of the self as informed by cultural contexts. Memory and nostalgia also emerge as consistent subjects of poetic interest and enquiry in *The Other Country*. Very often these themes are intertwined with those dealing with the search for the meaning of home and belonging, but they also crop up in relation to language and the genre of poetry. 'Weasel Words' and 'M-M-Memory' are the most notable examples of where Duffy explores the contingency of linguistic meaning by revealing the 'palimpsest' layering of language as a medium. Here Duffy is able to show off the most idiosyncratic feature of her poetic voice: a witty but nevertheless pertinacious exploration of an image or metaphor which is probed at and illuminated with verve and intellectual curiosity from a variety of perspectives. Lightheartedness and inquisitiveness are always balanced, opening up the structure of the poem to an active and creative reading experience.

However, some of the most poignant poems gathered in *The Other Country* exude a sense of despair and hopelessness when dealing with the state of the nation and its inhabitants. 'Mrs Skinner, North Street', 'Job Creation' and 'Losers' paint a bleak picture of a country where greed, consumption and moneymaking have become the main signifiers of contemporary culture. It is in particular the northern regions of Britain which emerge as places of cultural and economic dearth with their inhabitants stigmatised by a politics that has no moral qualms to eradicate historical traditions and infrastructures. These are places where people may lose their bearings because 'Britishness' is now conflated with the traditions and lifestyle of the more affluent, southern parts of the country. However, these poems manage successfully to avoid an overall tone of propaganda and moral indignation because of the attention paid to structure and form. Fragmented text, gaps in the semantic weaving and a staccato-like language ask the reader for intellectual participation based on empathy and understanding. Britain emerges here as the other country for a vast part of its subjects but these poems also fire the imagination for the possibilities of another country where national identity is constructed in a different and more inclusive manner.

*The Other Country* also contains some of the poems which established Duffy's reputation as one of the most innovative voices of contemporary British poetry. 'Translating the English, 1989', 'Poet For Our

Times' and 'Making Money' are typical examples for her talent to parody the language of Thatcherite England, investing it with an ironic twist to create a poetry which takes issue with the contemporary culture of the late 1980s and early 1990s. In these poems Britain, and in particular England, is represented as a consumer society where commercialisation has become the major denominator of national culture. Alcoholism, drug culture, soap operas, corrupt politicians and criminality dominate the country in 'Translating the English, 1989', and have an effect on every other aspect of culture by turning Shakespeare, Charles Dickens, Wordsworth and British history and art into commodities, thus brandishing British culture as a market place where the right amount of money can buy you anything. By presenting national culture as a list of merchandise the poem points out the underlying emptiness of life in a country where only the language of monetary exchange provides a grammar and semantics of understanding and intelligibility. The poem is written in a kind of pidgin English, using short sentences and media-speak and parodying the discursive structures of the tabloid press which became so typical for the Britain of the late 1980s. Whereas the linguistic structure of the poem as such is based on monologue and exclusion, dominated by one autocratic voice, the poem emerges as a dialogue, since it demands to have its gaps filled in and its randomness made sense of by the process of reading. By doing so the text makes a strong point about national identity since, as David Kennedy puts it so aptly, the

> reader, as a consequence, is prompted to consider his or her own relation to and identity in a culture whose confusions, gaps and apparent randomness suggest a debasement or perhaps even total loss of coherent national identity.[56]

However, rather than nostalgically mourning the loss of a coherent national identity which might once have existed and included all inhabitants of the country, the poem develops a rather different trajectory. Culture, it seems to suggest, is never a fixed, historically transcendent entity but always embedded and dialectically connected to political power. Its language of exclusion is never completely successful since its very structure always provides the means for a counter-discourse which works against its presumed intentions. By focusing on language and analysing its intricate relationship to political and social issues, Duffy is able to develop here a poetry which is highly critical of contemporary living, but avoids falling into the trap of nostalgia. As these poems demonstrate, language is for Duffy never a medium that simply represents and reflects reality and subjectivity; on the contrary, her poetry insists on a non-representational status of language with the effect that whatever is signified can only ever be provisional and contingent on the discursive reality of the cultural and political fabric of society. Therefore, one could argue, Duffy's poetry is at its most political when it is, in terms of its content, at its most postmodern.

Whereas *The Other Country* offers a balance of political, personal and satirical poems, the 1993 volume *Mean Time* focuses on the plight of the self. The major frame of reference is indicated by the title: Michael Woods demonstrates in this book how *Mean Time* is concerned with capturing and renovating experience from 'mean' time, the inevitable process that is intent on robbing us of our being. When she discusses the volume in the *Poetry Book Society Bulletin*, Duffy points out how time features in her fourth major collection:

> The poems in *Mean Time* are about the different ways in which time brings about change or loss. In the collection, I mean to write about time. The effects of time can be mean. Mean can mean average. The events in the poems can happen to the average man or woman. The dwindling of childhood. Ageing. The distance of history. The tricks of memory and the renewal of language. The end of love. New Love. Luck. And so on.[57]

The ambiguity of the title indicates already the many faceted images and thoughts on time which shape the different poems collected in this volume. As Duffy explains, the compound 'Mean Time' can give rise to a variety of interpretations: time can be mean in the sense of 'bad times'; 'mean times' refers to the fact that time is not a metaphysically fixed entity but linked to language and its temporal positions of past, present and future which allow us to think of being 'between times' (and thus also introduce the subject of memory which features in several poems of the volume). Mean, as already indicated by Duffy, can also be understood in the sense of 'average', suggesting that time, as Woods points out, 'averages out our experience by framing our existence within a continuum that finally reduces each of us to nothing more than a brief interruption in the world'.[58] Last but not least, there is of course also the connection between time and mean(ing) which foregrounds the extent to which the production of meaning is deeply related to time. If we consider meaning as continually moving along the chain of signifiers, it is simultaneously only ever possible as a temporal movement, and as timeless, since the goal – a final meaning – is never reached. Many of the poems collected in *Mean Time* reflect on this complex relationship between time and signification, in particular when focusing on memory, and how time in its particularisation of past, present, future impacts on identity and our sense of being in the world.

In titles such as 'The Captain of the 1964 *Top of the Form* Team', 'Nostalgia', 'Before You Were Mine', 'Never Go Back', 'First Love', 'The Biographer' and 'Mean Time' the subject matter of time is already clearly announced. Other poems, as for example, 'Litany', 'Stafford Afternoons', 'Confession', 'Caul', 'Small Female Skull', 'Crush' and 'Havisham' reveal their themes in a more conceptual manner. The common denominator of all these poems is their exploration of temporality, or, to be more precise, how we experience time and, simultaneously, how our experience as a self is shaped by it. The opening poem, 'The Captain of the 1964 *Top of the Form* Team', introduces one of Duffy's favourite modes of poetically examining the subject of time: the childhood memory. The persona remembers a specific moment in the 1960s when he felt at ease, and could provide the answers to all questions: 'I want it back. The captain. The one with all the answers' (*MT*, p. 7). The poem is developed in the form of a collage, interspersing the shreds of memory with evocative signifiers of the decade, in particular titles of popular songs. By doing so personal memory is inextricably linked with the public and cultural sphere, thus making a point that the history of the self is always a contiguous one. In that respect the poem is also a proof of what could be called the failure of memory: the more we attempt to assemble a unified self, the more we are reminded that such an enterprise can only be an illusion since 'the outside', in the form of culture, constantly intervenes. The poem with its italicised elements, its half-sentences and disjointed semantic structure emphasises fragmentation as underlying the concept of subjectivity, thus making a point that any recognition of a self in memory can only ever be a mis-recognition, since the personal self is always already deflected into a social self. The perceptible disappointment of the persona at the end of the poem who feels lost in the present and tries to re-create his sense of self by placing it in a specific point in the past is thus not only the personal disappointment of a frustrated man unhappy with his life, but also the result of realising that this very process is a futile one. Even a lost self might still indicate its previous existence, but the persona can never pinpoint this moment, the only sign of a self is the frantic search for it. The poem thus plays cleverly with the opposition between question and answer, the very essence of the quiz, by disqualifying any answers as illusions and privileging questions as the only methodological path to the mystery of subjectivity. In that respect the persona is not dissimilar to Oedipus who addresses the chorus with the question 'Where would a trace / of this old crime be found' when he attempts to decipher his present existence by looking back into the past.[59] It is precisely this kind of Oedipal quest, one could argue, that emerges as the dominant framework underlying this volume as a whole.

In 'Litany', again framed as a childhood memory, this theme is ✕ continued by adopting the religious litany, and using it as a discursive vehicle to explore the relationship between meaning and language. The hierarchical concept of the litany – a form of public prayer, usually penitential, consisting of a series of petitions in which the clergy lead and the people respond – is here transposed into the working-class home, where women recite the contents of a catalogue:

> The soundtrack then was a litany – *candlewick*
> *bedspread three piece suite display cabinet –*
> and stiff-haired wives balanced their red smiles,
> passing the catalogue.
>
> (*MT*, p. 9)

This litany of desirable objects is rudely interrupted by the young child who informs the assembled group of women that '*A boy in the playground . . . told me to fuck off* '. The child, after delivering a litany of apologies to the present housewives, is then punished by having her mouth washed out with soap. Similarly to the preceding poem, 'Litany' utilises interspersion in a visual sense (italicisation) to underline the idea that language works on a level of disruption, fragmentation and silences. A word is not simply a word but also always a potential social time bomb. The painful learning experience of the child is here symptomatic of the way in which life is a continuous experience of the fact that we are the effect of language rather than its autonomous creators.

In the poem 'Nostalgia' Duffy approaches the subject of memory and time from a different perspective by creating a direct relationship between language, writing and memory. The dominant theme here is the despair created by the knowledge of the unreliability of remembering and the simultaneous urge to deny this, which of course is precisely what nostalgia denotes. How can something be the same and yet changed, the final lines of the poem seem to ask:

> It was spring when one returned, with his life
> in a sack on his back, to find the same street
> with the same sign on the inn, the same bell
> chiming the hour on the clock, and everything changed.
>
> (*MT*, p. 10)

Poignantly, the poem is not written in the style of a dramatic monologue and does not refer to an individualised persona. By doing so the text de-personalises the process of memory and wants to be read as a reflection on it rather than an example of it. Furthermore, by erecting a barrier of suspicion between the self and its memories the poem indicates that remembering the past is never a direct process, but that it is always and already interfered with from a location outside the control of the self. It is the process of perception: 'the wrong taste, / . . . and the wrong sounds, / the wrong smells, the wrong light, every breath – / wrong' which does not allow an unmediated relationship between self and reality and thus makes it impossible to remember a state of subjectivity uncontaminated by culture. Thus it is the feeling of loss which is susceptible in every line of the poem which becomes its most dominant subject:

> But the word was out. Some would never
> fall in love had they not heard of love.
> So the priest stood at the stile with his head
> in his hands, crying at the workings of memory
> through the colour of leaves, and the schoolteacher
> opened a book to the scent of her youth, too late.

Nostalgia could be described as a state of melancholia, which Sigmund Freud distinguished from mourning: 'In mourning it is the world which has become poor and empty; in melancholia it is the ego itself.'[60] This sense of melancholia is simultaneously the subject and the effect of the poem, generated by the presence of exact and detailed images of the past ('where maybe you met a girl, / or searched for a yellow ball in long grass, / found it just as your mother called you in') and the impossibility of placing them in time and in relation to the present state of the self. The process of (nostalgic) remembering, the poem seems to suggest, does not allow us to revisit a known past but, on the contrary, reminds us that time and our notion of subjectivity are constructed in a framework of temporal relations which themselves are the closest to what we could know as a self. This sense of melancholia pervades the volume *Mean Time* as a whole. In some poems it is embedded in personal memories ('Stafford Afternoons'), in others it takes the form of a deliberate distancing ('Never go back'). 'Havisham' approaches it from the perspective of the famous character in Dickens's *Great Expectations*, the jilted bride who stubbornly refuses to live according to the scheme 'past-present-future', and thus also kills memory by living it every moment of her life. But perhaps it is the fourth stanza of 'Moments of Grace' which summarises the underlying theme of *Mean Time* best: memory is a 'caged bird' that 'won't fly'; this leaves the poet with mundane 'adjectives, nouns', but also, more importantly, verbs, 'the secret of poems' (*MT*, 26).

### 'I've seen my fair share of ding-a-ling': *The World's Wife* and *Feminine Gospels*

Although gender, and in particular the subject of femininity, features often and in various forms in Carol Ann Duffy's poetry, her 1999 volume *The World's Wife* is the one which is entirely based on feminine voices. Apart from 'The Kray Sisters', which consists of the composite voice of twins, all other poetic texts gathered here are dramatic monologues written from the point of view of one female persona. Most of the female voices poetically imagined here draw on the lives of wives of famous historical, fictional or mythical males: Frau Freud, Mrs Darwin, Mrs Midas, Anne Hathaway, Delilah, Penelope (to name but a few). The poems are often witty and tongue-in-cheek, as in 'Mrs Icarus' or 'Mrs Darwin'. Others throw light on the ways masculinity has dominated history, fiction and myth by silencing femininity and/or the ways femininity has been imagined and defined by male voices. *The World's Wife* is certainly committed to feminism, but not one based on a politics of binary oppositions. Duffy suggests that the relationship between the genders and the sexes is not one defined by a hierarchical structure of power, resulting in the impression that men are always oppressors with women as their helpless victims. 'Little Red-Cap', for example, renders its heroine as a strong young woman who is not threatened by the beast, and is able to help herself without the assistance of the hunter in its fictional source: 'I took an axe to the wolf / as he slept, one chop, scrotum to throat, and saw / the glistening, virgin white of my grandmother's bones' (*TWW*, p. 4). Delilah, by cutting Samson's hair, does him a favour by helping him to get in touch with his feminine side: 'And, yes, I was sure / that he wanted to change, / my warrior' (*TWW*, p. 29). Frau Freud, addressing a female audience, adds one synonym for a penis after another, thus demonstrating to what extent psychoanalysis by talking about femininity is actually much more eloquent about masculinity and its anxieties. The poem can be read as a witty reply to Freud's famous essay 'Femininity', in which he is preoccupied with the 'riddle of the nature of femininity' and where he addresses his audience in the following way: 'Nor will *you* have escaped worrying over this problem – those of you who are men; to those of you who are women, this will not apply – you are yourselves the problem.'[61] Duffy, rather than producing a polemical counter-argument to Freud's view, engages with the father of psychoanalysis by taking him at face value: yes indeed, the poem seems to say, femininity is worrying for men, and no, this does not constitute so much a problem for women, because it is a problem intrinsic to the construction of masculinity.

Myth, in its social as well as its literary sense, is one of the major areas Duffy re-views from a feminine, and often feminist, perspective in this volume. A notorious discursive site of gender conflict, myth and mythologies often rely on the naturalisation of a hierarchical relationship between men and women: men are wronged by treacherous women and femininity is accepted only if it is lived according to patriarchal law. In poems such as 'Thetis', 'Mrs Midas', 'Medusa', 'Eurydice' and 'Penelope' Duffy reflects on how, as Roland Barthes put it so aptly, myth 'transforms history into nature'.[62] Medusa, that famous emblem of the threat of feminine sexuality to masculinity, has lost all her original 'gorgonesque' qualities when she laments her fate as a woman: rejection and lost love have turned her into the personification of the grotesque and abject. Eurydice retells the Orpheus myth from the point of view of a woman stalked and harassed by the famous poet who traps her 'in his images, metaphors, similes, / octaves and sextets, quatrains and couplets, / elegies, limericks, villanelles, histories, myths', and cunningly tricks him into turning around by appealing to his vanity as a poet (*TWW*, p. 60). Similarly, Penelope, rather than waiting longingly for the return of her heroic husband Odysseus, discovers in his absence her own talent, and instead of taking up embroidery as a means of passing the time, it becomes a creative passion. In all these examples, Duffy unravels myth not only from a narrative point of view but simultaneously demonstrates to what extent every story and every discourse achieves social intelligibility by silencing other versions. By reading between the lines of history, literature, science and myth, the poems collected in *The World's Wife* can be read as shedding the light on the unconscious of texts and the extent to which they function as a creative and politically productive disturbance of socially accepted truths. And so typical for Duffy, the volume's last poem, 'Demeter', finishes these poetical reflections with a ray of hope for change and new beginnings as an intrinsic element of a new way of living sexual identities. When Demeter's daughter approaches her mother 'the air softened and warmed as she moved, // the blue sky smiling, none too soon, / with the small shy mouth of a new moon' (*TWW*, p. 76).

Just as this introduction was completed, *Feminine Gospels* was published, Duffy's sixth major volume. Whereas the monologues in *The World's Wife* constitute, as Avril Horner and Antony Rowland demonstrate in this book, a tirade on masculinity in all its various forms (apart from female masculinity), *Feminine Gospels* chooses simply, for the most part, to ignore men, and concentrate on the fairy-tale stories of 'The Long Queen', 'The Map-woman', 'Beautiful', 'The Diet', 'The Woman Who Shopped' (etc.). In an interview in 2002, Duffy stated that she would probably not 'now write a poem in the male voice', such as the earlier 'You Jane' from *Standing Female Nude*.[63] 'The Laughter of Stafford Girls' High' epitomises both this concentration on female narrators in the last two volumes and the switch to third-person narration in *Feminine Gospels*, as she celebrates lesbian relationships between some of the teachers, and the pupils' carnivalesque, if inexplicable, bursts of merriment. The final poems, 'Wish', 'Northwest' and 'Death and the Moon', offer a teasing return to the lyrical voice so predominant in *The Other Country* and *Mean Time*, where issues of gender identity are temporarily suspended. Sharon Olds's poem 'Son' ends Duffy's recent anthology *I Wouldn't Thank You for a Valentine* with a more utopian vision of men's future than is experienced anywhere in *The World's Wife* and *Feminine Gospels*. 'Coming home from the women-only bar', the mother peeps in at her sleeping son, and concludes: 'Into any new world we enter, let us / take this man.' Perhaps nothing is as conventionally idealist as the metaphor of a child. This would be a pedantic retort in the context of Olds's eulogy, however. 'Son' forms a precursor of 'Demeter', which completes *The World's Wife* with a hopeful image of femininity ('a new moon') as the daughter returns from her incarceration in the underworld. The mother is 'choosing tough words' as she laments her absence at the beginning of the poem, just as Duffy chooses 'tough words' to affirm a world in which identity politics still matter. In her work as a whole, the 'tough words' about gender politics demand responses, however awkward and compromised the ensuing voices might be.

## Notes

1 In Manchester's Waterstones, *Selected Poems* (London: Penguin, 1994) sold 266 copies in a year (October 2000 to October 2001); *The World's Wife* (London: Picador, 1999) sold 157 copies, and *Mean Time* (London: Anvil, 1993) 236 in the same period. The popularity of *Mean Time* may be due to the fact that it has been chosen as an A-level text as much as the *Selected Poems*.

2 Sean O'Brien, 'A Stranger Here Myself', *The Deregulated Muse* (Newcastle: Bloodaxe, 1998), pp. 160–70, p. 167.

3 www.bris.ac.uk/Depts/English/journals/thumbscr.

4 Simon Brittan, 'Language and Structure in the Poetry of Carol Ann Duffy', *Thumbscrew*, 1:1 (winter 1994–95), pp. 58–64.

5 Ibid., p. 64.

6 *Robert Browning*, ed. Colin Graham (London: Everyman, 1997), pp. 6–7.

7 Brittan, p. 59.

8 Ibid., p. 64.

9 Letter from Gunn to Ted Hughes (3 February 1990), held in the archives at Emory University, Atlanta.

10 Mark Reid, 'Near Misses Are Best', *Magma*, 2 (June 1994), pp. 34–8.

11 Duffy implicitly makes this separation in an interview with Vicci Bentley when she says that she 'can't do' performance poetry in the same way as Benjamin Zephaniah or Liz Lochhead (*Magma*, 3 (winter 1994), pp. 17–21, p. 21).

12 Carol Ann Duffy, *Feminine Gospels* (London: Picador, 2002).

13 Michael Hulse, David Kennedy and David Morley (eds), *The New Poetry* (Newcastle: Bloodaxe, 1993). It must be noted that Duffy went on record as being not overly fond of this anthology owing to the lack, as she regarded it, of women poets and performance poets. In 'New Generations, Same Old Story' (*Agenda*, 34:1 (1996), pp. 185–91), Kiernon Winn refers to the New Generation poets touted by *The New Poetry*, a South Bank Show special and

*Poetry Review* as 'overly reliant on personal anecdote, descriptive physical detail, and a kind of defensive wit' (p. 185). He suggests that most of them should 'try to get down to something more serious than random youthful twitchy jammings' (p. 187). Instead, their free verse is 'usually straggly, their treatment of deliberately "low", "unpoetic" matter flogging a dead horse by now, their attempts to shock with sharp wit exhausted' (p. 191). Glyn Maxwell and Robert Crawford are singled out for particular criticism, but the critic might wonder whether Duffy is included in his allusions to anecdotal, anti-poetic, lowbrow and self-consciously witty writing. The alternative Winn offers of a poetry that 'reaches the level of the timeless and universal', one that expresses honest feeling, is equally troubling. Aside from the outdated concepts contained in the quotation (universal to whom?), one fears for the dramatic monologue if personal experience correctly rendered becomes a criteria for literary criticism.

14 Robert Sheppard, 'Further Thoughts on Poetry Anthologies', *peggy's blue skylight* 3 (2000), (no pp.).

15 Philip Larkin, *Collected Poems* (London: Faber, 1988), p. 180; Carol Ann Duffy, *Standing Female Nude* (London: Anvil, 1985), p. 14.

16 www.guardian.ac.uk/archive.

17 John Osborne, 'Postmodernism and Postcolonialism in the Poetry of Philip Larkin', in James Booth (ed.), *New Larkins for Old: Critical Essays* (Basingstoke: Macmillan, 2000), pp. 144–65.

18 Carol Ann Duffy (ed.), *I Wouldn't Thank You for a Valentine* (London: Penguin, 1995); *Stopping for Death: Poems of Death and Loss* (London: Penguin, 1996).

19 Linda Kinnahan, '"Look for the Doing Words": Carol Ann Duffy and Questions of Convention', in James Acheson and Romana Huk (eds), *Contemporary English Poetry*, (New York: State University of New York Press, 1996), pp. 245–68. The collection *The World's Wife* has been read as a conservative project in its seeming return to militant, first-wave feminism, but a more subtle reading of the switch in Duffy's work from the more 'literary' early and middle volumes to the politicised jokiness of the 'wife' poems might attest to an alternative view. Perhaps she is subtly responding to a recent trend in which women 'return' to feminism in motherhood, or in their thirties, as their awareness increases of tangible gender inequalities.

20 In *Carol Ann Duffy* (Plymouth: Northcote House, 1999), Deryn Rees-Jones lists Duffy's main influences as Jacques Prévert, Pablo Neruda, Aimé Césaire, Wordsworth, Browning, Auden, Larkin, Dylan Thomas, Hughes, Eliot, the Liverpool Poets, the Beats and W.S. Graham (p. 1). André Breton, Adrienne Rich and Sylvia Plath could be added to the list.

21 Carol Ann Duffy, *Selling Manhattan* (London: Anvil, 1987).

22 Carol Ann Duffy, *The Other Country* (London: Anvil, 1990).

23 Carol Ann Duffy, *Fleshweathercock and Other Poems* (Walton-on-Thames: Outposts, 1973). Deryn Rees-Jones gives Duffy's age as 18 when she published the collection (p. 5), but in an interview in 1999, the age quoted is 16 ('Metre Maid', *The Guardian Weekend*, 25 September 1999, pp. 20–6, p. 24). Duffy

was born in 1955, so she would have been 17 or 18 when *Fleshweathercock* was published in 1973.

24 'Metre Maid', p. 24. In an interview with Jane Stabler in 1991, Duffy states that her first influence was 'Keats and my poems were addressed to "thee" etc.! Then Dylan Thomas . . . Ted Hughes. Eliot' (*Verse*, 8:2 (summer 1991), pp. 124–8, p. 125).

25 Carol Ann Duffy and Adrian Henri, *Beauty and the Beast* (Liverpool, c.1977). There are no page numbers in the pamphlet.

26 Duffy argues in the 1999 interview that 'Little Red-Cap' from *The World's Wife* is not Based on Henri, and yet it could be argued that it re-writes the earlier pamphlet. The beast becomes the wolf. Sixteen years old in the poem, the girl meets him at a poetry reading: these details mirror Duffy's meeting with Henri. The 'magic bird' in *Fleshweathercock* - which the young narrator fears 'will never / come / again' – represents a fear of rejection (p. 6). In 'Little Red-Cap' it becomes the 'white dove' which the 'flew, straight, from my hands to [the wolf's] open mouth. / One bite, dead. How nice, breakfast in bed, he said': innocence is corrupted by an ageing poet who lures the girl with the 'magic' of words. Duffy's denial that the poem was autobiographical may have been due to an understandable attempt to protect Henri at the time of publication of *The World's Wife* in 1999: he was ill at the time, and died in December 2000.

27 In September 2001, a copy was on sale at the Poetry Bookshop in Hay-on-Wye for £25. As with *Fleshweathercock*, a copy has been deposited in The British Library.

28 Kathleen Gough, 'The Origin of the Family', in Rayna Reiter (ed.), *Toward an Anthropology of Women* (New York: Monthly Review Press, 1975), pp. 60–70.

29 Duffy was to return to this fairy tale twenty years later with 'Mrs Beast', published in *The World's Wife* (pp. 72–5). The doting Beast in the original story is used as a vehicle for the narrator's feminist verve: Mrs Beast prefers to be the 'less-loving one', and commands her husband to suffer for the sins of all men, at the same time at satisfying her sexually, but only when she requires it (p. 75).

30 Carol Ann Duffy, *Fifth Last Song* (West Kirby: Headland, 1982).

31 Rees-Jones, pp. 5, 6.

32 Rees-Jones, p. 5

33 Barbara Charlesworth Gelpi and Albert Gelpi (eds), *Adrienne Rich's Poetry and Prose* (London and New York: W.W. Norton and Co., 1993 [1975]), p. 77.

34 Carol Ann Duffy, *Thrown Voices* (London: Turret, 1986), pp. 10, 11. These two pieces form parts two and three of 'Common Prayer' (pp. 9–12). The fourth part is reprinted in *Selling Manhattan* as a separate poem ('An Old Atheist Places His Last Bet') (p. 16). Most of the other poems in *Thrown Voices* are republished in *Selling Manhattan*; exceptions are the first three parts of 'Common Prayer', and the peculiar 'Vienna 1900'. In the latter, a Scottish narrator attacks the Edinburgh festival as an event where 'those wi' nae talent gather / ti delude thirselves' (p. 13).

35  Rees-Jones, p. 21.
36  Antony Rowland, 'Patriarchy, Male Power and the Psychopath in the Poetry of Carol Ann Duffy', in Daniel Lea and Berthold Schoene-Harwood (eds), *Male Order* (Amsterdam: Rodopi, due to be published in 2003).
37  Alan Sinfield, *Dramatic Monologue* (London: Methuen, 1977).
38  Ibid., p. 6.
39  As in many of Duffy's poems, the gender of the narrator is indeterminate, but the familiarity with which the teacher addresses the pupils as 'girls' suggests that she is female.
40  For an excellent essay on this topic, see Kai Merten, 'Scholastic Performances: Seamus Heaney and Tony Harrison (Back) at School', *Critical Survey*, 14:2 (2002), pp. 101–12.
41  This reading might be supported by the interview with Jane Stabler. Duffy notes that, 'As far as going into schools is concerned, I dislike – as all poets do – being shoved in front of 60 bored, embarrassed 4th formers. If the English teacher who invites me seems sympathetic – you can always tell if they're inviting you only because they've got £60 from their L.E.A. – I'm generally happy to go' (p. 125). Regrettably, at one such reading in Merseyside, the children were asked by the teacher whether they had any questions: a cheeky lad piped up, and asked Duffy why she had such a boring voice.
42  Rees-Jones, pp. 21, 22.
43  Ibid., p. 15.
44  Quoted in Jean Leymarie, *Georges Braque* (New York: Prestel, 1988), p. 15.
45  Leymarie, p. 21.
46  Larkin, p. 149.
47  Rees-Jones, p. 26.
48  Tony Harrison, *V* (Newcastle: Bloodaxe, 1987 [1985]), p. 17.
49  Gough, 'The Origin of the Family'.
50  Adrienne Rich, 'Compulsory Heterosexuality and Lesbian Existence', in Barbara Charlesworth Gelpi and Albert Gelpi (eds), *Adrienne Rich's Poetry and Prose* (London and New York: W.W. Norton, 1993 [1980]), pp. 203–23, p. 208.
51  Judith Halberstam, *Female Masculinity* (Durham and London: Duke University Press, 1998). Rich, p. 217.
52  Andrew McAllister, 'Carol Ann Duffy Interview', *Bête Noire*, 6 (winter 1988), pp. 69–77, p. 71.
53  Kinnahan, p. 256.
54  David Kennedy, *New Relations: The Refashioning of British Poetry 1980–94* (Bridgend: Seren, 1996), p. 230.
55  Neil Roberts, *Narrative Voice in Postwar Poetry* (Harlow: Longman, 1999), p. 184.
56  Kennedy, p. 229.
57  Reprinted from the *Poetry Society Bulletin* (summer 1993), in *Poetry Review*, 84:1 (spring 1994), 111.
58  Michael J. Woods, *Carol Ann Duffy: Selected Poems* (London: York Press,

2001), p. 40.

59  Sophocles, 'Oedipus King', trans. David Greene, in *Sophocles, I: The Complete Greek Tragedies* (Chicago: University of Chicago Press, 1954), p. 15.

60  Sigmund Freud, 'Mourning and Melancholia', in Sigmund Freud, *On Metapsychology: The Theory of Psychoanalysis*, eds Angela Richards and Albert Dickens, The Penguin Freud Library, 11 (Harmondsworth: Penguin, [1915]), p. 254.

61  Sigmund Freud, 'Femininity' in *New Introductory Lectures on Psychoanalysis*, eds Angela Richards and Albert Dickens, The Penguin Freud Library, 2 (Harmondsworth: Penguin, 1991 [1933]), p. 146.

62  Roland Barthes, *Mythologies*, trans. A Lavers (New York: Hill and Wang, 1972), p. 120.

63  Peter Forbes, 'Profile: Carol Ann Duffy', *The Guardian Review* (31 August 2002), pp. 20–4, p. 20.

# I

# Duffy, Eliot and impersonality

NEIL ROBERTS

IN THE 1992 'Bookmark' programme *Love in a Cold Climate*, directed by Daisy Goodwin, a number of British poets are filmed reading their own love poems. In most cases they do so in the presence of their partners. In this sentimentally naturalising context by far the most memorable performance is that of Carol Ann Duffy. She is filmed through a window, apparently alone, and the poem she reads is 'Warming Her Pearls'.

When asked in a 1988 interview about influences Duffy spoke most enthusiastically about T.S. Eliot: 'If I had to pick one who devastated me and made me shiver and want that it would be Eliot, and still it would be Eliot.'[1] Seemingly casual allusions to Eliot are scattered through her earlier work: 'A hard coming / we had of it' ('It Has Come', *FLS*, p. 26), 'a wicked pack of cards' ('Naming Parts', *SFN*, p. 21), 'the dull canal' ('Psychopath', *SM*, p. 29). Her evocations of bleak urban scenes persistently echo 'Preludes' (for example, 'Morning / in this street awakes unwashed; a stale wind / breathing litter', 'Mrs Skinner, North Street', *TOC*, p. 9). Even in her least Eliot-like book *The World's Wife*, the words of 'Queen Herod' 'The pungent camels / kneeling in the snow' (*TWW*, p. 9) recall 'And the camels galled, sore-footed, refractory, / Lying down in the melting snow' of 'Journey of the Magi',[2] though this poem could be seen as a riposte rather than a homage.

In 1959 Hugh Kenner famously, if slightly ironically, dubbed Eliot 'The Invisible Poet'. Eliot's most notorious critical essay, 'Traditional and the Individual Talent', is the classic statement of a sophisticated distaste for the relationship between poetry and personality implied by most of the performances in 'Love in a Cold Climate'. As Kenner wrote, 'Eliot deals in effects, not ideas; and the effects are in an odd way wholly verbal, seemingly endemic to the language.'[3] Even in 1959, however, 'the man who suffers'[4] in Eliot was not wholly invisible, as Kenner implies when he discusses the effect of the title, 'The Love Song of J. Alfred Prufrock':

> It was genius that separated the speaker of the monologue from the writer of the poem by the solitary device of affixing an unforgettable title. Having done that, Eliot didn't need to fend off his protagonist with facile irony; the result was a poised intimacy which could draw on every emotion the young author knew without incurring the liabilities of 'self-expression'.[5]

The device of the title is so brilliant precisely because it is so slight. It does not prevent the critic from confidently attributing the poem's feeling to 'the young author', but it allows him to do so without, on his own or the poet's behalf, falling into the 'self-expression' that Eliot, and the literary culture he partly created, despised. In the wake of confessionalism, and the publication of *The Waste Land Facsimile and Transcript* in 1971,[6] a later generation of readers could indulge in the directly personal resonance of lines such as 'By the waters of Leman I sat down and wept'[7] and 'On Margate sands. I can connect / Nothing with nothing'[8] without worrying about 'incurring the liabilities of "self-expression"'. Thus the poetry adapts to a changed literary culture.

The title of 'Prufrock' plays with the reader's uncertainty – and desire for certainty – about the relationship between poet and speaker. It defines as 'dramatic monologue' what might otherwise be taken as direct lyric utterance. Duffy's performance in 'Love in a Cold Climate' plays on the same readerly fix in a different way. In this case the poem on the page does not seem at all to invite a 'confessional' reading. No reader is likely to suppose that the poet is a maidservant who sleeps in an attic. It is more securely a 'dramatic monologue' than 'Prufrock'. At the same time the poem's subtle but powerful eroticism, longing and desire, in a same-sex context, could well prompt some such phrase as Kenner's 'draw on every emotion the young author knew'. Choosing to read 'Warming Her Pearls' in a programme of love poems seems to reinforce this, as does Duffy's solitary presentation of a poem in which the object of desire is so absent: 'At night I feel their absence and I burn' (*SM*, p. 56).

All this is fairly obvious. A slightly more searching reflection on Duffy's performance reveals more subtle implications. In choosing to read 'Warming Her Pearls' she has of course chosen *not* to read other poems that might seem more obviously to suit the requirements of the programme, such as 'Words, Wide Night'. There is an implicit refusal to identify herself as the protagonist of such apparently straightforward love poems, to simplify the relationship between author and speaker in the way that other poets appearing on the programme do.

Eliot's most famous formulation of impersonality was 'The more perfect the artist, the more completely separate in him will be the man who suffers and the mind which creates'.[9] Kenner's 'effects [that] are in an odd way wholly verbal, seemingly endemic to the language' are an important aspect of Eliot's means of achieving this separation. Duffy's way of speaking about the separation is less provocative than Eliot's, but probably very similar in substance:

> I don't think you do feel exposed in poetry, because it's a made thing. It's a crafted piece of writing, rather than a diary extract or letter. All the work that goes into a poem pushes it away from your own vulnerable moment. I feel quite hard-hearted towards a poem when I've finished it.[10]

Alan Robinson has spoken of the 'linguistically self-generating'[11] character of much of the language in Duffy's poem 'Naming Parts'; I suggest that this is not an effect peculiar to a single poem, but a signature of a great deal of her work, her equivalent of Eliot's 'wholly verbal' effects that are 'seemingly endemic to the language', and similarly a means to impersonality. In neither case, of course, does 'impersonality' mean that the poetry is not rooted in personal experience, and in neither case is the poet really 'invisible', but in both cases the reader is deterred from substituting a voyeuristic interest in the poet's personal life for a reading of the poetry.

The most extreme example of this effect is her use of cliché. Again she has spoken of this in interview:

> I think often the most tragic or joyous moments are expressed in cliché. So if I was to write a love poem which said 'When I look at you I am over the moon, let's go to bed and make a spoon', which are things I do say in real speech, as a poem it would look banal or awful. But if you can bring things into a poem at a particular stage, almost ordering it musically, you can perhaps bring out what you hear in

35

them anyway. So I would often put a cliché in italics, or a fragment of speech that seems very ordinary, next to something else in the hope that it would nudge the reader into seeing it the way I do.[12]

This device is most extensively and strikingly used in the poem 'The Brink of Shrieks', collected in *Selling Manhattan* and unfortunately not reprinted in *Selected Poems*. Apart from the title-phrase, this poem consists almost entirely of what would usually be considered cliché. But the effect is far from banal: it is vivid and emotionally compelling. Cliché is normally banal and deadly because it epitomises an inert, unquestioning, taken-for-granted notion of the relation between signifier and signified. Reading the poem, however, one struggles to interpret the situation that it refers to. The speaker is complaining vehemently about having 'fetched up / living with him'; 'he' is either mentally or physically disabled, or very eccentric, or some combination of the three: the vehemence of the speaker's complaint obliterates any clear sense of the situation (*SM*, p. 23). The experience of reading the poem is very like overhearing a conversation: no clues are provided to supplement the speaker's exasperated words. It is not even possible to say how justified the speaker is in feeling like this. If the poem consisted entirely of phrases like 'Up to the back teeth' and 'the tip of the iceberg' it might be considered simply as an exercise in the representation of this kind of speech. The last line, however, 'And me? I'm on the brink of shrieks', has a completely different quality. It is just as demotic as the rest of the poem; there is no sense of its having been infiltrated by the poet. But it also seems to have been forged in the feeling of the moment: it sways the reader's response in the speaker's favour and influences the reception of the rest of the poem's language in the way described by Duffy in the interview. This makes the poem different from the comparatively rare cases where Duffy merely represents language (the speech of the white children in 'Comprehensive' for example). In his essay 'Discourse in the Novel' Bakhtin speaks of words that are 'treated completely as objects, that is, deprived of any authorial intentions – not as a word that has been spoken, but as a word to be displayed'.[13] This is the most common way in which cliché is incorporated into literary texts, and it is the way Duffy uses language in the 'white' sections of 'Comprehensive'. 'The Brink of Shrieks' is an extreme example of Duffy's technique for rescuing the language that people actually speak from being 'treated completely as objects'.

In her excellent short monograph Deryn Rees-Jones valuably emphasises Duffy's early interest in surrealism which 'is in many ways symptomatic of her wish to revitalize language in a way which does not depend on a notion of the authority of a speaker or the authenticity of experience'.[14] 'The Brink of Shrieks' exemplifies one way in which Duffy does this, by literally constructing the speaker out of fragments of discourse. Another, more frequently used technique, on which many critics have commented, is the erosion of the boundary between the voice of the fictive persona and that of the poet. In 'Standing Female Nude' for example the artist's model who is nominally the speaker says,

> I shall be represented analytically and hung
> in great museums. The bourgeoisie will coo
> at such an image of a river-whore.
>
> (SFN, p. 46)

Her monologue concludes,

> These artists
> take themselves too seriously. At night I fill myself
> with wine and dance around the bars. When it's finished
> he shows me proudly, lights a cigarette. I say
> Twelve francs and get my shawl. It does not look like me.

There is, at least, a tension between these discourses. In Rees-Jones's terms, the intellectual critique of the first does not issue straightforwardly from an 'authenticity of experience' represented by the plebeian assertiveness of the second. This latter might seem more naturally to align itself with the most obvious, philistine interpretation of 'It does not look like me': a demand for photographic realism in art. However, the presence of the other discourse in the poem discourages the reader from settling conclusively on this interpretation, allowing room for speculation such as that of Linda Kinnahan:

> The 'me' of the poem is a self shaped by economic systems of exchange and by a set of discourses (moral, aesthetic and so on) that keeps this system in place. Rather than evoking an essentialized self or enacting a reification that excludes the material and discursive constituents of the 'self,' the dramatic monologue subverts its own conventional expectations and assumptions in dispersing the self.[15]

The erosion of the boundary between discourses not only reinforces this resistance to 'an essentialized self' but also helps to avoid the impression that the model is being straightforwardly 'represented' by the poet.

The model in 'Standing Female Nude' is one of a number of personae in Duffy monologues who speak with tremendous force and confidence. I suggest that this is partly because of the device I am discussing: the fact that her speech is not 'merely' represented, and that the discourse one might more readily ascribe to 'the poet' does not stand aloof but is combined with her voice. One might say that the poem endows her with this discourse. Partly for this reason most readers feel a strong balance of sympathy with the speaker even if they might feel that another view of the artist's work than hers is possible. (Indeed, the device I am describing is closer to the Cubism of the poem's artist 'Georges' – assumed by several critics to be Braque – than to the naive realism of 'It does not look like me'.)

Another poem whose persona speaks with great confidence is 'Psychopath'. This poem however works very differently from 'Standing Female Nude' and of course most readers respond very differently. One might say that the construction of this persona combines the methods of 'Standing Female Nude' and 'The Brink of Shrieks'. His speech is peppered with clichés – 'Let me make myself crystal', 'you feel like a king', 'Some little lady's going to get lucky tonight', 'I hope you rot in hell', 'Jack the Lad', 'You get one chance in this life', 'she asked for it' – and with stereotypical 1950s cultural references (*SM*, pp. 28–9). However, as Ian Gregson has remarked, our attention is drawn to 'a poetic voice speaking alongside the psychopathic one':[16] 'my shoes scud sparks against the night', Eliot's 'dull canal', 'The streets are quiet, as if the town has held its breath' which less explicitly and more incongruously recalls Wordsworth's 'Dear God! The very houses seem asleep; / And all that mighty heart is lying still!' ('Composed Upon Westminster Bridge').[17] Rather than seeing the contrast between these 'voices' as the most significant factor, one might think that they are linked by a common citational character, which includes, as I have argued elsewhere,[18] the 'reminiscences' (of sexual humiliation by 'Dirty Alice' at the age of 12 and witnessing his mother's adultery with the rent man) that offer insight into his psychological condition. As I have also argued elsewhere[19], the title is deceptive, offering to label as an essential identity something that is 'linguistically self-generating'. Conventionally, if there is one word that is indisputably the author's, it is the title, but Duffy subtly withdraws from the title of this poem. As Ian Gregson has written, the poem gives 'self-reflexive prominence to problems of representation'[20] and this extends to the most assertively representational word of all. The speaker of this poem is much more obviously and self-consciously a linguistic and cultural construct than that of 'Standing Female Nude', but he speaks, as I have said, with just as much force and confidence. As with the earlier poem there is no separation between a representing and a represented voice: all the discourses in the poem belong to the speaker. Hence, although Deryn Rees-Jones is right to stress the importance of images of reflection, I would not agree with her that the persona 'fails to identify with his own reflection' when he says, 'My reflection sucks a sour Woodbine and buys me a drink. Here's / looking at you.'[21] There is undoubtedly a sardonic wit in the citation of a phrase that epitomises both classic Hollywood romance and its 'male gaze', when talking about looking at himself in a mirror, but to suppose that he does not identify with his reflection would be to attribute this wit to a superior representing voice that, I have argued, the poem excludes (at a more banal level, if he does not identify with his reflection how does he know that its Woodbine is sour?).

A similar claim can be made in respect of many other Duffy personae who might seem to be objectively 'represented'. The 'Captain of the 1964 *Top of the Form* Team' is another persona whose discourse is largely made up of time-bound cultural references. Not only is he obviously aware of this, but the most pungent 'authorial' comments are attributable to him. Perhaps the most brilliant of these is 'I look / so brainy [in the team photograph] you'd think I'd just had a bath' (*MT*, pp. 7–8), which Sean O'Brien describes as 'a historically perfect conflation of education and class aspiration'.[22]

There are extreme cases of poems so 'linguistically self-generating' that it is impossible to construct any speaker at all. Perhaps the only example in Duffy's *oeuvre* is '$' (*SFN*), which consists entirely of meaningless phonemes from pop songs. 'Poet for Our Times' (*TOC*), which consists largely of tabloid headlines, comes close. Here the speaker is a composer of such headlines, but he resembles Steve Bell's cartoon character Harry Hardnose rather than a human being, and in this case the poem's witty punchline, 'The instant tits and bottom line of art' (*TOC*, p. 50), definitely sounds like the satirical poet breaking in, rather than the speaker himself. Linda Kinnahan considers that 'Translating the English, 1989' (*TOC*) is such a poem, but I think it is a more interesting case.

Welcome to my country! We have here Edwina Currie
and The Sun newspaper. Much excitement.
Also the weather has been most improving
even in February. Daffodils. (Wordsworth. Up North.) If you like
Shakespeare or even Opera we have too the Black Market.
For two hundred quids we are talking Les Miserables,
nods being as good as winks.

(*TOC*, p. 11)

Kinnahan comments:

> Paratactically arranged, each phrase stands equally with others,
> although it is suggested that in the official version of 'the English,' a
> more hierarchically structured discourse would subordinate or elimi-
> nate the less savory details, such as 'plenty rape' (in the final lines) or
> 'Ireland not on.' The parataxis works to 'translate' the official version
> of England – the nationalism of 'my country' – into a form encourag-
> ing us to make connections between Shakespeare or Opera and the
> Black Market. Although an 'I,' or more precisely a 'my,' speaks this
> poem, it is neither unified nor singular. Rather, the poem seems spo-
> ken or produced by various discourses: tourism, nationalism, high
> culturalism, journalism, the vernacular.[23]

Kinnahan's point about parataxis is excellent, and I would add that, as
the date in the title suggests, the parataxis is allied to synchronicity, so
that comparatively ephemeral events, such as Edwina Currie's gaffe
about eggs, appear on the same level as matters of more enduring
importance. It is also true that, like 'Psychopath', 'The Captain of the
1964 *Top of the Form* Team', 'Poet for Our Times' and '$', it is largely
the product of pre-existing discourses. However, we have seen that the
possibilities of an imaginable subject of such a poem vary consider-
ably. In this case the idea of translation is crucial, and in more than the
metaphorical sense suggested by Kinnahan. As well as the pre-existing
discourses, 'language' in a more technical sense contributes to the
effect of the poem. It is full of non-idiomatic peculiarities such as the
inappropriate use of the continuous present, redundant definite articles and plurals where the singular is the norm. These are combined
with slightly stylised idiomatic expressions such as 'we are talking',
'Squire' and 'plenty' (as in 'plenty rape') (*TOC*, p. 11). Bizarrely, given
the subject matter, it reads as if it were translated into English from
another language by a non-native speaker who has learned English
idioms from a book. The poem's epigraph is '. . . *and much of the poetry,*

*alas, is lost in translation',* another piece of anonymous 'discourse', and I would agree with Kinnahan that what is lost, the 'poetry', is the ideological cloak of Englishness stripped away by the paratactical arrangement. But Kinnahan does not mention that the poem is very funny, and the humour derives from these other linguistic peculiarities. It is a comic 'turn' like (to take an example contemporary with the poem's date) Harry Enfield's Greek take away owner, Stavros. The point is not to laugh at the expense of foreigners, but it is a classic satirical defamiliarisation device, an 'innocent-eye' view provided by the peculiarities of the speaker's command of English.

Deryn Rees-Jones has written of an 'anxiety' in Duffy's poetry 'concerning not only female power but the representation of female subjectivity' which enables her 'to position herself in her dramatic monologues as both self and other'.[24] I agree with this, and would add that not only is it a feature of dramatic monologues but it problematises the distinction between dramatic monologue and lyric utterance. The erosion (or obscuring) of the boundary between self and other is partly achieved by Duffy's characteristically slippery use of personal pronouns. These words' character as 'shifters' has been, via Jakobson and Barthes, central to the development of post-structuralist theory, and Duffy's exploitation of this partly explains the attraction of many explicitly post-structuralist critics, such as Jane E. Thomas,[25] Linda Kinnahan and Deryn Rees-Jones to this ostensibly 'accessible' poet. Alan Robinson has written illuminatingly of the way the pronouns 'vacillate indeterminately' in 'Naming Parts', 'compounding the experiential turmoil that compels the reader to undergo the stressful breakdown in communication that is the poem's subversive technique as well as its theme'.[26] This is not a peculiarity of this particular poem. The speaker in a Duffy poem might use 'I', 'we', 'she' or 'you', and any of these pronouns may have an indeterminate relationship to a reader's sense of an authorial position. To take a simple example, most readers will feel that the 'she' of 'Postcards' (*SM*) or 'Crush' (*MT*) is closer to the author than the 'I' of 'Education for Leisure' (*SFN*) or 'Psychopath', and not only for reasons of gender. Most characteristic and interesting is Duffy's use of 'you' which, in addition to the shiftiness characteristic of all pronouns, may be a distanced way of saying 'I', a more informal version of 'one', or a direct address to an interlocutor, either singular or plural. It is obviously the most powerful pronoun for implicating the reader. There are many examples in Duffy's poetry, but I will focus on three very different ones, 'Foreign' (*SM*), 'Adultery' (*MT*) and 'Practising Being Dead' (*SM*).

I have discussed 'Foreign' elsewhere[27] as a prime example of what Bakhtin calls 'sympathetic co-experiencing':

> Sympathetic co-experiencing of the hero's life means to experience that life in a form completely different from the form in which it was, or could have been, experienced by the *subiectum* of that life himself. Co-experiencing in this form does not in the least strive toward the ultimate point of coinciding, merging with the co-experienced life ... A sympathetically co-experienced life is given form not in the category of the *I*, but in the category of the *other*, as the life of *another* human being, another *I* ... [It] is essentially experienced *from outside*.[28]

The poem begins,

> Imagine living in a strange, dark city for twenty years.
> There are some dismal dwellings on the east side
> And one of them is yours. On the landing, you hear
> Your foreign accent echo down the stairs.
>
> (*SM*, p. 47)

So far we seem to be asked to do no more than imagine ourselves in another situation. As the poem develops, however, it is filled with motifs which make it clear that 'you' is not the (educated, western) reader in a different situation but a migrant worker from the Third World displaced in Europe. Thus to hear 'Your foreign accent' shifts between hearing your own accent as foreign to others and imagining that you have an accent that is foreign to yourself: 'not in the category of the *I*, but in the category of the *other*' (Bakhtin's formulation chimes interestingly with Rees-Jones's). This effect is intensified in the poem's conclusion:

> Imagine
> That one of you says *Me not know what these people mean.*
> *It like they only go to bed and dream.* Imagine that.

I think the point of the last two words is that this is literally unimaginable. To do so would be to occupy a position that is simultaneously inside (to be 'one of you') and outside (to hear the speech of 'one of you' as a stereotypical representation of foreignness). This impossible position is one that Duffy's poetry often occupies discursively: this is the poem that pushes its contradictions to the furthest extreme.

'Adultery' is perhaps Duffy's most dialogic poem. It can be read as the utterance of a single subject (addressing her/himself as 'you') but it incorporates a range of sharply contrasting attitudes and subject positions. There is intimate recollection of sexual pleasure ('your face / on a white sheet, gasping, radiant, yes') where despite the second person only one subject seems to be involved (*MT*, pp. 38–9). But this is cut across by sharply hostile and sarcastic utterances: 'You're a bastard', 'You know all about love, / don't you', 'You're an expert, darling'. While the first discourse is fairly easily translatable into the first person, the second would become at best sickly self-blame and at worst meaningless. Thus within the same poem the second person functions both as intimate self-address and as the internalisation (or quotation) of another voice (at one point this becomes a literal dialogue: 'You did it. / What. Didn't you. Fuck. Fuck.').

In 'Practising Being Dead' 'you' are asked to perform an act of imagination as difficult as that of 'Foreign'. Imagining the relationship of the dead subject to her/his own life entails slippages of temporality as well as of person:

> Inside, the past is the scent of candles the moment
> they go out. You saw her, ancient and yellow,
> laid out inside that alcove at the stairhead.
>
> (*SM*, p. 9)

First person shifts to third as present shifts to past, and time is spatialised to represent the absolute futurelessness of death in a way that is reminiscent of 'Down the passage which we did not take' in 'Burnt Norton':

> It is accidental and unbearable to recall that time,
> neither bitter nor sweet but gone, the future
> already lost as you open door after door, each one
> peeling back a sepia room empty of promise.[29]

This destabilisation of time, space and person epitomises Duffy's resistance to what Rees-Jones calls 'an authenticity of everyday lived experience'.[30] The reader is asked to engage with an act of imagining precisely what could not be grounded in such an authenticity. This is an extreme and special case, but nearly all Duffy's poems make the reader engage with what is going on in the text, rather than leaning on a facile referentiality.

This is the quality above all that Duffy shares with Eliot, though it is probably not what she was thinking of when she spoke of him as 'one who devastated me and made me shiver': that sounds like a more 'visceral' response to Eliot's language, oddly similar to that of F.R. Leavis when he first read poems such as 'Portrait of a Lady', returning traumatised from the trenches.[31] I want to conclude by returning to the comparison with Eliot, to make the final point that, while the two poets share this impersonality, it is achieved by each of them in a very different way.

When one reads lines like the following from 'Portrait of a Lady', it is hard to believe that Eliot succeeded in constructing himself as an impersonal, invisible poet:

> I take my hat: how can I make a cowardly amends
> For what she has said to me?
> You will see me any morning in the park
> Reading the comics and the sporting page.
> Particularly I remark
> An English countess goes upon the stage.
> A Greek was murdered at a Polish dance,
> Another bank defaulter has confessed.
> I keep my countenance,
> I remain self-possessed
> Except when a street-piano, mechanical and tired
> Reiterates some worn-out common song
> With the smell of hyacinths across the garden
> Recalling things that other people have desired.
> Are these ideas right or wrong?[32]

It is true that a certain air of impersonality is acquired from the borrowed Laforguian manner, but the passage goes far beyond Laforguian dandyism and indeed the concluding lines from 'Except' rebuke the brittleness of the foregoing lines (a superb example of Eliot's 'visceral' effect, achieved largely by rhythmical means). Although the speaker begins by 'performing' his persona and inviting the reader to take an external view of him, the final effect is one of intense *interiority*, and it is this very interiority, the speaker's 'own voice', that delivers judgement. At the same time, classic Eliot effects such as 'the smell of hyacinths across the garden' are completely textual; they owe nothing to an imputed 'authenticity of lived experience'; their power would be diminished by biographical reference.

Compare these lines from 'Adultery', also about guilt.

> You know all about love,
> don't you. Turn on your beautiful eyes
> for a stranger who's dynamite in bed, again
> and again; a slow replay in the kitchen
> where the slicing of innocent onions
> scalds you to tears. Then, selfish autobiographical sleep
>
> in a marital bed, the tarnished spoon of your body
> stirring betrayal, your heart over-ripe at the core.
> You're an expert, darling; your flowers
> dumb and explicit on nobody's birthday.

In one sense this is more determinate than Eliot's poem. While it is never clear exactly how his speaker has betrayed the lady, this poem is brutally explicit. Where it is less straightforward is that it does not commit itself to a single subject-position and therefore to interiority. This *could* be construed, like Eliot's persona reading the paper, as a speaker performing her / his self-judgement. However, almost every word could equally be attributed to another subject-position, that of the betrayed partner. For all the emotional intensity of the poem, the reader remains outside, 'sympathetically co-experiencing' but not identifying. This is the distinctive character of Duffy's impersonality.

### Notes

1   Andrew McAllister, 'Carol Ann Duffy: An Interview with Andrew McAllister', *Bête Noire*, 6 (winter 1988), pp. 69–77, p. 73.
2   T.S. Eliot, *Collected Poems 1909–1962* (London: Faber, 1963), p. 109.
3   Hugh Kenner, *The Invisible Poet: T.S. Eliot* (London: Methuen, 1965 [1959]), p. 4.
4   T.S. Eliot, *Selected Essays* (London: Faber, 1951), p. 18.
5   Kenner, p. 4.
6   Valerie Eliot (ed.), *The Waste Land Facsimile and Transcript* (London: Faber, 1971).
7   Eliot, *Collected Poems*, p. 70.
8   Ibid., p. 74.
9   Eliot, *Selected Essays*, p. 18.
10  Katharine Viner, 'Metre Maid', *The Guardian Weekend*, 25 September 1999, pp. 20–6, p. 20.
11  Alan Robinson, *Instabilities in Contemporary British Poetry* (Basingstoke: Macmillan, 1988), p. 201.
12  McAllister, p. 75.

13 M.M. Bakhtin, 'Discourse in the Novel', in Michael Holquist (ed.), *The Dialogic Imagination*, trans. Caryl Emerson and Michael Holquist (Austin: University of Texas Press, 1981), p. 321.

14 Deryn Rees-Jones, *Carol Ann Duffy* (Plymouth: Northcote House, 1999), p. 12.

15 Linda Kinnahan, '"Look for the Doing Words": Carol Ann Duffy and Questions of Convention', in James Acheson and Romana Huk (eds), *Contemporary British Poetry: Essays in Theory and Criticism* (Albany: State University of New York Press, 1996), p. 260.

16 Ian Gregson, *Contemporary Poetry and Postmodernism: Dialogue and Estrangement* (Basingstoke: Macmillan, 1996), p. 97.

17 *The Oxford Authors: William Wordsworth*, ed. Stephen Gill (Oxford: Oxford University Press, 1986 [1984]), p. 285.

18 Neil Roberts, *Narrative and Voice in Postwar Poetry* (Harlow: Longman, 1999), p. 190.

19 Ibid.

20 Gregson, p. 99.

21 Rees-Jones, p. 22.

22 Sean O'Brien, *The Deregulated Muse: Essays on Contemporary British and Irish Poetry* (Newcastle-upon-Tyne: Bloodaxe, 1998), p. 163.

23 Kinnahan, p. 254.

24 Rees-Jones, p. 43.

25 Jane E. Thomas, '"The Intolerable Wrestle with Words": the Poetry of Carol Ann Duffy', *Bête Noire*, 6 (winter 1988), pp. 78–88.

26 Robinson, *Instabilities in Contemporary British Poetry*, p. 201.

27 Roberts, pp. 185–6.

28 M.M. Bakhtin, 'Author and Hero in Aesthetic Activity', in Michael Holquist and Vadim Liapunov (eds), *Art and Answerability: Early Philosophical Essays by M.M. Bakhtin*, trans. Vadim Liapunov (Austin: University of Texas Press, 1990), p. 82.

29 T.S. Eliot, *The Four Quartets* (London: Faber, 1959), p. 13.

30 Rees-Jones, p. 3.

31 Ian Mackillop, *F.R. Leavis: A Life in Criticism* (London: Allen Lane, 1995), p. 50.

32 Eliot, *Collected Poems*, pp. 20–1.

# 2

## Female metamorphoses:
## Carol Ann Duffy's Ovid

### JEFFREY WAINWRIGHT

> I talk
> to myself in shapes, though something is constantly changing
> the world, rearranging the face which stares at mine.[1]

AT READINGS, Carol Ann Duffy regularly explains the curiosity that her poem '*from* Mrs Tiresias' bears that prefix because 'an academic' had once condescendingly pointed out that there was 'of course' more to the Tiresias story than her poem allowed. The subsequent addition of '*from*' to a poem that has no other parts is her tongue-in-cheek response to pedantry. It might also be taken as warning-off ponderous dissection of poems that she introduces as 'entertainments', and certainly any consideration of them needs to keep in mind the lightsome satirical tone that dominates *The World's Wife*. None the less, in this discussion of the poems from that volume which, like '*from* Mrs Tiresias', re-work stories from Ovid's *Metamorphoses*, I want to suggest that there is indeed 'more' to the Tiresias myth, and that a good part of that is explored in the other Ovidian poems in the book.

Duffy's predilection for the subjects and styles of myth and fable has been marked from her earliest published work. *Standing Female Nude* includes 'Girl Talking' and 'Comprehensive', both of which use the direct statement and naive voice of traditional story-telling. The truth of the naive vision of the child-speakers of 'Comprehensive' is perceived via the ironic gap between what they say and what we the readers know, or think we know. In the satirical mode of *The World's Wife* it is the voices that are usually knowing and their men-folk naively or obtusely ignorant, but there is the same use of the place-ment of voice and the same liking for folk-tale elements as can be found at the opening of 'Dies Natalis' – 'When I was cat, my mistress tossed me sweetmeats' (*SM*, p. 10) – or in 'Model Village', which jux-taposes stanzas in a childlike voice – 'Cows say *Moo*' (*SM*, p. 21) – with the haunted voice of a secret matricide. Sartre wrote of searching myths 'for stories so sublimated that they are recognizable to every-one, without recourse to minute psychological details'.[2] Duffy puts to use that quality of recognition, and the stripped, elemental character of folk tale and myth in poems that might be said to inhabit the ground evoked in the phrase from the opening poem of *The World's Wife*, 'Lit-tle Red-Cap': 'At childhood's end'.[3]

'At childhood's end', as that poem's variation of the Little Red Rid-ing Hood fable shows, is a treacherous, uncertain, obscure and *trans-forming* place and time. It involves the metamorphosis – Ovid's great eponymous theme – from child to adult, and the progressive realisa-tion that changeability and confusion, especially regarding gender and sexuality, do not end there. Indeed, although fairy stories are sup-posed to begin 'once upon a time' and end 'happily ever after', through his twelve books Ovid's tales have no self-enclosed openings and end-ings but wind one continuous thread in which everything is connected, one story merging immediately into the next. Italo Calvino writes of

> a proliferation of tales and cycles of tales. Earthly forms and stories repeat heavenly ones, but both intertwine around each other in a double spiral. This contiguity between gods and humans – who are related to the gods and are the objects of their compulsive desires – is one of the dominant themes of the *Metamorphoses*, but this is simply as a specific instance of the contiguity that exists between all the fig-ures and forms of the existing world, whether anthropomorphic or otherwise.[4]

Thus there is always 'more', and when Carol Ann Duffy selects her portion of the Tiresias myth, and the novel invention of telling it through the voice of the seer's spouse, so much of the rest of the story is implied.

Duffy's Tiresias is a self-important cove, a creature of habits – remembering his stick, walking the dog, writing to *The Times* – con-ceivably an academic, imaginably, with his 'open-necked shirt, / and a jacket of Harris tweed I'd patched at the sleeves myself' (*TWW*, p. 14),

F.R. Leavis. The stick will be the one which, in Ovid, he shook impatiently at two copulating snakes in his path resulting in his being suddenly changed into a woman. The poem then enjoys itself satirising ham-fisted masculine helplessness as Tiresias grapples with the novel problems of blow-drying his hair, shopping and periods. The self-importance carries over into new pontifications such as 'telling the women out there / how, as a woman himself, he knew how we felt'. He is however asexual. When, 'after the split', Mrs T. sees him escorted by 'powerful men', she knows 'there'd be nothing of *that* / going on / if he had his way'. It is here that Duffy makes her most radical revision of the myth. In *Metamorphoses*, Tiresias' first interference with the snakes is followed by a repeated occasion when he gets changed back into a man. But Ovid sets this in the context of a quarrel between Jupiter and Juno as to whether the man or the woman derives the greater pleasure from sex. It is Tiresias' transsexual experience which makes him the perfect witness to resolve the argument, and when he does so by reporting in favour of Jupiter's contention that the greater pleasure is woman's, the indignant Juno strikes him blind. Why so? Roberto Calasso in his remarkable book on the myths, *The Marriage of Cadmus and Harmony*, offers this explanation:

> Tiresias was trespassing upon a secret, one of those secrets sages are called upon to safeguard rather than reveal. . . . [he] confirmed an antique doubt, a fear at least as old as the ruttish daughters of the sun. Perhaps woman, that creature shut away in the gynaceum, where 'not a single particle of true eros penetrates' knew a great deal more than her master, who was always cruising about gymnasiums and porticoes.[5]

All of this may or may not be in the unwritten portions of 'Mrs Tiresias', but most likely not since her Tiresias is surely too sensually obtuse to gain any such knowledge himself. Changed to a woman, he yet remains incorrigibly a man. Only belatedly does something begin to dawn as his erstwhile wife introduces him to her lover and he becomes transfixed by her physical beauty and sexual allure. He pictures 'her bite at the fruit of my lips' and hears 'my red wet cry in the night'. Here, in Duffy's revision, is Juno's secret and it is a lesbian one.

This glimmering apprehension might be Duffy's glance at the foresight granted Tiresias by Jupiter as consolation for Juno's vindictiveness. In Ovid the first prediction of that foresight also bears upon love and lovemaking in his reply to the question about the beautiful child Narcissus who he predicts will indeed live long – if he does not come to know himself. Of course it is Narcissus' love for his own image in the pool that annihilates him, an off-stage, more tragic trope of the masculine self-absorption that is the object of Duffy's robust satire. Besides her Tiresias, her characterisations of Orpheus, Sisyphus and Midas all share something of Mrs Icarus' estimate of her husband: 'a total, utter, absolute, Grade A pillock' (*TWW*, p. 54) – all men of futile action. This type of masculine obsession and self-obsession is often specified as an artist. Ignored to 'lie alone in the dark', Mrs Sisyphus likens herself to 'Frau Johann Sebastian Bach' and it is the poet Orpheus' vanity which proves his undoing. The wolf in 'Little Red-Cap' is the symbol of masculine poetry who must be slain. Pygmalion is another such figure, and in Duffy's radical re-writing of this myth instead of being deservingly triumphant he is confounded by his own discovery of Juno's secret.

In Ovid, Pygmalion's story begins with the Propoetides, a race of women who deny the divinity of Venus and whom she therefore turns into hardened prostitutes. It is the repulsion Pygmalion feels for them, and thus for the female sex, that draws him away to create the perfect, but utterly remote beauty of his statue. In his version of the myth in his *Tales from Ovid* Ted Hughes makes the progress of Pygmalion's disgust from the Propoetides to all women particularly emphatic. Whilst most of his versions hold close to the literal translations of Ovid, here he embellishes by adding his own metaphor which sees the transformation of

> Every woman's uterus to a spider.
> Her face, voice, gestures, hair became its web.
> Her perfume was a floating horror. Her glance
> Left a spider-bite. He couldn't control it.[6]

Hughes's elaboration has a Shakespearean ring to it reminiscent of the mad Lear's ravings: 'Down from the waist they are Centaurs . . . there's hell, there's darkness, / There is the sulphurous pit –' (*King Lear*, IV.vi). This is the misogynstic context of the Pygmalion story, but Duffy bides her time. 'Pygmalion's Bride' begins:

> Cold, I was, like snow, like ivory.
> I thought *He will not touch me*,
> but he did.
>
> (*TWW*, p. 51)

As Duffy's Pygmalion falls in love with his statue, his perfect woman, he courts her just as Ovid's does, except that 'his words were terrible' and the presents he thinks of as *girly things*'. Although she does not respond, he 'jawed all night' and will not desist. Traditionally the statue grows warm and comes to life and this is Pygmalion's reward for his skill and his pure faithfulness. Duffy's bride does the same, melts, kisses back:

> began to moan,
> got hot, got wild,
> arched, coiled, writhed,
> begged for his child,
> and at the climax
> screamed my head off –
> all an act.

> And haven't seen him since.
> Simple as that.
>
> (*TWW*, p. 52)

Pygmalion, an early worshipper in the long tradition of poetic and artistic idealisation of the feminine, cannot cope with the fleshly, sexual reality: simple as that.

This is one of the victories of liberation won by Duffy's 'wives'. Another is won by Eurydice, though this has a darker implication. There is local satire in the portrayal of 'Big O' with his 'poem to pitch' (*TWW*, p. 59) and the way that Eurydice speaks as though to friends gossiping on a hen-night. But in presenting him as an all-too-recognisable type of the contemporary career-poet, vain, fallible and insecure, Duffy debunks the idealisation of Orpheus as *the* type of the poet whose perfect mastery charms all of creation. The revelation that Eurydice *wants* to stay in the Underworld, and then contrives a way to exploit his vanity to make Orpheus turn so that she might sink back, undercuts one of the most enduring of hero-myths. The author's relish at this inversion is evident enough, but perhaps more interesting is the implication of Eurydice's preference for Hades – for death indeed. Wittily, this is the place of 'Eternal Repose', of resting in peace, more meaningfully, 'a black full stop, a black hole / where words had come to an end'. The living world is the world of language and the world of men which makes its opposite blissfully – and, as embodied in the poem's last lines – *lyrically* desirable:

51

> The dead are so talented.
> The living walk by the edge of a vast lake
> Near the wise, drowned silence of the dead.
>
> (*TWW*, p. 62)

Earlier in the poem, Eurydice has said 'I'd rather speak for myself / than be Dearest, Beloved, Dark Lady. . .', and in telling it like it was to her female friends she is. But in these last lines there seems to be a more profound voice, defiant, somewhat wistful, perhaps lonely but self-contained, suggestive of a quite different interior mode of being that can have an element of death-longing. It can be caught in other poems, perhaps even fleetingly in Mrs Sisyphus lying 'alone in the dark' as her husband toils mindlessly on. It is certainly mysteriously present at the end of 'Circe'. Again the leading voice in the poem belongs in the discourse of 'girls together', this time, inspired by the characterisation of Circe as the sorceress who turned men into swine, an acerbic parody of cookery advice: 'When the heart of the pig has hardened, dice it small' (*TWW*, p. 47). But immediately upon this lip-smacking climax the tone changes abruptly:

> I, too, once knelt on this shining shore
> watching the tall ships sail from the burning sun
> like myths; slipped off my dress to wade,
> breast-deep, in the sea, waving and calling;
> then plunged, then swam on my back, looking up
> as three black ships sighed in the shallow waves.
>
> (*TWW*, p. 48)

Then the tone switches back, just as brusquely, and dismisses this reverie as the mood of youth when she was 'hoping for men'. There are two possible ways of reading those lines. Either they are a parody of girlish romanticism which is promptly skewered by the wised-up voice of the man-eating cook, or they evoke a lost and lamented eroticism. Either way the two modes of sensuality in the poem lie against each other in an intriguing way. 'Breast-deep, in the sea, waving and calling' inevitably brings the echo of Stevie Smith's 'not waving but drowning'[7] and the black ships also speak of thanatos, that ancient association of the sea with oblivion and death. In Ovid 'no one had a heart more susceptible to love than Circe'.[8] Hence, perhaps, the hardening of heart and the sharpening of knives.

The Medusa is another female figure whose power and tragedy are inextricably bound together. Traditionally, the beautiful Medusa has been made hideous by the vengeful Athene after Poseidon has slept with her. In Duffy's account ('Medusa', *TWW*, pp. 40–1) her petrifying visage emerges from within the beautiful creature, a psychological distortion made manifest as a result of brooding upon 'A suspicion, a doubt, a jealousy' about masculine betrayal, the 'perfect man, Greek God', who will 'go, betray me, stray / from home.' Hence her inverting herself into not only the antithesis of beauty but the power that can turn everything she looks upon, even a buzzing bee, to stone. Characteristically the 'perfect man' comes 'with a shield for a heart / and a sword for a tongue' but as she draws him towards her there is an ironic ambiguity in her seduction: 'Wasn't I beautiful? / Wasn't I fragrant and young? / / Look at me now.' Look at me now and you too will be turned to stone, except that we readers know the end of the story and the stratagem of the shield as mirror which will enable Perseus to avoid her gaze and decapitate her. But 'Look at me now' is also a sorrowing cliché of the once beautiful woman. Thus is this apparent female power turned to tragic defeat.

There is something Bacchic, Dionysian, that is shared by Medusa, Circe, Eurydice, Mrs Tiresias and the bride of Pygmalion. All represent what men fear: the released, primarily sexual energy of the Dionysian band that, as Tiresias foretold, destroyed Pentheus; the same 'rout that made the hideous roar' who ripped the singing Orpheus' head from his shoulders in Milton's lament 'Lycidas'. In their superior knowingness and common sense, if not their agency, Thetis, Mrs Midas, Mrs Sisyphus and Mrs Icarus also have powers lacking in their stolid, blinkered men-folk. In both dimensions, this latter group's pragmatic appraisal of the realities of the world and the divinest sense that is the others' Dionysian madness, Duffy's Ovidian women, though only occasionally victorious, are the real Greek heroes.

The madness – if we must term it so – is largely to do with the death-longing perceptible in Eurydice, Circe and possibly Medusa. According to Roberto Calasso, citing Heraclitus, '"Hades and Dionysus are the same god"'.[9] Thus there is a connection between the pleasuring associated with Dionysus and the darkness of the Underworld, even the bliss of oblivion. In *The Marriage of Cadmus and Harmony*, Calasso writes:

> Some early poets suggest that Persephone felt a 'fatal desire' to be car-
> ried off, that she formed a 'love-pact' with the king of the night, that
> she shamelessly and willingly exposed herself to the contagion of
> Hades. Kore [Persephone] saw herself in Hades' pupil. She recog-
> nized, in the eye observing itself, the eye of the invisible other. She
> recognized that she belonged to that other.[10]

Persephone appears once in *The World's Wife* in the volume's last and
perhaps most uncharacteristic poem, 'Demeter', which with its four-
teen lines and closing couplet lightly brushes the sonnet form, takes
her mother's voice and it is one of great maternal tenderness. Much of
the story is implied, opening on a winter scene whose frozen hardness
Demeter tries to break with 'tough words' (*TWW*, p. 76). Her efforts
are unavailing for this is the drear half of the year in which Persephone
dwells with Hades. When, at line 7, Persephone does return with the
Spring, she simply appears, unbidden, 'from a long, long way'

> walking,
> my daughter, my girl, across the fields,
> in bare feet, bringing all the spring's flowers
> to her mother's house.

This image, so reminiscent of the picture of Spring in Botticelli's *Pri-
mavera* painting, achieves great delicacy through its pauses, the rein-
forcement – 'my daughter, my girl' – exactly carrying the goddess's
surge of relief and pride at her daughter's appearance. As the myth has
it that the world is transformed with the return of Persephone and
Spring, so is the human feeling of the mother at the return of her
daughter. Duffy succeeds here in melting together story and recognisable occurrence in a way that humanises the myth. That this is happening 'none too soon' with the familiarity of the phrase a part of this
humanisation, carries the implication of the long, preceding, barren
loneliness and that the interval of her visit will end all too soon. There
is of course nothing here ascribed to Persephone that could imply her
attraction to the Underworld. Indeed Demeter's emotion is the
warmest, most positive feeling to be seen among any of Duffy's Ovidian heroines. None the less, there is a remoteness in this Persephone
that comes of her passivity. Her presence is quietly but wholly joyous
for everything about her, yet she is given no word or action. She could
– as she will – drift equally smoothly, and indifferently, away.

The other image of motherhood in the Ovidian poems comes at the end of 'Thetis'. Here the shape-changing goddess flails and writhes through one creature and another in an effort to shake off the rapacious Peleus who will father the warrior Achilles upon her. Nothing she can do can make Peleus let go,

> So I changed, I learned,
> turned inside out – or that's
> how it felt when the child burst out.
> *(TWW, p. 6)*

Quite what this change, this learning *is* that comes with the child's birth I am not sure. The physical image is clear enough, and the implication must be that this turning 'inside out' is the one successful, truly transformative change of shape that Thetis makes. Or so she felt at that moment. Perhaps the suggestion lies here that while Thetis' and Demeter's motherhood is transforming and joyous beyond anything else, its joy will be limited by loss: the failure of Thetis finally to protect her son and Persephone's annual return to the 'drowned silence of the dead.' The strut of masculinity is mocked throughout *The World's Wife*, but the mother and child – seen here as the life force – are poised to withstand its more formidable face, war and death. To do so will require a further metamorphosis: changing the future.

## Notes

1  Carol Ann Duffy, 'Dies Natalis', in *Selling Manhattan* (London: Anvil, 1987), p. 10.
2  Quoted in Michael Grant, *Myths of the Greeks and Romans* (New York: Mentor, 1962), p. 280.
3  Carol Ann Duffy, *The World's Wife* (London: Picador, 1999), p. 3.
4  Italo Calvino, 'Ovid and Universal Contiguity', trans. Martin McLoughlin, in *Why Read the Classics?* (London: Vintage, 2000), pp. 25–6.
5  Roberto Calasso, *The Marriage of Cadmus and Harmony*, trans. Tim Parks (London: Vintage, 1994), p. 81.
6  Ted Hughes, 'Pygmalion', in *Tales of Ovid* (London: Faber, 1997), p. 145.
7  Stevie Smith, 'Not Waving but Drowning', *Collected Poems of Stevie Smith* (London: Allen Lane, 1975).
8  Ovid, *The Metamorphoses*, trans. Mary M. Innes (Harmondsworth: Penguin, 1981 [1955]), p. 11.
9  Roberto Calasso, *Literature and the Gods*, trans. Tim Parks (London: Vintage, 2000), p. 64.
10  Calasso, *The Marriage of Cadmus and Harmony*, pp. 209–10.

# 3

# Love and masculinity
# in the poetry of Carol Ann Duffy

ANTONY ROWLAND

THIS CHAPTER explores the shift in Carol Ann Duffy's poetry from the exuberance of the love lyrics in *Standing Female Nude* to the rejection of masculinities in the satirical poems of *The World's Wife*.[1] Male subjects are inextricably tied to the production of amorous poems in Duffy's first collection, whereas the later book *The Other Country* offers universalist accounts of sexual encounters in which love is primarily depicted as a linguistic phenomenon.[2] *The World's Wife* marks a critical departure from the earlier poetry in that men and masculinity are attacked constantly by more abrasive female narrators. This tendency is augmented by the more overtly homoerotic relationships between women in the collection, a sisterly bonding that, in poems such as '*from* Mrs Tiresias', is complemented by a celebration of lesbian sexuality. Duffy has often been pigeonholed as a lesbian poet, particularly by the media in the furore over the identity of the new Poet Laureate. Such a label might create a particular expectation for the love poetry: an engagement with relationships between women might be anticipated in the tradition of Adrienne Rich and Daphne Marlatt, whereas Duffy's early amorous lyrics depict the agonies of errant, or neglectful, male partners; even *The World's Wife* demonstrates that men and masculinity remain a site of (albeit critical) negotiation for the amorous subject. By following the development of Duffy's amorous poetics across the various collections since *Standing Female Nude*, a discursive trend can be detected in which men are, at first, desirable, but equally dangerous or pathetic, then negated, and paradoxically perpetuated, in the universal love poems of *The Other*

*Country*, and then rejected as irritating presences in the later poetry. By tracing this narrative, it becomes clear that Duffy is attempting from the outset, as Angelica Michelis has argued, to subvert classical traditions of the male (voyeur) poet and female muse.[3] A sensibility reigns in Duffy's work that is suspicious of the fact that, even in supposedly universal renderings of the elusive concept of *amor*, the subject has tended to remain male, or, at least, masculine. When the theorist Roland Barthes unveils a series of keywords to unpack the supposedly transcendent nature of love, the key figures are still male, such as Goethe's Werther and the narrator who shaves his head when jilted; his work is still rooted in the homosexual delights of Paris's gay scene rather than women's experience of male or female lovers.[4]

Although Duffy's later love poems grate against the celebrations of homosexual relationships in Barthes's treatise, her work is certainly responsive, and often resistant, to recent trends in critical theory. Owing to an interest boosted by her studies in modern philosophy at the University of Liverpool, her amorous lyrics are rooted in debates over the function of language, and the difficulties in formulating 'experience'; so much so that, as Linda Kinnahan has argued, her work has more in common with avant-garde poets in the USA and Canada than might at first be expected when a critic glances at the traditional forms of the vast majority of the texts.[5] The subject matter of Duffy's poems can be distinguished from the tradition of the western love lyric through her engagement with amorous situations in the modern world; her poems are littered with lovers who struggle to formulate their alienation amongst urban cityscapes. This may account for the vast number of amorous texts in which love is figured as an oppressive terror rather than erotic release. The amorous *flâneur* of critical theory might delight in the infinite erotic possibilities lurking in the crowd, but Duffy's narrators often respond to the metropolis as if it were a form of pornography, offering, but constantly delaying, fulfilment.[6] Amorous commitment is celebrated, rather than postmodern romance, with its parasitic relationship to consumer culture. Surrealist influences inform this loyalty: bourgeois culture is potentially upset by the exuberant celebration of the amorous in the middle of office blocks, phone booths and railway stations. Within this cityscape, Duffy analyses amorous linguistics: she mirrors Roland Barthes's *Fragments d'un discours amoreux* in her post-structuralist investigation of stock phrases such as 'I love you'. Romance in Duffy's work is composed of duplicitous *texts* in which lovers can be heroes as well as 'bastards'.[7] 'Bastard', with its peculiarly gendered etymology, marks out the usurper of the idealist, amorous moment as an errant male.[8] Apart from the texts depicting overt lesbian eroticism, masculinity, particularly in the early poems, functions as an unsettling force that exasperates the surrealist lover's search for subversive *jouissance*. Indeed, the poetry gradually moves from frustration to rejection as the number of love poems decreases across Duffy's *oeuvre*. This dissipation is encouraged by her deployment (influenced by Robert Browning, T.S. Eliot and Sylvia Plath) of the dramatic monologue: when men are (ostensibly) given the opportunity to express desire, the result is not the tender machinations of a writer such as Hugo Williams. Across the collections as a whole, a polymorphous love poetry ensues in which the sexual conquests of a psychopath vie with explorations of lesbian eroticism. When Duffy attempts to depict masculine desire, disturbed narrators tend to ensue rather than more 'normative' amorous discourses, which is why I compare her work to that of Ian McEwan in another essay; McEwan has a similar predilection for the perverse in his early fiction.[9] However, whereas McEwan persists in his engagement with men and masculinity in his later texts, they gradually disappear from view in Duffy's. Compared to the fifteen or so love poems addressed to men in *Standing Female Nude*, *The Pamphlet* contains two, one of which presents an allegory of men as pigs who would be less harmful if allowed to sizzle on a spit.[10] In *The World's Wife*, with its relentless attack on different forms of negative masculinity, men are cradle snatchers, obnoxious poets, hunters, bad lovers, greedy capitalists, whingers, jealous, spiteful or boring husbands, obsessives, penis worshippers, emotionless strongmen, adulterers, Viagra-wielding sex pests, libertine princes, devils, apes and, again, pigs.

## Love and the city

Love, like religion, might appear anti-ideological, since it creates a sense of collectivity which seems naturally anti-institutional, but sex, desire, eroticism and the amorous are contingent, and this dependency is reflected in cultural products such as poetry. In contrast, Sasha Weitman has explored socioerotic life by listing its universal laws and rules, such as the romantic connotations of a log fire, but such signs are unstable: most of her examples are clearly cultural stereotypes of western romance to be found in many Mills and Boon and Harlequin novels.[11] They invite agency: such signs may be rejected or endorsed (or ironically endorsed) by amorous subjects, or regarded quizzically by cultures in which a handful of roses has no pre-ordained meaning. Krafft-Ebing has written of more perverse amorous signs outside poetry, such as the fetish of the handkerchief.[12] According to this writer, gangs of giddy Victorian men cruised the streets in an attempt to steal the handkerchiefs of unassuming ladies. Such peculiar signs are not limited to Victorian history. During the Renaissance, even the lowly prune had the potential to function in love poetry as an amorous sign: in George Wither's 'A Love Sonnet', the subversive lovers sneak off into a boat loaded with cream, cakes and prunes.[13] Other, more traditional, poetic signs include doves (Swinburne's 'The Leper'), birds in general (Spenser's 'Epithalamion'), spring, summer and nature (Shakespeare's sonnets), flowers (Robert Burns's 'A Red, Red Rose'), eyes (William Barnes's 'White an' Blue'), fire (Sidney's 'Dear, why make you more of a dog than me?') and storms (Wyatt's 'The Lover Compareth his State to a Ship in a Perilous Storm Tossed on the Sea').[14] In Duffy's early love poems, the amorous signs are reproduced from western culture, particularly from the English and French traditions of the love lyric. For example, in 'This Shape', roses, sheets, doves, blood, pearls, smoke, tongues, hearts, the sea, sleep, storms and stars are associated, conventionally, with amorous desire (p. 17). In the later poem 'Adultery' from *Mean Time*, however, the amorous signs are markedly different (pp. 38–9). Strangers, dark glasses, money, phones, a clock, cabs, lunch, restaurants, alcohol and a gift of flowers are deployed to forge a modern, urban version of the love lyric.

'Adultery' clearly demonstrates that amorous signs are contingent. Indeed, Mike Featherstone has argued that contemporary urban life requires a specific code of love, which might include an exaggerated eyebrow or a lingering chink of wine glasses as possible preludes to sex.[15] In 'Adultery', this code includes the errant hand on the thigh that 'tilts' the restaurant (p. 39). However, as opposed to the triumphant celebrations of postmodern love in recent amorous theory, Duffy's poetry is wary of a dialectic between love and the city. In contrast, Jeffrey Weeks has celebrated the fragmentation of traditional amorous relationships, and the subsequent 'becoming' of an androgynous sexual citizen.[16] Amorous somatic pleasure is theorised as anti-consumerist in time and space: it is mainly experienced during the evening or at the weekend, in the home or a hotel; hence the office affair functions as a potential site for transgressive sexual activity. Such idealism needs to be tempered with a dialectic in which love is dependent on, and supportive of, late capitalism: in this context, shenanigans over the photocopier can be regarded as the most conservative of amorous encounters. Late nineteenth-century employers provided the full weekend as an opportunity for excursions: within such patent constraints, the amorous then appears to flourish in the twentieth-century phenomenon of the 'dirty weekend'. As with the amorous possibilities inherent in the concept of leisure time, the modern city tends to be depicted as an erotic marvel, in which sexual fantasies flourish in the crowd; Zygmunt Bauman refers to this as 'free-floating eroticism'.[17] Different levels of pornography draw on this phenomenon by depicting supposedly transgressive sex in cash-machine booths, cars, aeroplanes and so on; hence the recent furore over a hard-core sex flick which was being filmed in the car park of a major airport. Such films exploit the postmodern telecity, in which the urban crowd mirrors the strangers seen daily on television. Constantly mixing fantasy and reality, amorous excitement is generated in the telecity by the mere 'glance of someone in the crowd, or the glimpse of a face on an advertising poster'.[18] In contrast, when the philosopher Theodor Adorno gazes at a model's beautiful teeth in an advert, he can think only of the victim's grimace in a torture chamber.[19] Adorno's response in *Minima Moralia* highlights the undialectical nature of many recent sociological accounts of the city, and supports Duffy's critique in her poetry; eroticism *passim* cannot be positive. Bauman refers to its prevalence as leading to a 'rapid emaciation of human relations': sexual advances are now commonly detected in friendly conversations at work, and abuse in family photographs of children cavorting naked in paddling pools.[20]

Modernist concerns over the encroaching metropolis inform Adorno's *moralia*. Duffy's wariness of the city as a site of erotic marvels is informed in her early poetry by Modernist poetry rather than philosophy: idealist theories of urban love clash with the amorous despair illustrated in 'I Remember Me' and 'Telephoning Home'; both texts are influenced in particular by the writing of T.S. Eliot. Aesthetics of erotic teeth in Adorno form symptoms of a process in which eroticism is deployed by mass culture as a kind of terror. Duffy's 'I Remember Me' thus proves to be a committed work of art in its late-modernist attempt to separate the erotic from the city, and its rejoinder to amorous identity as fickle flexibility rather than an on-going process.[21] In its prosaic descriptions of the amorous subject on a platform, it engages with unrequited *amor*. Modern narratives of marriage and romance denigrate the individual who cannot, or who may not wish to, love: here, non-identity with these 'universal' concepts leads to a double alienation from both the city and the amorous in general. 'Despair stares out from the tube-trains at itself / running on the platform for the closing door': the metrical break instigated by the internal rhyme (Despair / stares), and the echo of vowel sounds (platform / for) stresses the hermetic nature of modern urban life (*SFN*, p. 16). Being 'safe' on the tube is considered alongside the process of running desperately for the train; Duffy's poem mirrors Adorno's detection of 'an impression of terror' when watching people run in the streets.[22] Lovers also pass in the rain and do not know you 'when you speak' in 'I Remember Me': the neurosis explored in the surreal dream reflects the urbanity of strangers in which the amorous object can easily revert to the seemingly autonomous *flâneur*; urban love in this poem is depicted as a kind of enforced onanism with the alienated self (p. 16). Late capitalist society is based on the fantasy of individual autonomy in a world of strangers. In Philip Larkin's poetry, this proves exciting, as the faces of strangers start 'The whole shooting-match off' in 'Wild Oats'.[23] But this co-exists with a paradoxical desire for security, a tension explored throughout Larkin's work. Strangers pervade Duffy's work too: the word appears in 'Telephoning Home', in which 'The stranger waiting outside [the phone box] stares / through the glass that isn't there', and in other texts such as 'Plainsong', 'Saying Something' and 'Mrs Skinner, North Street' (*SM*, p. 52). Postmodern love mirrors economic exchange by emphasising short-term amorous contracts between strangers, and the intensity of the affair (as in 'Adultery'). Consumer culture as a whole proves hostile to amorous commitment: orgasm mirrors the sound investment package as the ultimate stake, which Viagra seeks to democratise. This process is reflected in an article from a 1998 edition of *The Times* entitled 'Sex Drug Turns Aged Tycoon into Errant Stud', in which a 63-year-old woman sued Viagra for two million dollars on grounds that their relationship broke up after his sexual potency was restored.[24] There is a direct link here to Duffy's poem 'Mrs Rip Van Winkle', in which an elderly woman enjoys artistic pursuits until the husband returns, 'rattling Viagra' (*TWW*, p. 53). Duffy produces poems which attempt to thwart the increasing capitulation of sex to a form of capital, and hard-core pornography's celebration of intercourse as an encounter with strangers: against urban alienation, she presents the supposed authen-ticity of the lover's discourse.[25] She attempts, in the early poetry, to produce transcendent love lyrics that might be anti-urban. In 'Tele-phoning Home', a phone conversation with the amorous object takes place in the alienating space of a railway station; it ends with the con-fident declaration that 'This is me speaking' (*SM*, p. 52). Having been pigeonholed by this time as a poet of the dramatic monologue, here Duffy renounces ventriloquism to give way to a supposedly unmiti-gated exposure of the amorous self.[26]

## Love and surrealism

This lack of mitigation can be further explicated by looking at Duffy's early interest in French surrealism. *Standing Female Nude* marks the high point of the amorous poetry in terms of its celebration of surreal-ist love. Sean O'Brien has argued that 'I Remember Me' from this col-lection is a promising (love) poem, but does not contain her 'most successful lines'.[27] Eliot's or Baudelaire's influence is hinted at; André Breton's first principles of surrealism, the Liverpool Poets, Larkin, and surrealist elements of modernist writing might be added to the list. Breton's first *Surrealist Manifesto* demonstrates Freud's influence on French surrealism by stressing that dreams and unconscious life, cou-pled with poetry, 'contain solutions to the gravest problems of human existence'.[28] Pure 'psychic automatism', he argued, expresses 'the real functioning of thought'.[29] In 'I Remember Me', the first two stanzas depict Duffy's attempt to peruse urban love through a nightmare in which neurosis is explored through refined automatic writing, com-posed in tranquillity.[30] Dreams, the narrator argues, define identity; they 'make us different' even though humans have a 'common (the same shaped?) skull' (*SFN*, p. 16). Aesthetic definitions of surrealism usually consist of the juxtaposition of opposites to evoke marvellous absurdity, as in the infamous example of Dalí's lobster telephone; hence in the first stanza the poet's face is planted on 'someone else' who uncannily 'gapes back'. Following the first manifesto's edict to dis-rupt the tyranny of the rational, the poem attempts to disrupt any possibility of a fixed reading. Instead of the stranger's face reflecting the poet's, the opening lines might depict members of a crowd who resemble the narrator, but are slightly different; they are, after all, 'paler'. This reading privileges narcissistic love, but here the amorous object refuses to recognise the poet; 'I Remember Me' is a love poem in the sense that the unrequited narrator mourns the fact that the amorous is poignantly absent in the urban cityscape. Duffy's elegiac tone mirrors that of the Liverpool Poets when the city and its suburbs evoke despair, as in Brian Patten's 'Near the factory where they make the lilac perfume'.[31] Urban banality in 'I Remember Me' also recalls the poetry of Larkin, as in the epiphanic moment in 'Dockery & Son' when the melancholic poet stares out across Sheffield's railway lines after eating an awful pie, and contemplates procreation as 'dilution'.[32] Similar moments occur in Duffy's poetry when the narrator fixes on the 'The wet platform' that 'stretches away from me towards the South and home' in 'Telephoning Home', and the calling of a child in 'Prayer' as though it signalled a 'loss' (*SM*, p. 52; *MT*, p. 52). Instances of a platform, faces and a crowd in 'I Remember Me' are reminiscent also of Ezra Pound's 'In a Station of the Metro', with its surrealist juxtaposition of petals with the 'apparition' of faces on the underground network.[33] Pound's haiku certainly connects with Duffy's espoused desire in 1988 to present the object 'as it is' rather than cloud it with emotional slither.[34] In *Standing Female Nude*, the imagist chimera of objectivity results in a love poetry that strives to present the amorous 'in itself', as a simultaneous affirmation of Bretonian psychic life amongst the alienating cityscape.[35]

'In a Station of the Metro' might be surreal*ist*, but a grave difference between surreal*ism* and high Modernism can be detected in the former's celebration of 'mad' love as anti-bourgeois. Deryn Rees-Jones analyses Duffy's relationship to surrealism, and provides an illuminating commentary on the influence of the female surrealist Méret Oppenheim in relation to the overt lesbian eroticism in 'Oppenheim's Cup and Saucer' from *Standing Female Nude* (p. 48).[36] Duffy's appropriation of 'first' surrealist principles can also be seen in her commitment to giving a (ventriloquised) voice to the underprivileged, and her anti-capitalist poetics. Surrealism has been regarded in the popular imagination as a purely aesthetic movement which lauds (*à la* Dalí) outrageous silliness, and yet Breton constantly stressed the early French surrealists' adherence to the cause of the proletariat, which occasioned a brief alliance with the Communist Party in the 1930s.

Duffy would have been well aware of this, since in 1978 she appears to have bought a book by Franklin Rosemont entitled *André Breton and the First Principles of Surrealism,* which emphasises throughout the revolutionary potential of the movement.[37] Mad love is presented in this text as wary of sex and eroticism. Procreation is regarded as a possibly commodified entity, whereas the amorous, practised preferably between two passionate, committed heterosexuals, attains transgressive potential with the possible 'irruption of desire into ordinary existence which could lead to the transformation of our being'.[38] After the first manifesto, surrealism became synonymous with love, and poetry: Breton commented that the latter is 'made in a bed' like the amorous; one of the early slogans for French surrealists was '*Si vous aimez l'amour vous aimerez surréalisme*' ('If you love love, you'll love surrealism').[39] 'This Shape' from *Standing Female Nude* can be read as an exercise in amorous derangement, and as an antidote to the urban nightmare in 'I Remember Me', owing to its appropriation of pastoral signs of desire. Dreams and anti-capitalist verve also pervade the poem: the amorous object comes to the lover only 'in sleep'; the subject moves 'through a vast world without goodness', and returns to childhood in the final stanza after orgasm (*SFN*, p. 17). In the first manifesto, innocence and the amorous are inextricable, since Breton contends that 'It is perhaps childhood that comes closest to true life.'[40] In an interview in 1991, Duffy recalls this remark: 'André Breton said, I think, that childhood is the only reality'.[41] This links to Duffy's exploration of origins as a contested site of 'truth' in *The Other Country*. Love and childhood become metaphysical sites of exploration in the early poetry: the structuralist Duffy searches there for meanings which are, tantalisingly, just beyond her reach.

'This Shape' confirms a commitment to the surrealist concept of 'mad' love in Duffy's early work. This utopian notion elides gender difference, whereas elsewhere in *Standing Female Nude* masculinity constitutes an opposite pole in an amorous dialectic. At its extreme point, in Duffy's next collection, *Selling Manhattan*, this results in the poem 'Psychopath', in which an adolescent character seeks sexual favours from a minor. Lesser symptoms of masculine, amorous discourse contribute to the diminishing prevalence of amorous lyrics in Duffy's later works, but *Standing Female Nude* already signals the difficulty of reconciling heterosexual love poetry with pragmatic representations of men. Hence a contradiction persists in the collection: utopian, 'mad' love vies constantly with expositions of male violence. 'This Shape' promises the *jouissance* of a surrealist pairing early on in this collection, but by the nineteenth and twenty-second poems of *Standing Female Nude* ('A Clear Note' and 'You Jane'), the equating of violence with masculinity upsets this possibility. Even the twelfth poem, 'Where We Came In', presents an end to the defining (and unnamed) amorous tie in the collection, if 'I Remember Me', 'This Shape', 'Saying Something', 'Jealous as Hell', 'Naming Parts', 'Till Our Face' and 'Lovebirds' are read as the script of a developing relationship. 'Where We Came In' is followed by 'Free Will', a poem on abortion, and 'Alliance', in which Duffy aborts the cycle of love poems by depicting men as drinkers, Scrooges and unemotional retrogrades. In 'Alliance', the husband's paradoxical empowerment and bitterness through his status as breadwinner is figured by the moment in which he returns from the pub and 'plonks his weight down' on both the wife's tired and unresisting body, and her life in general (*SFN*, p. 26). Love has capitulated to the scourge, for surrealism, of disastrous marital sex by the half-way point of *Standing Female Nude*. This trope is repeated in 'You Jane', in which Duffy depicts a perceived aspect of proletarian masculinity with the thuggish 'Man of the house' who farts 'a guinness smell against the wife / who snuggles up to [him] after [he's] given her one / after the Dog and Fox' (*SFN*, p. 34). It is as if Duffy cannot equate the French surrealists' desire to encourage 'mad' love and working-class emancipation with her sense of tangible gender inequalities. Masculine imperatives frustrate Breton's idealist search for *jouissance*: the erection shoved into the wife in 'You Jane' is linked to the 'purple vein' which 'throbs' in the 'master's' neck. It is as if Duffy argues that the patriarch's identity is essentially constructed by the violent male body; equally, she might be indicating that the masculine penchant of violence produces culturally determined expressions of desire. Whether nature or nurture is to blame, the amorous behaviour of masculine, working-class men is ultimately presented in this poem as analogous to the articulations of the clumsy ape-man referred to in the elided part of the title.

## Post-structuralist love

Although Duffy does not explicitly state this in the poetry, the body count of errant men in *Standing Female Nude* indicates that ensuing problems of male addressees in her love poems are not just products of her conception of working-class masculinity. Nevertheless, her surrealist poems in this collection still mark the zenith of her continuum of amorous poetry in terms of their sheer idealism, even if they are negated with hindsight by a number of texts which present masculinity as intolerable. In Duffy's next book, *Selling Manhattan*, the nadir of the amorous lyrics is reached in the form of the poem 'Psychopath', from which the idealist thrust of the early love poetry never recovers: it depicts hysterical masculinity as a product of the amorous, but also a negation of it. 'Psychopath' should not be read as a direct exposition of 'normative' masculinity; nevertheless, a critique is implicit, since paedophilia forms the extreme point of a continuum of the infantilising of women in male discourses of desire. Amorous narrators or addressees in *Standing Female Nude* are clearly not directly comparable to the psychopath in *Selling Manhattan*, but, if even a tenuous connection can be made, the logic of the poetry suggests, then they are not to be trusted. Hence men are, for the most part, elided as objects of erotic contemplation in *The Other Country* in favour of female lovers, as in 'Girlfriends', or universalist love poems. 'Two Small Poems of Desire' reflects the latter trend. Since 'Girlfriends' is situated next to these two pieces in the collection, an exposition of lesbian eroticism might be expected, but the title is deliberately vague: 'Desire' suggests that amorous utterance somehow transcends gender difference. As in many of Duffy's love poems, the identity of the subject and object remains a mystery; the phrase 'these things' in the first piece refers to sexual endeavours, but their exact nature persists in obscurity (*TOC*, p. 42). Daphne Marlatt's collection *Touch to My Tongue* struggles to forge a new amorous language to articulate lesbian experience: Duffy does not appear to be attempting this in *The Other Country*; if she is, then the attempt has failed.[42] As with Marlatt's poems, the slippery signs of erotic encounter point either to the ambiguous gender identity of the lovers or to a metaphysics of genderless amorous subjects. A distancing effect helps to augment this ambiguity: the text is only about sex *prima facie*; its real concern is desire. Since the object is absent, the narrator fondly remembers the latter's presence through a series of metaphors which close with the rendering of amorous desire as 'tiny gardens / growing in the palms of the hands'.

Duffy is perfectly aware of the constructed nature of her linguistic devices: hence the gardens are 'invisible, / sweet, *if* they had a scent' (my italics). This sense of artifice does not undermine the potency of the amorous situation, since the poet functions in post-structuralist mode here, arguing that desire is a pre-existing linguistic system which must be acquired over time. Thus, at the beginning of the poem, the lover becomes an 'animal learning vowels' during sex. Jane Thomas has argued persuasively for Duffy as a post-structuralist poet, even as she correctly notes that a structuralist desire for a metaphysics of order and presence persists in the poetry. '[T]he language we acquire in early infancy obviously pre-dates us – its meanings have already been constituted through the history of articulate human experience': by applying Thomas's comment to the amorous lyric, it can be seen that, in a similar way to discourses of, say, law, lovers are constituted as such only through an identity modulated by a pre-existing linguistic system; in this case, the historical category of desire.[43] By entering this exciting realm of language they become, as in Thomas's quotation, babies; hence, perhaps, the proliferation of babyish ur-speech in the lover's discourse. Instead of an adult/infant paradigm, Duffy figures desire in terms of an animalistic linguistic system that grates against more 'human' discourses in 'Two Small Poems of Desire'. She intends the amorous to be regarded, still following her early surrealist principles, as potentially subversive if juxtaposed with more dominant social discourses, such as the previously mentioned one of law. Desire fuses with the genre of poetry as a potentially anarchistic challenge to the semiotic, but the totalising aspect of the latter category is revealing, since these are not particularly seditious poems in terms of literary form or tradition. Indeed, the first piece can be read as a (loose) fourteen-line sonnet in the sub-genre of the *blason*, which contemplates various sites of the (woman's) body, with the conventional *volta* after line 8. Part two self-consciously echoes Wordsworth's 'Daffodils': the 'inward eye' which seeks solace in imagined nature becomes the amorous object in Duffy's text; when the amorous subject starts 'staring inwards' in the midst of 'a busy street' it is unclear whether the loved object is present, putting down a drink, or, as with the flowers in Wordworth's lyric, poignantly absent.[44] Perhaps it could be contended that Duffy negates the pastoral tradition by replacing daffodils with sexual desire, but the surrealist predilection for woods as well as naked bodies surely cancels out this possibility. If the sex act is read as lesbian, then perhaps the reversion to tetrameter in the first sonnet, even dactyls in line 7, could be interpreted as a subversion of the sonnet form to present a region of women's experience elided in literary tradition. This prospect is immediately rendered dialectical by the framing device of two pentameters in lines 1 and 14. Hence the paradox of the sonnet as a whole: a post-structuralist version of the love lyric is offered in the conventional form of the metrical *blason*.

One of the most problematical instances of language for post-structuralist writers and critics of amorous desire is the phrase 'I love you'. It cries out for a deconstruction of its evasive metaphysics, at the same time as its prevalence within the lover's discourse invites recognition of its currency as a self-referential, and self-perpetuating, linguistic device. If it is merely lauded as outside 'normative' social discourses, as Duffy seems to suggest it should be in this poem, it becomes subversively 'bad' language, appertaining to an aesthetics of awkwardness that challenges the semiotic. Virtuous language in the first piece might refer to the former discourses, or a stricture in which the metaphysics of 'I love you' surpasses the logic of an explanatory sentence such as 'I love you because . . .'. It is 'tough' and 'difficult', but somehow 'true' for the poet to laud the conventional enunciation, but this 'truth' remains obscure (*TOC*, p. 42). At this point, Duffy veers from Roland Barthes's deconstruction of '*je-t'-aime*'. If the third stanza enacts the first utterance of 'I love you', then the amorous theorist would not be displeased, since his text argues that it forms a linguistic device that can only be used once effectively. (He also suggests that '*je-t'-aime*' might alternatively be expressed through other signs which would render its affirmation redundant.) However, the present tense in Duffy's poem ('when you do . . .') suggests that the annunciation is ongoing, whenever the amorous object enacts her miraculous 'things'. In contrast, there is no truth in iteration, according to Barthes, because its divagation increases with repetition. Without going into the immense subtleties of Barthes's argument, which take eight pages to denounce 'the avowal', it might be facetiously retorted that his lovers were obviously not trying hard enough. A one-off proffering smacks of the male orgasm, or of brief amorous encounters that might have little to do with the enduring, if brittle, relationships celebrated by Duffy in her love poetry. At base level, she is a poet, not a theorist: the elision of the masculine in 'Two Small Poems of Desire' creates a universalist love poem that does not require an eight-page justification of the metaphysics of presence.

'Adultery' continues the trend for universal personas who are constructed through amorous discourse; it also perpetuates the split between love and the urban explored in both part two of 'Two Small Poems of Desire' and the earlier texts of *Standing Female Nude*. It primarily recalls 'I Remember Me' rather than the love poems from *The Other Country*, however, owing to its pessimistic tone: indeed, *Mean Time* as a whole seems to signal the end of a relationship so joyously celebrated in the previous collection. The narrator is 'older', 'sadder' and wiser in 'Adultery'; as in 'I Remember Me', the city just as much as an errant amorous object appears to be to blame for this amorous situation (*MT*, p. 38). 'Adultery' supports Henning Bech's declaration that 'Modern sexuality is essentially urban'; more specifically, the list of amorous signs in this poem consists of fetish objects associated with the lover, which form an integral part of the erotic contemplation of the past.[45] Within this cityscape, romantic love and marriage are presented as separate, but connected, linguistic systems. Each of these categories is inextricably connected in western thought: the former exists when the latter fails; each are products of the other. Bell hooks discusses this as one of the most tragic paradigms for gender studies.[46] If marriage arises out of a romantic encounter then it is inherently flawed, she argues, since the next object of erotic contemplation will inevitably threaten it. Hence the submerged censure in Duffy's poem vies with an acceptance that adultery arises out of the flawed scripts of romance and nuptial bliss. However, although adultery is ultimately lambasted, there is still a narrative thrill evident in the recounting of amorous details. And although the tone overall is elegiac, the reader might relish the paradoxical empowering of the woman through the affair. Her marriage breaks up; freed from possibly tyrannical (or plain boring) husbands, it is only fairly recently that western women have been allowed to talk about their *own* adultery openly.[47] In contrast, the narrator of 'Adultery' appears as a kind of damaged, but all-knowing, and therefore empowered, urban lover; hence the appeal in the first stanza for the innocent reader to wear dark glasses in the rain, and regard 'what was unhurt / as though through a bruise' if they ever find themselves in a similar amorous situation (*MT*, p. 38). A double-time narrative presents love, in the form of the passionate affair, as an aesthetic experience both within, and outside, the text. Duffy operates in post-structuralist mode here by presenting adultery itself as a pre-ordained 'script' (*MT*, p. 39). Three layers of text mix in the poem: the elegy itself, the relationship recounted within 'Adultery' and the texts of affairs and marriage in general.

These 'scripts' disintegrate towards the closure: question, and exclamation, marks are elided in the interrogative lines 'You did it. / What. Didn't you. Fuck. Fuck. No.'; consequently, the reader does not know who is speaking to whom. Urban love functions as discourse in this poem: the 'flowers / dumb and explicit on nobody's birthday' are included as conventional and modern amorous signs, like the earlier phrases 'You're a bastard' and 'You know all about love, / don't you'. The latter, as in the lines from the last stanza, is devoid of the expected question mark: it is as if the omnipotent, jaded lover is quoting from the 'script' without bothering to complete the syntax sense. Three voices then blend in the closure. The cuckold accuses the adulterer ('You did it?' 'Didn't you?'), who replies ('What?' 'Fuck?'). (Another possibility remains: the lines might be self-accusatory; the narrator's split self may be engaging in dialogue over the nature of the affair.) After the cuckold affirms the amorous crime ('Fuck'), the narrator enters denial by arguing that this is the 'wrong verb': it is 'only an abstract noun'; in other words, instead of fucking, he or she just 'fucked up'. Duffy's voice also enters the text here with the possibility that the author persona takes a step back from the poem after the second fuck and comments self-referentially that she has got the verb wrong herself. If read in this way, 'This is only an abstract noun' offers multiple interpretations. Perhaps drawing on Larkin's tendency to create syntactic confusion with abstract pronouns, Duffy provides a pun on 'This', which, as a demonstrative pronoun or adjective, is unlikely to (but could) constitute a noun phrase in itself. 'This' might refer to the fuck of the previous line, or the 'fuck up' of the whole poem itself, in the sense of its depiction of urban love rather than an overly modest evaluation of its aesthetics. Another possible pun is contained within the final word 'noun', which is itself another possible referent of the 'abstract noun' referred to by 'This'. Whichever interpretation is adhered to, urban love in the form of the affair is ultimately depicted as a nightmare of broken communication, in which pre-ordained scripts fragment, leaving only the 'terror' of an abstract 'fuck up'.

### Rejecting the male: *The World's Wife*

If *Standing Female Nude* entertains a dialectic between the instigation and simultaneous dissipation of love poetry, 'To the Unknown Lover' from *The Pamphlet* negates it, since this poem rejects even the possibility of a future affair. And if *The Other Country* and *Mean Time* both elide and perpetuate masculinity in the ambiguous gender identities of the amorous subjects, then, to twist the end of 'Telephoning Home', *The World's Wife* makes it quite plain that this is a woman speaking, and she does not tolerate errant men. As the last text in the collection, 'To the Unknown Lover' provides a precursor to the satirical poems in *The World's Wife*, in which only Shakespeare survives relatively unscathed. As a counterpoint to misbehaving men, lesbian relationships are more visible in the last two collections. 'Oppenheim's Cup and Saucer' and 'Warming Her Pearls' from *Standing Female Nude*, and 'Girlfriends' from *The Other Country* prove to be forerunners of the lesbian eroticism in the later love poems, such as 'Queens' from *The Pamphlet* and '*from* Mrs Tiresias' in *The World's Wife*. The latter endorses Germaine Greer by presenting men who have sex changes as travesties of femininity.[48] When Tiresias is transformed into a woman he can only copy female traits to produce a parody of women. Reduced to a grotesque drag figure, he cannot imitate a woman's voice, and emits the memorable transferred epithet of a 'cling peach slithering out from its tin', which makes his wife grit her teeth (*TWW*, p. 17). Duffy rewrites the characters of Tiresias depicted in both 'The Waste Land' and *The Odyssey*.[49] As Jeffrey Wainwright outlines in this book, the Theban seer was turned into a woman for killing the female of two coupling snakes; he was also blinded by an enraged Hera in classical myth for proclaiming that heterosexual sex gave women ten times more pleasure than men. Hera's act can be read as either anti- or pro-feminist, since she denies that women are allowed to enjoy copulation, but also contends that they cannot possibly gain as much delectation from penetrative sex as men. In Duffy's poem, Tiresias's possibly pro-feminist statement is derided when he attempts to mimic femininity on Vanessa-style television shows. The poem's closure then abandons the jealous Theban for a celebration of the wife's lesbian lover. A traditional amorous sign, fruit, is re-written as a symbol of lesbian eroticism when the woman chews the 'fruit of [the wife's] lips'. Such poems negate any requirement for an amorous masculinity in *The World's*

*Wife*. 'Little Red-Cap' depicts the 'ten years' the narrator had to spend in the shadow of a male poet (an exaggerated version of Adrian Henri, perhaps) before she rejected 'Lesson one' of the love poem in order to forge an unmitigated lyricism in a tradition of female poets (*TWW*, p. 3). Rosemont quotes Breton as arguing that 'poetry is made in the woods' of youth, but here the figure of the surrealist male poet is abandoned.[50] When the poet / wolf's belly is ripped open, the grandmother, a symbol of occluded women writers, is revealed.

In contrast to 'Little Red-Cap', the early love poems in Duffy's work retain masculinity as a possible antidote to urban capitalism through the transcendent union of sexual bodies. As her work progresses, however, the traditional love lyric's attack on women's waywardness as the scourge of the amorous is turned on its head. Instead of the inconstant females in Donne's 'The Apparition', Thomas Carew's 'Song: to my Inconstant Mistress' and George Meredith's *Modern Love*, in *The World's Wife* Herod's decision to kill male babies is explained through the queen's desire to save her daughter from '*Him. The Husband. Hero. Hunk. / The Boy Next Door. The Paramour. The* Je t'adore. / *The Marrying Kind. Adulterer. Bigamist. The Wolf. / The Rip. The Rake. The Rat. / The Heartbreaker. The Ladykiller. Mr Right*' (*TWW*, p. 8). Such sentiments distinguish the narrators of Duffy's later poems from those of comparable women writers. Wendy Cope's rejection of 'old-fashioned masculinity' in her poetry always contains a nostalgic, erotic bond with balding charmers. For example, in 'My Lover', the satirical list of the amorous object's quirks is tempered by the amused tone of the besotted subject.[51] Similarly, in 'From June to December', the amorous subject remains trapped within her own heterosexual paradigm: despite the lack of interest displayed by the male addressee, the female lover cuddles 'the new telephone directory / After I found your name in it' (p. 33). As with Duffy's verse, the tone of much of the poetry about men is scathingly ironic, as in her subversive renderings of male poets' material; the latter is epitomised by the Larkinesque 'Strugnall'. However, Cope offers no alternative to the charming dotard in 'My Lover' (a potential site of an heroic *telos* for the New Lad), who insists on making the noise of several trains, ruminating over the delights of Tottenham Hotspur, and reacting with puzzlement when team mates introduce talcum powder into the changing room (p. 38). In contrast, Duffy's later love poems are refreshing in their total rejection of the heterosexual male.

# Notes

1 Carol Ann Duffy, *Standing Female Nude* (London: Anvil, 1985); *The World's Wife* (London: Picador, 1999). An earlier version of this chapter appeared in *English*.

2 Carol Ann Duffy, *The Other Country* (London: Anvil, 1990).

3 Angelica Michelis, 'The Pleasure of Saying It: Images of Sexuality and Desire in Contemporary Women's Poetry', in Detler Gohrbandt and Bruno von Lutz *Seeing and Saying: Self-referentiality in British and American Literature* (Frankfurt: Peter Lang, 1998), pp. 59–72.

4 Roland Barthes, *Fragments d'un discours amoreux* (Paris: Éditions du Seuil, 1977).

5 Linda Kinnahen, '"Look for the Doing Words": Carol Ann Duffy and Questions of Convention', in James Acheson and Romana Huk (eds), *Contemporary British Poetry* (Albany: State University of New York Press, 1996), pp. 245–68.

6 I am echoing Angela Carter's comment in the introduction to *The Sadeian Woman* (London: Virago, 1979) that pornography appears to sate sexual desire, but actually postpones fulfilment, since 'however much he wants to fuck the willing women or men in his story, he cannot do so but must be content with some form of substitute activity' (p. 14).

7 See, for example, the opening of 'Havisham' from *Mean Time* (London: Anvil, 1993), in which Dickens's jilted character addresses the lover as 'Beloved sweetheart bastard' (p. 40).

8 The *OED* (2nd edn) cites the word as referring to both sexes of illegitimate children, but almost all of the examples refer to male children. Owing presumably to the historical predilection for the first-born male in terms of heritage, the colloquial meaning of 'bastard' (first used in the nineteenth century) appertains solely to men in the citations.

9 Antony Rowland, 'Patriarchy, Male Power and the Psychopath in the Poetry of Carol Ann Duffy' in Berthold Shoene-Harwood and Daniel Lea (eds), *Male Order* (Amsterdam: Rodopi, due to be published in 2003).

10 Carol Ann Duffy, *The Pamphlet* (London: Anvil, 1998), pp. 28–31.

11 Sasha Weitman, 'On the Elementary Forms of Socioerotic Life', *Theory, Culture & Society: Love and Eroticism*, 15:3–4, (London: Sage, 1998), pp. 71–110.

12 Richard von Krafft-Ebing, *Psychopathia Sexualis* (Stuttgart: Enke, 1907).

13 Geoffrey Grigson, *The Faber Book of Love Poems* (London: Faber, 1973), pp. 156–60. A brief cultural history of this dried fruit demonstrates that it has descended from this lofty amorous height to a sign of coarseness. In the nineteenth century it was derided as a laxative; by the mid twentieth century it was associated with a plebeian lifestyle. Geoffrey Willans and Ronald Searle's account of schoolboy life in 1953 includes a chapter entitled 'Nightmare: the Revolt of the Prunes'. Normally, the schoolmasters disappear from the canteen to devour the more aristocratic strawberry, whereas the boys are left to chew on the 'tribe of savvage prunes who lived in a blak mass in the skool pantry' (*Molesworth* (London: Penguin, 1999 [1953]), p. 96).

14 All these poems have been taken from Grigson, pp. 331–7, 59–63, 367, 100, 86, 155, 160.

15 Mike Featherstone, 'Introduction' in *Theory, Culture & Society: Love and Eroticism*, pp. 1–18, 5.

16 Jeffrey Weeks, 'The Sexual Citizen' in *Theory, Culture & Society: Love and Eroticism*, pp. 35–52.

17 Zygmunt Bauman, 'On Postmodern Uses of Sex', *Theory, Culture & Society: Love and Eroticism*, pp. 19–34.

18 Featherstone, p. 12.

19 Theodor Adorno, *Minima Moralia*, trans. E.F.N. Jephcott (London: Verso, 1978 [1951]), p. 141.

20 Bauman, p. 31.

21 It may be potentially contentious to label Duffy's early love poetry as late modernist. By doing so I wish to stress the gulf between theoretical explications of postmodern love and her illustration of alienated lovers in her poems from *Standing Female Nude*, which are influenced primarily by modernist poetry and the French surrealists.

22 Adorno, p. 162.

23 Philip Larkin, *Collected Poems* (London: Faber, 1988), p. 143.

24 *The Times*, 15 May 1998, p. 1. This article is quoted by Featherstone, p. 16.

25 Not all hard-core pornography celebrates sex between strangers, of course, given the recent interest in amateur films.

26 Barthes critiques this in *Fragments d'un discours amoureux* by arguing that 'I love you' invites a tautological answer; he concludes that the phrase should never be used (pp. 147–54).

27 Sean O'Brien, 'Carol Ann Duffy: *A Stranger Here Myself*', in *The Deregulated Muse* (Newcastle: Bloodaxe, 1998), pp. 160–70, p. 162. O'Brien critiques the flatness of tone, and the prosaic style, but these may be regarded as positive, rather than as aesthetic deficiencies, in terms of the poem's depiction of urban love.

28 Franklin Rosemont, *André Breton and the First Principles of Surrealism* (London: Pluto Press, 1978), p. 24. I am quoting from Rosemont rather than the primary source; the reason for this will become clear later in this chapter when I suggest this book's influence on Duffy.

29 Ibid., p. 23.

30 There are similarities between Wordsworth's exposition of poetry as spontaneous emotion reflected in tranquillity and psychic automatism (*The Oxford Authors: William Wordsworth*, ed. Stephen Gill (Oxford and New York: Oxford University Press), p. 598). Misreadings of both have led to the lauding of outpourings of a supposedly unmitigated self in Romantic and surrealist writing. Breton famously derided any sense that automatic writing is beyond value.

31 Brian Patten, *Love Poems* (London: Unwin Hyman, 1984 [1981]), p. 73. A flatness of tone pervades the poem, such as the less-deceived narrator's contention that the perfume is a 'manufactured lie / one that makes women's flesh and their graves / smell sweeter'.

32  Larkin, *Collected Poems*, pp. 152–3. 'Dockery & Son' contains an echo of Tennyson's *In Memoriam* when the narrator attempts to recapture the excitement of his college days by entering his old room, which is locked (p. 152). In LXXXVII, Tennyson passes 'the rooms in which [Arthur] dwelt [at university]. / Another name was on the door: / I lingered; all within was noise' (ed. Christopher Ricks, *The Poems of Tennyson in Three Volumes*, 2nd edn (Harlow: Longman, 1987 1969) pp. 403–4).

33  Peter Jones (ed.), *Imagist Poetry* (Harmondsworth: Penguin, 1972), p. 95.

34  Andrew McAllister, 'Carol Ann Duffy Interview', *Bête Noire*, 6 (winter 1988), 69–77, p. 72; T.S. Eliot (ed.), *Literary Chapters of Ezra Pound* (London: Faber, 1960 [1954]), p. 12.

35  Deryn Rees-Jones notes the influence of T.S. Eliot in *Carol Ann Duffy* (Plymouth: Northcote House, 1999), p. 2. It is particularly evident in *Standing Female Nude*; for example, in the love poem 'Naming Parts', male seduction is likened to Madame Sosostris's 'wicked pack of cards' from 'The Waste Land' (p. 21; T.S. Eliot, *Selected Poems* (London: Faber, 1954), p. 52). The amorous piece 'Till Our Face' in *Standing Female Nude* is reminiscent of H.D.'s 'Oread' (p. 22; *Imagist Poetry*, p. 62). Pools of fir in H.D.'s surrealist depiction of violent sexuality become the masculine 'drift of pine needles' in 'Till Our Face'. Nevertheless, in the McAllister interview, Duffy stresses that 'if I had to pick [just] one [influence] who devastated me and made me shiver it would be Eliot' (p. 73).

36  Rees-Jones, pp. 6–8, 30–6.

37  Rosemont defines surrealism as 'an unrelenting revolt against a civilisation that reduces all human aspirations to market values, religious impostures, universal boredom and misery' (p. 1). In 1998 I bought this treatise from a bookshop in Chorlton. It is inscribed 'Carol Ann Duffy, 15-ii-78'. Of course, this does not prove that Duffy read the book, but the association of surrealism and 'mad' love with revolutionary potential in *Standing Female Nude* would suggest that she might have done.

38  Featherstone, p. 15. This utopian bent of the surrealists mirrors the theories of 'becoming' lauded by many of the sociologists in *Love and Eroticism*. Through my use of Adorno earlier in this piece, I have tried to present a brief critique of such idealism.

39  Rosemont, pp. 65, 26.

40  Ibid., p. 9.

41  Interview with Jane Stabler, *Verse*, 8:2 (summer 1991), 124–8.

42  Daphne Marlatt, *Touch to my Tongue* (Edmonton: Longspoon Press, 1984).

43  Jane E. Thomas, '"The Intolerable Wrestle with Words": the Poetry of Carol Ann Duffy', *Bête Noire*, 6 (1988), 78–88, p. 78.

44  *The Oxford Authors: William Wordsworth*, p. 304.

45  Henning Bech, 'Citysex: Representing Lust in Public', *in Theory, Culture & Society: Love and Eroticism*, pp. 215–42, p. 215. As Matthew Pateman has pointed out to me, this assumes that modern lovers are of a certain age and sexual persuasion, and that they occupy a designated geographical space. Bech's declaration balks at, say, an elderly homosexual, who might

encounter more prejudice in most parts of the city as opposed to young, male heterosexuals. A rural inhabitant with a predilection for goats would be even more marginalised by Bech's assertion.

46  bell hooks, 'Food for Love', www.guardianunlimited.co.uk/Archive/Article/0, 4273, 3962944, 00.html. hooks argues that love is not the same as romance; the latter is a subset of the former category. There is no agency in romantic love: we 'fall' into love as if caught in a trap; this leads to an unnecessarily lauded lack of responsibility in amorous affairs. She proposes instead a more agonising, but potentially fruitful, concept of the amorous in which the subject and object labour constantly to maintain a relationship of longevity, instead of giving in to the alterior pressure of romance.

47  Cas Wouters, 'Balancing Sex and Love since the 1960s Sexual Revolution', in *Theory, Culture & Society: Love and Eroticism*, pp. 187–24, p. 198.

48  Germain Greer, *The Whole Woman* (London: Anchor, 2000 [1999]), p. 88.

49  Homer, *The Odyssey* (London: Penguin, 1991 [1946]).

50  Rosemont, p. 9.

51  Wendy Cope, *Making Cocoa for Kingsley Amis* (London: Faber, 1986), pp. 36–8, p. 58.

# 4

## 'Me not know what these people mean': gender and national identity in Carol Ann Duffy's poetry

ANGELICA MICHELIS

It is noteworthy that the first foreigners to emerge at the dawn of our civilization are foreign women – the Danaïdes.[1]

W HAT DOES it mean to belong to a country, to identify with a nation's supposed peculiarities and idiosyncrasies? The meaning of national identity and what it entails has always been a major subject of British poetry. One might even go so far as to say that the development of British poetry as a genre has been inextricably linked to feelings of national belonging. These have left their traces in the open and unashamed celebrations of imperialism and colonialism of late Victorian and Edwardian poetry as well as in the simplistic parochial and pantheistic notions of an England in Georgian poetry. Many aspects of postwar poetry can be viewed as a revision of earlier poetic expressions of national identity by introducing a much more complicated and complex relationship to Englishness and Britishness. Political developments in Northern Ireland, the progressing devolution of Scotland and Wales and the changes brought about by a multiculturally structured society have had a lasting effect on contemporary poetry and forced the genre to respond poetically to a concept of national identity defined by heterogeneity and hybridity. Compared to the beginning of the last century the idea and image of Britain as a country, the question of what it means to be British and the extent to which the poet's national identity plays a role in the kind of poetry he or she produces have turned into complex issues.

There is, of course, no such thing as a universal concept of what constitutes a nation or what exactly is meant by national identity and how it can be defined. The meaning of Englishness or Britishness has experienced profound changes over the centuries and the discourse of poetry has played a major part in constructing and giving expression to the historically and politically motivated shifts in the meaning of national identity. It is also important to point out here that the idea of belonging to a nation is certainly not the only type of collective identity relevant in relation to the constitution of subject positions. However, I would go along with Anthony Smith when he argues: 'Other types of collective identity – class, gender, race, religion – may overlap or combine with national identity but they rarely succeed in undermining its hold, though they may influence its direction.'[2]

Whether we like it or not, national identity seems to exercise an overwhelming allure in the way we see ourselves and how we relate to the country we come from, 'our country'. But how exactly do we relate to the country of our birth, whose language we speak and whose culture we live? And is 'we' an appropriate pronoun in this case? Virginia Woolf famously stated in *A Room of One's Own*, 'As a woman, I have no country' because her country was 'the whole world'.[3] And what about John Lucas's observation, '"Englishness" turns out to be a largely, or even exclusively, male affair'[4] when commenting on the relationship between gender and national identity in poetry?

In this chapter I will be exploring the relationship between gender and identity in the poetry of Carol Ann Duffy. By looking at a selection of her poems and particularly focusing on her aptly named collection *The Other Country* I want to investigate how, and to what extent, the aspect of gender influences the direction and construction of the meaning of national identity. How exactly does Duffy approach and discuss the relationship between national and gender identity? What kind of England and / or Britain emerges from her poems and how do these imaginations of national belonging comment on the meaning of Englishness and Britishness in cultural and poetic discourses? In order to pursue these questions I will situate my enquiry in the context of ideas of displacement and the notion of the foreigner and their particular relationship to femininity and gender identity in general.

## Who are we (1)?

In 1963, in defence of the Movement poets, Robert Conquest argued that 'British Culture is receptive to immigration, if not invasion; but it remains highly idiosyncratic. It is part of our experience, and for that no one else's experience, however desirable, can be a substitute.'[5]

Whose experience does the author refer to here? Conquest seems to have no qualms about evoking an idea of a homogeneously structured Britain that is undivided by gender, ethnicity, race and religion. But conjuring up the illusion of inclusiveness is of course part of a notoriously ideological rhetoric based on a hierarchical division of society. 'Our experience' in relation to poetry and national belonging refers traditionally to the experience of being white, male, educated and (southern) English and thus imagines a country whose culture is inextricably linked to the values of this particular segment of British society. If you cannot share Conquest's experience you are not British and your experience is someone else's; it might be a desirable one but certainly can not act as a substitute for the 'real thing'. Compare to this James Fenton's comment of 1990 on the relationship between poetry and national identity in poetry: 'Englishness, for a poet, is almost a taboo subject. Britishness is altogether out. Whereas an American poet may speak to, or on behalf of, his nation, this is hard for an English poet, now that it is not clear what his nation is.'[6]

Whereas Conquest can situate himself with authoritative confidence as the centre of British culture and voice without doubt what it means to experience it, Fenton seems to have lost his sense of national belonging, and according to his statement poetry has become a place void of a voice that can speak for, and on behalf, of the nation. What has happened in the (nearly) thirty years that separate these comments?

From the 1970s onwards, beginning with the so called 'middle generation' including Douglas Dunn, Tony Harrison and Seamus Heaney, British poetry has opened itself to new voices and experiences that not only questioned the truth and validity of Conquest's statement but, furthermore, initiated a discursive process that laid open and challenged the underlying and implied cultural and nationalistic arrogance and bias in his statement. In the years between 1960 and 1990 that apparently so stable and homogeneous reference point of the 'experience of being British' turned into a hollow spectre which instead of providing a safeguard of cultural and national identity now haunted the empty space in poetry once occupied by 'the nation'. As David Kennedy put it so aptly: 'It is as if, as the 1980s opened, a new generation of poets no longer felt obliged, or, perhaps, no longer felt able to write as citizens of "the society of the poem".'[7] Kennedy's as well as Fenton's comments on the demise of the nation as a stable concept in British poetry could be read as a nostalgic longing for better times with their rhetoric of loss and uncertainty. However, the shifting of margins and the concomitant process of redefining the meaning of national identity and its relevance for the works of individual poets, the poetic voice, the social and political place of the poet and the genre of poetry as such, had a far-reaching impact on the qualitative output, topics and narrative voice of poetry in years to come. The deconstruction of England and Britain as unifying and inclusive concepts (and as a consequence the new positioning of national identity in its relation to poetry) is a phenomenon which became typical for postwar British poetry but, I would argue, it is from the 1980s onwards that this poetical preoccupation gained a particular momentum. This development is inextricably linked with the politics of Thatcherite Britain which, as David Kennedy argues, 'resulted in an "England of the mind" that became narrower, single-perspective and exclusive of many'.[8] Many poetic works produced in those years when concerned with questions of national identity can be seen as a direct reaction to the political situation created by eleven years of a reactionary Conservative government and its politics of exclusion. But the role of any cultural and literary discourse can of course not be reduced to a one-way mirroring of historical reality. What is of much more interest and relevance here is the fact that many of these poems produced what could be called a counter-discourse to the dominant imaginations of Britain based on nostalgia and apparently traditional values. Precisely by incorporating the language of commodification, the 'free market', the fierce individualism of 'looking after number one' and the (tabloid) media, poetry of the 1980s not only contributed to a critique of political reality but, furthermore, produced alternative notions of the meaning of nation and national identity. By dismantling the Thatcherite myth of 'one Britain' and by transforming the political concept of alienation into a discursive poetic strategy, many poetic works were able to critically comment on the extent to which British poetry – generically and thematically – has always been intertwined with ideas of Englishness. And by doing so poetry of that period is often portrayed, as Neil Corcoran has pointed out, as 'a coming to terms among English writers themselves with a national individuality newly and differently defining itself in relation to a vastly altering historical circumstance and political status'.[9] As we shall see later on, the poetry of Carol Ann Duffy played an important and path-breaking part in this process.

## Who are we (2)?

Concluding from the above comments by Conquest and Fenton one could argue here with Lucas that Englishness and concomitantly the issue of national identity have largely been the preserved preoccupation of male poets. In her introduction to the anthology *Kicking Daffodils: Twentieth-century Women Poets* Vicki Bertram even suggests 'that women poets are less interested in questions of nationhood than their male counterparts'.[10] Although I agree that the relationship between national identity and poetry can be viewed as being part of a particular masculine tradition, contemporary poetry by women does certainly not circumnavigate the problematic connections between nationhood and its role for the genre of poetry. I would argue that the way nationality is discussed in contemporary women's poetry from the 1980s onwards appears to be as an issue of gender and thus gains a different quality in contradistinction to the problematisation of national identity in male poetry. For Peter Childs 'the querying of what it means to be British or English is underlaid by the extent to which national identity has always been localised and gendered' by the fact that 'Women are explicitly included but implicitly excluded'[11] which thus puts them into the vicinity of the position of the foreigner. However, it is always problematic to speak in a generalised way of 'women's poetry'. Gender as well as national identity cannot be regarded as unified concepts: aspects of race, ethnicity, class and sexuality play an important and modifying role to the extent to which gender is relevant as a lived identity. Although the aspect of gender difference, and therefore access to a different kind of experience compared to the one of male poets, has an important impact on what is traditionally referred to as 'women's poetry', the work produced by female poets cannot (and should not) be reduced to them just adding a 'female voice' to the body of poetry emerging from the 1980s onwards. Apart from the rather difficult and complex relationship between lived (female) experience and poetic discourse, poetry written by women during the last two decades is at its most interesting where it interweaves different, and sometimes contradictory, aspects of the construction of subjectivity in order to question the notion of a stable fixed self, be it one based on gender or on national identity. Rather than offering just an alternative view of reality, many of the poems published in anthologies and single-author volumes explore and lay bare the very processes of identity construction, and by doing so examine the genre of poetry as a discursive space where nationality is constructed and the particular ways it offers positions of exclusion and inclusion. This becomes particularly apparent in the work of female poets from Scotland and Northern Ireland. The poetry of Medbh McGuckian and Liz Lochhead, for example, shows how femininity

> is cut across by questions of national and political history forcing a relationship which produces gendered and sexual bodies whose genealogy is inextricably linked to the politics of national geography . . . ; the public allegory of the nation, on the other hand, depends on a specific body politics relying on the gendered terminology of private and public languages filtered through sexualised bodies.[12]

It does not come as a great surprise that poetic works from Northern Irish and Scottish poets should be preoccupied with questions of national identity considering their often tempestuous relationship with England/Britain. The interweaving of questions of femininity with those of national identity emerge as a poignant feature in the poetical works of female poets who are situated in a relationship to the British motherland and mother tongue which oscillates between inclusion and exclusion. As Cairns Craig argues when exploring Liz Lochhead's poem 'Inter-City':

> By the identification of her own condition with the country's, she makes redemption of the feminine equivalent to redemption of the nation; construction of a *feminine* speech is a means to recovering an obliterated Scottish speech.[13]

But how does the relationship between gender and national identity feature in the works of a poet who is usually regarded as a British poet, who has spent most of her adult life and education in England, and a poet who was short listed for the most English position of Poet Laureate?

To present Carol Ann Duffy as a British or English poet could be regarded as highly contentious. She was born in Glasgow and spent her childhood years in Scotland, from where she moved to Stafford-shire, then studied at Liverpool University, lived and worked for some time in London until she moved back to the north of England, to Manchester where she lives now. This problem of placing and categorising the poet and her work does not only pose difficulties in regard to the question of national identity, as Deryn Rees-Jones points out:

> Do we read her as a Scottish poet? A Scottish woman poet? A feminist poet? A working-class poet? Is she a political poet, a dramatic poet, or a lyric poet? Of course, she is all of these things and none of them, testimony to the fact that the value of the neat pigeonhole is undoubtedly suspect.[14]

This resistance to clear and unquestionable identification of the poet and her work, I would argue, rather than forming an impediment to a critical reading of Duffy's poetry, already indicates some of the major elements of her poetic voice, that of alienation, displacement, transition and translation. In the following section I will look at some of her poems in *Selling Manhattan* and *The Other Country* by focusing on the impact of the above-mentioned issues on the discursive con-struction of national and gender identity in the poetry gathered in these volumes.

## Foreign in the other country: alienation and displacement in *Selling Manhattan*

One of the most striking qualities of the poems collected in *Selling Manhattan* is their tentative tone, resulting in a body of poetic works whose common feature consists of a probing of the possibilities and limitations of language. But it is never just the linguistic side: the ques-tioning of language as a communicative tool which promises trans-parency and understanding is extended to a critical inquiry into the politics of identity and belonging. Many of the poems collected in this volume use metaphors which are directly related to language, such as 'Dies Natalis': 'They are trying to label me, / / translate me into the right word.'[15] 'Strange Language in Night Fog': 'although they told themselves / there must be a word for home, / if they only knew it' (*SM*, p. 17). 'Money Talks': 'I am the authentic language of suffering'

(*SM*, p. 33). 'Selling Manhattan' refers to the colonial appropriation of America and its concomitant eradication of Native American culture. As a dramatic monologue the poem is divided into the voice of the coloniser in the first stanza and that of the Native American who speaks the remaining six stanzas. This hierarchical division of poetic space is already highly significant in relation to the way the poem problematises home, national identity and the question of belonging. In traditional history it is of course the white man and his version of the 'discovery of America' that fills the history books and thus established itself as the dominant voice of 'historical truth'. An important element of this truth consists of the notion that there is such a thing as an inherent national identity bestowed on the 'proper' inhabitants of a particular country. By commenting on the transition of America from Native American country into the home of the coloniser, and by structuring it poetically as a discursive dialogue between appropriator and displaced, the poem comments on the fictionality of such a version of national identity. This aspect is further underlined by the differences in tone between the white man and Native American. This is the white man speaking:

> *All yours, Injun, twenty-four bucks' worth of glass beads,*
> *gaudy cloth. I got myself a bargain. I brandish*
> *fire-arms and fire-water. Praise the Lord.*
> *Now get your red ass out of here.*
>
> (*SM*, p. 34)

By putting the coloniser's speech in italics, the poem comments on and reverses the process of 'othering' underlying the history of colonialism and imperialism. It is the white man's voice that is made strange, indicated not only by the italicisation of his enunciation but also by the ironic contrast between '*All yours*' at the beginning of the stanza and its final sentence. The phrase '*Praise the Lord*' adds a further cynical element to this irony, commenting not only on the complicity between the colonising power and its dominant religion but also on the semantic emptiness of a religious discourse that has become only meaningful as a cynical comment. One could go even further here and read 'Lord' in its gendered sense, which refers to the implicit masculinity of the figure of God in almost all western religions and, furthermore, constructs the coloniser as a figure who presents himself as a godlike figure who creates the world and men in his image.

In contrast to the staccato-like phrases of the first stanza, the speech of the Native American is structured in eloquent sentences thus indicating a more tentative grasp of the meaning of home, country and belonging. The second and third stanza both open with 'I wonder', thereby introducing a mode of philosophical questioning. The world as defined by greed and possession is counter-balanced with an alternative notion of what the relationship between men and world should and could be. By privileging the voice of the 'other' from a spatial as well as from a moral point of view, the poem shifts the boundaries between centre and margin and it is the discourse of the norm, of the white coloniser, that appears strange and questionable. By doing so 'Selling Manhattan' not only comments critically on an allegedly 'natural' concept of national identity but also shows – in a very Brechtian sense – how identity, rather than being a inherent feeling of natural belonging, is the result of a political and historical process. It is as if the dramatic monologue of the Native American makes audible and visible everything that is repressed and annihilated in the short first stanza. Whereas the relationship between land and inhabitants is presented in the language of ownership by the coloniser, the now displaced and alienated subject is able to offer a different view based on the idea that his sense of identity only comes into being by seeing himself as part of the environment he inhabits:

> I wonder if the spirit of the water has anything
> to say. That you will poison it. That you
> can no more own the rivers and the grass that own
> the air. I sing with true love for the land;
> dawn chant, the song of sunset, starlight psalm.
>
> (*SM*, p. 34)

To a certain extent, this can also be read as a comment on language, questioning the 'adamic', masculine idea of naming and owning as it is part of the myth of creation in western religion. The language of the diasporic and marginalised subject is one of dispossession in the widest sense: in the same way that man cannot own the land, words cannot own meaning. This is enforced by the transformation of the coloniser's alliteration '*I brandish fire-arms and fire-water*' which becomes 'I have learned / the solemn laws of joy and sorrow, in the distance / between morning's frost and firefly's flash at night' in the monologue of the Native American. The short brutal sentence of the white man encapsulating the politics of colonisation and greed based on the idea of a subject of active agency (subject-verb-object) is counter-balanced by a much more complex structure which presents the subject as not outside and acting on the environment but as being part of it and thus implicated in the way it is treated. The pathetic fallacy of the final stanza emphasises this climactically: the subject has disappeared completely and can be comprehended only as inextricably linked to the environment in which it is situated.

'Deportation' offers another variation of the theme of the foreigner and his or her precarious place in an alienated space. Outspokenly political, the poem refers to the situation of a worker who leaves his native environment in order to find employment in a more economically affluent country so he can support the family he left behind. Like 'Selling Manhattan' the poem is a dramatic monologue emphasising the linguistic alienation of the narrative voice emanating from a world where language cannot be conceived as dialogic. The utter loneliness of the speaking subject is underlined by the fact that 'they', referring to the inhabitants of the 'guest country', and the 'I' of the narrative voice never appear in a sentence together, as if there is no space which can accommodate both:

> They have not been kind here. Now I must leave,
> the words I've learned for supplication,
> gratitude, will go unused. Love is a look
> in the eyes in any language, but not here,
> not this year. They have not been welcoming.
>
> (*SM*, p. 59)

Framed by the parallel structure of the first and final sentence of the poem, the speaker is literally in an 'in-between' space, excluded from the sphere where 'they' reside. The only connection between the two is provided by 'supplication' and 'gratitude' which define the existence and the self of the foreigner in a hierarchical dependence on the natives, thus denying the foreigner a position of subjectivity. The foreigner is thus placed in a paradoxical space: his identity is one of non-existence; he cannot be where 'they' are, and the place where he is does not exist, which effectively produces the position of the foreigner as an empty space. In *Strangers to Ourselves* Julia Kristeva describes this phenomenon in the following way:

This means that, settled within himself, the foreigner has no self. Barely an empty confidence, valueless, which focuses his possibilities of being constantly other, according to others' wishes and to circumstances. I do what *they* want *me* to, but it is not 'me' – 'me' is elsewhere, 'me' belongs to no one, 'me' does not belong to 'me', . . . does 'me' exist?[16]

However, this 'in-between' space of the foreigner can also be considered as a productive force since it is precisely his mode of being which in effect makes the notion of beginning and end (or in a more philosophical sense that of ontology and teleology) visible as discursive formations that narrative structure simultaneously is based on and produced by. 'They' can only be at the beginning and at the end of the stanza because 'I' is between them; we can only notice them/'them' because the empty position of the foreigner ensures that beginning and end do not collapse into each other. This reverses to a certain extent the situation of dependency between 'them' and 'I', since it is now those who can be sure of their national identity, those who apparently belong, who are rendered as being in a precarious space which is threatened by emptiness. The speaking subject's state of emergency caused by the movement of exclusion from the space that 'they' occupy, is therefore also the moment of its emergence.

The second stanza takes this issue even further when it adds a temporal component to the one of space:

> I used to think the world was where we lived
> in space, one country, shining in big dark.
> I saw a photograph when I was small.
>
> (*SM*, p. 59)

'Space' takes on a plurality of meaning here: it can denote the universe, time and duration and an expanse. According to the *OED* space can also mean a 'void or empty place' as well as an 'interval or blank between words, or lines, in printed or written matter'. The stanza resonates with all these different meanings here, thus emphasising signification as a constantly ongoing relationship between the levels of signifier and signified, and by doing so comments on meaning itself as a spatial process, an impression which is formally underlined by the semantic uncertainty created by the enjambement between its first and second line. In addition, the stanza also plays with notions of perspective and the visual in relation to space when the world is perceived as 'one country shining in big dark' a vision which is remembered from 'a photograph when I was small'. Perspective, of course, relies on a

87

certain moment of distance and displacement: to see something requires one to be spatially and temporally removed from the object that is perceived. It is precisely because of his non-presence that the foreigner is able to speak and (re-)present an image of himself and the world; he substitutes an eye for an I, thus indicating that the position of identity is possible only because of an inherent alterity, an otherness which simultaneously negates and constitutes subjectivity. The position of the foreigner is thus bound by the logic of the supplement in a Derridean sense:

> If it represents and makes an image, it is by the anterior default of a presence. Compensatory and vicarious, the supplement [evil eye] is an adjunct, a subaltern instance which *takes – the – place*. As substitute . . . [missing person] . . . it produces no relief, its place is assigned in the structure by the mark of an emptiness. Somewhere something can be filled up of itself . . . only by allowing itself to be filled through sign and proxy.[17]

This is encapsulated in the opening sentence of the third stanza: 'Now I am *Alien*.' Indeed 'I', denoting the subjectivity of the foreigner as well as identity as such, is a position of displacement and alienation inhabited by an alterity that never allows it/I to *be*. This moment of non-presence and non-being of the foreigner works also on the level of gender. It is only in reference to his lover and their child whom he left behind that the foreigner gains his masculine identity:

> My lover
> bears our child and I was to work here, find
> a home. In twenty years we would say This is you
> when you were a baby, when the plum tree was a shoot.
>
> (*SM*, p. 59)

It is interesting, however, that the speaker's masculinity is never indicated by the personal pronoun 'he' in this poem. His gender identity only emerges in relation to his feminine lover (whose femininity is positioned as a 'she' in the last stanza) and his position as a father to their child and is thus always the product of interpretation and construction. 'I' merges into 'we' and thus indicates subjectivity and gender identity as simultaneously and paradoxically defined by a moment of splitting (negativity) and unity. Masculinity, the poem seems to suggest, is possible only in its difference to femininity but this difference is at the same time sublated (destroyed *and* preserved) and negated in the plural position of 'we'. The state of alienation and displacement defining the space of the foreigner in the other country is thus not overcome and annihilated in his relationship to woman, but redefined in a productive sense: alienation and difference are envisaged as positive states of being as the very state of identity. In her text *Shadow of the Other* Jessica Benjamin theorises this position as intersubjectivity which she defines as following: 'The intersubjective perspective is concerned with how we create the third position that is able to break up the reversible complementarities and hold in tension the polarities that underly them.'[18]

Difference and sameness, belonging and being estranged are not cast as binary oppositions but imagined as a mode of being envisaging identity as a constant process of oscillating and negotiating between the two terms. Whereas being different and other in the foreign country throws the foreigner into a state of subjection, alienation and displacement allow him to gain a position of subjectivity and being in relationship to his lover and his child. But this concept of subjectivity is not based on an undoing of 'our ties to others but rather' on the possibility 'to disentangle them: to make of them not shackles but circuits of recognition'.[19] In the other country the foreigner becomes invisible and non-existent, he is not *recognised* and thus pushed to the realm of death:

> I have felt less small
> below mountains disappearing into cloud
> than entering the Building of Exile. Hearse taxis
> crawl the drizzling streets towards the terminal.
>
> (*SM*, p. 59)

However it is precisely the moment of alienation and displacement which allows him not only to be recognised by his lover but also to recognise her in her femininity when the mother of his child emerges as a 'she' in the final stanza:

> Go back. She will embrace me, ask what it was like.
> Return. One thing – there was a space to write
> the colour of her eyes. They have an apple here,
> a bitter-sweet, which matches them exactly. Dearest,
> without you I am nowhere. It was cold.
>
> (*SM*, p. 59)

However, the femininity of his lover is not configurated as an essential state but emerges as a figure of fantasy. The temporality of the verbs switches constantly between future, past and present and endows this stanza with a dreamlike quality, we are never sure if he is really back in his home country or if he imagines what it might be like being reunited with his lover. Furthermore, the distance from her created a space which allows him to encounter her on a different level, a level of difference which recasts her identity as the product of his experience of otherness in the foreign country. Both masculinity and femininity merge into a state of interdependency; they perform each other fuelled by an ongoing process of recognition and reinvention or writing.

One could argue here that 'Deportation' is in danger of slipping into a moment of nostalgia for unity by eliminating the negativity and violence of displacement and alienation, by overshadowing them with a concept of heterosexual love that is able to heal the wounds of the foreigner. But I do not think that this is the case. I would rather suggest that the poem develops different scenarios of otherness and estrangement by avoiding a reductive understanding of them as simply repressive and resulting in annihilation. Of course, the meaning of deportation is foremost one of forcible removal, thus suggesting a loss of agency and independence. However, being carried away can also be interpreted as a positive creative process which allows us to occupy new positions from which what seemed familiar and known emerges as strange and worth intellectual investigation. Duffy, it seems to me, neither idealises nor condemns otherness but explores it in its productive and creative function as an underlying force in the process of identity formation. 'Dearest, / without you I am nowhere' is thus meaningful in more than one sense: it denotes the fear of being lost and un-recognised, but without the notion of nowhere we are not able to imagine to transcend anywhere. The foreigner, Kristeva argues, is

> never simply torn between here and elsewhere, now and before. Those who believe they are crucified in such a fashion forget that nothing ties them there anymore, and, so far, nothing binds them here, Always elsewhere, the foreigner belongs nowhere.[20]

## Coming home? Alienation and otherness in *The Other Country*

*Yes, I only have one language, yet it is not mine.*[21]

Whereas many of the poems collected in *Selling Manhattan* are preoccupied with alienation and displacement from the perspective of the foreigner who is thrown into an unknown culture and thus forced to contemplate his / her state of identity, *The Other Country* explores these concepts from a different point of view. The volume, to a certain extent, continues to intersect questions of identity formation with political and social issues, similar to the trajectory of the previous collection, but now these questions are asked in a different context. England and Britain become the other country, a place which is defined by exclusion and division, be it on account of class, gender, age or geography. To set the tone, the volume starts off with the poem 'Originally' which interrogates questions of personal and national origin. Poignantly, the poem is very hesitant to use the personal pronoun 'I', which emerges only at the end of the first two stanzas, then to become a predominant signifier in the last stanza that concludes with the lines 'Now, *Where do you come from?* / Strangers ask. *Originally?* And I hesitate.'[22] Thus, although identity is thematically at the centre of the poem, there is a definite reluctance to use the personal pronoun as a fixed indicator to pronounce the idea of a self-existent subjectivity. This hesitant 'I' dominates the rest of this collection which as a whole explores in an inquisitive and often curious manner the state of the nation and the people that inhabit it. It is as if the position of the securely enunciating 'I' is in a state of dispersion and in danger of vanishing as the poem 'Hometown' suggests. Here, identity becomes deeply intertwined with space and time:

> Wherever I went then, I was
> still there; fretting for something else, someone else,
> somewhere else. Or else, I thought, I shall die.
>
> (*TOC*, p. 10)

To a certain extent, the poem disintegrates the position of identity by situating it as defined by simultaneously repetition and deferral. The persona is 'still there' but at the same time sublated into something, someone, somewhere else. The following two stanzas are even more outspoken about the conditions of this dispersal of identity by placing it firmly into a temporal framework:

And so I shall. Decades ahead of this, both of me,
then and now, pass each other like ghosts
in the empty market-place where I imagine myself

to be older and away, or remember myself
younger, not loving this tuneless, flat bell
marking the time. Or moved to tears by its same sound.

(*TOC*, p. 10)

Home and being at home are here presented not as a fixed state but as a process which could be described as deferred action, placing the individual in conditions of time and space which question the idea that personal history and history as such can be understood as a simple continuous and cumulative movement. Psychoanalysis refers to this state as 'afterwardsness' (*Nachträglichkeit*) which Freud describes in a letter to Wilhelm Fliess in the following way:

> I am working on the assumption that our psychic mechanism has come into being by a process of stratification: the material present in the form of memory traces being subjected from time to time to a *rearrangement* in accordance with fresh circumstances – to a *retranscription*. Thus what is essentially new about my theory is the thesis that memory is present not once but several times over.[23] (Freud's emphasis)

The theme of 'afterwardsness' is a ubiquitous one in *The Other Country*: the different poems in this volume oscillate thematically between past, present and future interconnecting the personal history of the poet who moved from Scotland to England with that of national history and identity. To define oneself in relation to home, rather than stating a secure and known position, is here developed as a journey in time ('All childhood is an emigration' as Duffy puts it in the poem 'Originally') which propels the subject backwards as much as forwards from a temporal point of view. The structural and thematic organisation of the poems collected in this volume can be understood in direct relation to its time of publication. The beginning of the 1990s marked the heyday of Conservative and reactionary politics, with their ideological emphasis of national and political confidence and self-knowledge epitomised in slogans such as 'Victorian values', 'family values' and 'back to basics'. The Conservative government promoted an often unashamed pride in everything British, endowing the term with apparent essential properties which suggested a natural existence of

national identity and belonging. *The Other Country* with its emphasis
on fragmentation, dispersal and the questioning of identity as a known
and fixed state, can be read as a direct and critical comment on the
public and official ideology of the time. Britain of the early 1990s is
problematised as the other country as a result of a politics of alienation
and marginalisation of certain social groups but, at the same time, the
emerging other country also becomes a place in which alternative concepts of identity – national and personal – can be developed and tex-
tually experienced. Thus, from a political perspective, the poems can
be read as a political critique without reducing the existing system of
power to a clear-cut division of oppressors and oppressed. Power and
official ideology are explored as being based on and executed as
repression but also as productive of new models of identity and subjectivity in radically anti-essentialist terms. In that respect *The Other
Country* offers an alternative view of national and personal history
when suggesting that the public as well as the private body are 'totally
imprinted by history and the processes of history's destruction of the
body'.[24] The meaning of destruction is here an ambiguous one since it
denotes the end of something as well as the possibility of the emergence of new models and understandings of identity. Thus Britain is
the other country but it is precisely this otherness resulting in alienation and marginalisation which constructs a position from which
another country and other possibilities of being can be perceived.

One of the most eloquent examples of the ambiguity of otherness
is provided by the poem 'Mrs Skinner, North Street' (*TOC*, p. 12). Here,
the reader is confronted with the monologue of a lonely old woman,
addressing a nameless cat, her only companion in a world which offers
no points of reference for her memories: 'Scrounger. Workshy. Cat,
where is the world / she married, was carried into up a scrubbed stone
step?' Her only contact with the outside world is reduced to a termin-
ology of abuse ('Strumpet', 'Slut', 'Scrounger'), reflected in her language which is as fragmented and negative as her own sense of being.
This is England's north where redundancy has become a byword for
existence and where words such as 'Good morning. Morning. Lovely
day' have lost their meaning living in 'A terrace of strangers'. The
poem's language is dominated by a scattered and fragmented language ('Breaking of glass. Chants. Sour abuse of aerosols') which often
leaves no space for verbs as symbols for connecting subjects with
objects or other subjects. The persona never refers to herself as 'I', only

as 'she', thus addressing herself as defined by a system of signs which she can never inhabit actively. Her only sense of identity is gained negatively by projecting her feelings of alienation and exclusion on to racially different people, thus endlessly revisiting her own empty existence as a xenophobia which determines her own condition as much as that of the other disenfranchised. The poem draws a map of a post-industrial England which is divided into 'us' and 'them', where national identity is defined purely by economic success based on 'Fear, morbid dislike, of strangers' and thus on a process of 'othering' inherent to the colonial and imperialist tradition underlying the feeling of national pride. Age, colour, class, gender and geography are shown as discrete sites of discrimination, defined by their specific cultural and political discursive history which shows them as interrelated in a complex way, but nevertheless as heterogeneous discourses of oppression which cannot be reduced to a simplistic, monolithically structured Other.[25]

The history of Mrs Skinner is dispersed in impressions, experiences and memory-traces resulting in a jigsaw of identity which is never complete since its different pieces are constantly rearranged in a new order. Like so many other poems in this volume, it is the accuracy of memory and its effect on how we imagine ourselves in the present and the future that are problematised here. Personal and national history, rather than to be understood as developing in a chronological manner (as the official version would like to have us believe), is here evoked as 'a process which continually undoes and rewrites the past'[26] in the sense of Freudian 'afterwardsness'. As mentioned before, this sense of 'afterwardsness' or deferred action is a dominant feature in *The Other Country*, a volume that is preoccupied with the state of the nation, national identity and the experience of feeling at home. Poignantly, many of the poems gathered here are rather reluctant and hesitant in their use of personal pronouns and in particular the personal pronoun 'I'. This is especially the case in poems which reflect directly on personal and individual experience such as 'M-M-Memory' and 'In Your Mind'. The indicated stutter in the title 'M-M-Memory' indicates already the moment of hesitance and insecurity as dominant when attempting to approach the subject of remembering. And rather than re-membering and reassembling a sense of identity, memory seems to work in the opposite way: the poem provides no space for a self-assured 'I' as an enunciating subject that is is in control

of its past. Identity in all its manifestations is envisaged as an archaeological formation which inhabits the subject via language:

> Kneel there,
> words like fossils
> trapped in the roof of the mouth,
> forgotten, half-forgotten, half-
> recalled, the tongue dreaming
> it can trace their shape.
>
> Names, ghosts, m-memory.
> (*TOC*, p. 36)

The concept of 'afterwardsness' with its emphasis on repression, repetition and the return of the repressed is conceptually related to the
image of the self as an archaeological site suggesting that (self-)knowl-
edge is not constituted by the human subject but rather that knowledge should be understood as 'an effect of primarily linguistic
discursive formation, i.e. a set of fundamental rules that define the discursive space in which speaking subjects exist'.[27] Thus any sense of
identity, be it on a personal, historical or national level, can only ever
be a transitional construct, the effect of narrative structures and recon-
structions, some of them dominant others inhabiting the margins of
social discourse. Remembering who we are, where we belong to and
which country is ours can only ever lead back to the answer: '*Originally? And I hesitate*' (*TOC*, p. 7).

## Moving on home

> Not belonging to any place, any time, any love. A lost origin, the
> impossibility to take root, a rummaging memory, the present in
> abeyance. The space of the foreigner is a moving train, a plane in
> flight, the very transition that precludes stopping.[28]

*Selling Manhattan* and *The Other Country* are both collections which
articulate otherness, alienation and the feeling of being excluded from
a sense of national identity as political issues which are deeply intertwined with the particular history of Britain between the 1980s and
1990s. But the poems gathered in these volumes are more than just a
purely political critique of English jingoism and nationalistic pride. By
linking questions of national identity with an enquiry into the concept
of identity as such, Duffy not only shows to what extent a sense of

national belonging is always inextricably connected to a gesture of exclusion but, furthermore, points out the inherent emptiness of the 'naturalness' of a given and known subjectivity. This emptiness emerges on different levels: poems such as 'Translating the English, 1989' (*TOC*, p. 11), 'Poet For Our Times' (*TOC*, p. 15) and 'Making Money' (*TOC*, p. 17–18) explore it linguistically by focusing on the 'media-speak' of everyday language which concomitantly produces the speaking subject as the effect of language rather than its creator. This results in a state of alienation and exclusion in which the home country is exposed as the Other Country in which we are foreigners and have lost our bearings. But this process of estrangement is also explored as an opportunity of gaining a new perspective allowing a re-vision of ourselves/our selves. Otherness and the state of being foreign, rather than being monolithically viewed as purely based on and resulting in, exclusion, derives a new meaning here: it is that which inhabits identity as a constantly present alterity which does not allow closure or certainty. Thus the relationship between inside and outside rather than being structured in a rigid binary is here presented as one of oscillation, questioning the possibility of any kind of identity as fixed and stable places in a cultural system. Being marginalised and forced to inhabit the peripheries of the social and cultural order are here imagined in their productive function, as that on which a nation's and culture's representational systems are founded on and conditioned by. In 'In Your Mind', the last poem in *The Other Country*, Duffy expresses this in a more poetical way when she concludes in the final stanza:

> Then suddenly you are lost but not lost, dawdling
> on the blue bridge, watching six swans vanish
> under your feet. The certainty of place turns on the lights
> all over town, turns up the scent on the air. For a moment
> you are there, in the other country, knowing its name.
> And then a desk. A newspaper. A window. English rain.
>
> (*TOC*, p. 55)

## Notes

1  Julia Kristeva, *Strangers to Ourselves* (New York: Harvester Wheatsheaf, 1991), p. 42.
2  Anthony Smith, *National Identity* (Harmondsworth: Penguin, 1991), p. 143.

3  Virginia Woolf, *A Room of One's Own* (Oxford: Oxford University Press, 1992), p. 313.

4  John Lucas, *Modern Poetry from Hardy to Hughes* (London: Batsford, 1986), p. 8.

5  Cited in Andrew Crozier, 'Thrills and Frills: Poetry as Figures of Empirical Lyricism', in Alan Sinfield (ed.), *Society and Literature, 1945–1970* (London: Routledge, 1983), p. 214.

6  James Fenton, 'Ars Poetica', *The Independent on Sunday Review*, 10 June 1999, p. 18.

7  David Kennedy, *New Relations: The Refashioning of British Poetry 1980–1994* (Bridgend: Seren, 1996), p. 22.

8  Ibid., p. 57.

9  Neil Corcoran, *English Poetry Since 1940* (Harlow: Longman Group UK, 1993), p. xvi.

10  Vicki Bertram, (ed.), *Kicking Daffodils: Twentieth-century Women Poets* (Edinburgh: Edinburgh University Press, 1997), p. 3.

11  Peter Childs, *The Twentieth Century in Poetry. A Critical Survey* (London: Routledge, 1999), p. 160.

12  Angelica Michelis, 'A Country of One's Own: Gender and National Identity in Contemporary Women's Poetry', *European Journal of English Studies*, 6:1 (2002), p. 67.

13  Cairns Craig, 'From the Lost Ground: Liz Lochhead, Douglas Dunn, and Contemporary Scottish Poetry', in James Acheson, and Romana Huk (eds), *Contemporary British Poetry: Essays in Theory and Criticism* (Albany: State University of New York Press, 1996), p. 355.

14  Deryn Rees-Jones, *Carol Ann Duffy* (Plymouth: Northcote House, 1999), p. 5.

15  Carol Ann Duffy, *Selling Manhattan* (London: Anvil, 1987) p. 12.

16  Kristeva, p. 8.

17  Jacques Derrida, *Of Grammatology*, trans. G.C. Spivak (Baltimore: Johns Hopkins University Press, 1976) p. 145.

18  Jessica Benjamin, *The Shadow of the Other: Intersubjectivity and Gender in Psychoanalysis*. (London: Routledge, 1998), p. xiv.

19  Jessica Benjamin, *The Bonds of Love: Psychoanalysis, Feminism and the Problem of Domination* (New York: Pantheon Books, 1988), p. 221.

20  Kristeva, p. 10.

21  Jacques Derrida, *Monolingualism of the Other, or The Prothesis of Origin* (Stanford: Stanford University Press, 1998), p. 2.

22  Carol Ann Duffy, *The Other Country* (London: Anvil, 1990), p. 7.

23  Sigmund Freud, *The Complete Letters of Sigmund Freud to Wilhelm Fliess 1887–1904* (Cambridge, MA, and London: Harvard University Press, 1985), p. 207.

24  Michel Foucault, 'What is Enlightenment?', in Paul Rabinow (ed.), *The Foucault Reader* (Harmondsworth: Penguin, 1984), p. 83.

25  See also Michelis, 'A Country of One's Own'.

26  Linda Ruth Williams, *Critical Desire: Psychoanalysis and the Literary Subject* (London: Edward Arnold, 1995), p. 129.

27  Lois McNay, *Foucault and Feminism* (Cambridge and Oxford: Polity Press, 1992), p. 26.
28  Kristeva, pp. 7–8.

# 5

## 'Small Female Skull':
## patriarchy and philosophy
## in the poetry of Carol Ann Duffy

### AVRIL HORNER

IN THIS CHAPTER I shall argue that much of Carol Ann Duffy's work engages with the central tenets of western philosophy and culture, wittily exposing their subjective nature and the often 'ludicrous views'[1] in which they result. This should not surprise us, given the nature of Duffy's work and the fact that she graduated with a degree in philosophy from the University of Liverpool in 1977. However, so far, work on Duffy in relation to philosophy has concentrated mainly on language-related issues, in an attempt to elucidate the complex nature of her wordplay.[2] I want to make the rather different claim here that Duffy's poetry tilts at the supposed objectivity of western philosophy in general and at the cultural legacy bequeathed by Cartesian dualism in particular. Her prime aim in making this challenge to the tradition of western philosophy is to show how it underpins particular forms of patriarchy and, as a consequence, how both sexes have been damaged by it in different ways. In this respect, Carol Ann Duffy can justifiably be described as a feminist postmodernist writer.

A close reading of 'Small Female Skull', from the acclaimed volume *Mean Time* will, I hope, begin to make the case. The opening stanza presents us with the first person-narrator, a woman, balancing 'my small female skull' in her hands. The skull is here an object, held up quizzically for inspection and comprehension: 'What is it like? An ocarina?'[3] Not surprisingly, it connotes mortality in a way that 'mildly' alarms the narrator, who presses her ear 'to its grin'. At the same time, its 'vanishing sigh' suggests the seductive mystery of what Shakespeare called 'The undiscovered country, from whose bourn / No traveller returns'.[4] For, of course, the parallels with *Hamlet* are deliberate: the mention of the ocarina (a musical instrument with a whistle-like mouthpiece and finger-holes) recalls Hamlet's castigation of Guildenstern when he presumes to 'play' upon the prince as if he were an instrument whose secrets and 'mystery' could easily be mastered.[5] The narrator's evocation of the dead woman's flesh and presence – her eye, her nose, her cry – suggests Hamlet's evocation of Yorick's humour and physical energy in the play's famous graveyard scene.[6] Haunting these first few lines, then, is the presence of Shakespeare's tragic prince as poet philosopher in the face of death.

These echoes of high art are quickly dissipated however by the next stanza, which presents us with the narrator sitting 'on the lavatory seat with my head / in my hands, appalled'. (Even here, though, it is difficult to resist the irreverent allusion to Rodin's 'The Thinker', whose similar pose signals the solitary male philosopher.) Appalled, presumably, by the experience of looking death squarely in the eye in this way, the narrator finds the inhumanity of the human relic 'Disturbing' and suggestive of a supernatural energy, 'as though it could levitate'. Yet there is an intimacy and a macabre humour here that expresses itself in the narrator's ventriloquist play with the skull in front of a mirror 'to ask for a gottle of geer'. But then, half-way through the third stanza, the poem changes mood yet again: the narrator washes the skull, handling it as gently as a 'firstborn', and sees (on the skull? In the mirror?) 'the scar where I fell for sheer love / down treacherous stairs, and read that shattering day like braille'. This leads us into the final stanza in which the memory of love is celebrated as indicative of life itself:

> *Love*, I murmur to my skull, then, louder, other grand words,
> shouting the hollow nouns in a white-tiled room.
> Downstairs they will think I have lost my mind. No. I only weep
> into these two holes here, or I'm grinning back at the joke, this is
> a friend of mine. See, I hold her face in trembling, passionate hands.
> (*MT*, p. 25)

The poem poses many riddles. Why is this 'A friend of mine'? Because she actually knew the owner of the skull? Because these intimate moments with a piece of bone have resulted in an acceptance of death itself? Because the skull reminds her of a (dead?) female lover? At the same time, the meaning of the poem is destabilised by the sense, running throughout, that the addressed skull is also that of the narrator herself. The use, for example, of the common phrase 'my head in my hands' suggests that the skull is the narrator's own, as does the seamless transition from washing the skull to seeing (on her own head) 'the scar where I fell for sheer love'.

In a sense, then, the narrator is addressing both an object, which represents an other, and a subject, who is herself. Indeed, the very act of appropriating Hamlet's pose when contemplating Yorick's remains enables Duffy's narrator to move through a deliberately ambiguous presentation of the skull as both her own and that of another. This, in turn, allows her to do several things. First of all, she presents what has become a clichéd moment of textual epiphany in a fresh light: the 'thinker' is here a woman, holding a female skull. That in itself alerts us to the fact that the western construction of the great lone philosopher is invariably male. How often have profound thoughts on death and mortality, presented from the female point of view, become canonised in western art? Far more common, as Elisabeth Bronfen has pointed out, is the reification of the female dead body as an object for male contemplation[7] or the portrait of the male thinker, inspired by the sight of a skull, dwelling on mutability and mortality. Georges de la Tour's paintings *The Magdalen* (circa 1625–28) and *Repentant Magdalen* (circa 1640) are rare examples of works that show a woman contemplating a skull;[8] they might even have been the inspiration for Duffy's poem. Secondly, the ambiguous nature of the female skull allows the narrator to switch between the notion of the woman as the subject (who thinks) and as an object (for contemplation by others). (This is also, of course, the dynamic which underpins the better-known poem, 'Standing Female Nude'.) Thirdly, the fact that the experience of love has been written as a scar on bone (of whichever skull) leads the narrator into a celebration of the living body as a feeling as well as thinking entity: a body which might have written on it signs of pain, love, despair, anger, desolation. What we see here, then, is a rejection of the mind/body split as conceptualised in the work of the French philosopher, René Descartes, which – in true Aristotelian mode – further privileged the mind over the body and rationality over emotion. In this light, of course, the narrator's 'philosophical' pose of holding her head in her hands whilst 'on the lavatory seat' can be seen as a critique of western philosophy's neglect of the body and its functions. Duffy's attack on the Enlightenment's embrace of Cartesian mind–body dualism thus flies in the face of western epistemology which, as Alison Jaggar notes, has tended to view not only the body but also emotion with hostility and suspicion. As Jaggar points out, in such a tradition:

> Not only has reason been contrasted with emotion, but it has also been associated with the mental, the cultural, the universal, the public and the male, whereas emotion has been associated with the irrational, the physical, the natural, the particular, the private and, of course, the female.[9]

Duffy's poem thus challenges the idea that the figure of the philosopher should be represented by a 'rational', 'objective' male whose enquiries supposedly transcend the body and emotion (which both then become seen as 'feminine') in a 'universal' engagement with death. It also challenges the nineteenth-century medico-scientific discourse which 'proved' the inferiority of woman as thinker by reference to the smallness of her skull in relation to that of the male. Instead, the poem presents us with a narrator who, by implication, recognises the fallacies underpinning much western philosophy and whose 'passionate' engagement with death reaffirms the validity of emotion as an aspect of thinking as well as different ways of being (a woman who loves other women). This is a poet who wants to suggest alternative ways of conceptualising the thinking process itself ('they will think I have lost my mind').

In such respects, the poem is deeply critical of western thought and the role that Aristotelian philosophy has played in shaping it. It demands that woman should find her own voice within the role of poet philosopher and present an alternative understanding of the world. In this respect, the narrator's ventriloquist use of the skull is both comic and serious: its moment of macabre humour poses questions concerning the right of anyone to speak for someone else, since the dummy or skull can 'speak' only through another.[10] Duffy used this metaphor earlier, in the poem 'The Dummy', where it allowed her to raise questions about the social, economic and political subordination – and consequent silencing – of one person or culture by another. Here, the ventriloquist's dummy gains a voice of its own through the poem's narrative and becomes assertive about its own 'separate' identity. Aggressively parodying the stance of the psychoanalyst who probes unconscious motivations for behaviour, the dummy even implies that the controlling figure envies its attributes:

Can you dance? No. I don't suppose
you'd be doing this if you could dance. Right? Why do you
keep me in that black box? I can ask questions too,
you know. I can see that worries you. Tough.

So funny things happen to everyone on the way to most places.
*Come on.* You can do getter than that, can't you?[11]

Appearing in *Selling Manhattan*, a volume that often 'speaks' for the disenfranchised, dispossessed and disempowered, the 'I' in this poem stands for all those suffering from some form of oppression. 'Small Female Skull' briefly retrieves the ventriloquist-dummy metaphor to raise questions about what has been, until recently in historical terms, the marginalisation of women within the philosophical discourse of the western world, a discourse that has always presented itself as an objective discipline based on the rigours of logic. Interestingly, a recent survey of more than a thousand philosophers, academics and students by the authoritative *Philosophers' Magazine* resulted in a list of the ten 'greatest philosophical works'.[12] Not one of these was by a woman, despite the enduring importance of female philosophers such as Mary Wollstonecraft, Hannah Arendt and Simone de Beauvoir. However, poststructuralism has enabled us to expose many influential discourses as essentialising and concealing a logic of domination. In particular, Hélène Cixous's deconstruction of the binary nature of patriarchal thought and Luce Irigaray's exposure of the biases underpinning western philosophy resulted in searing feminist critiques of the nature of philosophy itself.[13] It is unlikely that Duffy would have read the work of either Cixous or Irigaray whilst at Liverpool University in the mid-1970s, since their writing was not translated into English until the early 1980s, although, of course, she might well have read them since. However, it is more than likely that she would have studied the work of Kant, Adam Smith, Rousseau, Hegel and Nietzsche as well as that of Aristotle.[14] As Ellen Kennedy and Susan Mendus have pointed out, despite their differences in many areas, these philosophers make the same assumptions about women:

> Several themes recur throughout: the assumption that women's biological nature dictates and justified her lack of political status; the belief that woman's psychological nature is gentle, submissive, emotional, irrational; the insistence on confining women to hearth and home; the assertion that women are suited to rearing citizens but not

to being citizens themselves – all these views are either explicitly or implicitly adopted by philosophers otherwise completely at odds in their moral and political philosophy.[15]

During the 1980s postmodernists and feminist theorists argued vigorously that such masculinist assumptions (which had been lent a spurious respectability by their provenance within philosophic discourse) led to women being positioned on the negative side of a binary divide which always privileged one term at the expense of another. Hélène Cixous, for example, argued that men and women occupy very different positions in the symbolic order:

> *Where is she?*
> Activity/passivity,
> Sun/Moon,
> Culture/Nature,
> Day/Night,
>
> Father/Mother,
> Head/heart,
> Intelligible/sensitive,
> Logos/Pathos . . .
> <u>Man</u>
> Woman.[16]

As Andrea Nye has pointed out:

> Cixous does not view these as universal semantic structures necessary in any symbolic expression, nor does she undermine the rational order of the texts in which they are found only to restore it again. Instead she notes that the oppositions are 'couples'. In other words semantic structure mimics the human institution of the male/female couple. Further, she notes that the contrasts are kept in place only with violence, as in the contrast between rich/poor, master/slave, civilized/primitive. Semantics is not a neutral analysis, it corresponds to the power relations in the real world, relations that are maintained by force, a force applied by grammarians, linguists, and philosophers, as well as by police and armies. Semantic well-formedness does not reflect the power of the symbolic Father, so much as the power of men to establish and enforce hierarchical relations.[17]

The French thinker Luce Irigaray has also done much to explore precisely how such 'hierarchical relations' devalue and silence woman within western culture in the spheres of mythology, psychoanalysis and philosophy.[18] Following in Irigaray's footsteps, Judith Butler has pointed out that what has to be excluded from 'the economics of discursive intelligibility' is 'the feminine . . . the unspeakable condition of figuration . . . that which, in fact, can never be figured within the terms of philosophy proper, but whose exclusion from that propriety is its enabling condition'.[19] Such an exclusion, constituted within the symbolic order, results in a philosophic discourse that is far from objective; it also traps both men and women within masquerades of gender.

Duffy has always been recognised, of course, for poetry that shows a sharp awareness of how the social power dynamic between empowered and disempowered groups of people developed in Britain during and after the Thatcher regime. Her portrayal of contemporary society, in earlier volumes, through the viewpoints of children, immigrants or poorly paid or financially dependent women, offers us a sharply critical perspective of the ideological foundations on which it rests. As Linda Kinnahan notes, 'As a feminist attentive to divisions of power along lines of gender, class, race and nationality, she writes a poetry that continually contextualizes this fusion of the poetic and philosophical within the social'.[20] In *The World's Wife*, however, which ranges from Greek civilisation to the present day, Duffy is less concerned with a specific historical moment than with how western thought processes underpin a value system that has led to inequity and a damaging 'rigidification' of gender roles.

This is a book in which Duffy's feminist credentials are made absolutely clear; in which her great skill in the use of the dramatic monologue is harnessed to allow the anonymised 'wife' to speak; in which, with wit and irreverence, she truly 'think[s] back through our mothers', to use the words of Virginia Woolf.[21] Behind the light touch, however, there is not only a stripping away of the romance narrative which seduces so many women into collusion with patriarchal values, but also a deep engagement with a philosophic and cultural legacy that has resulted in women's dispossession. Mrs Aesop's irreverent dismissal of her husband's saws and fables – 'By Christ, he could bore for Purgatory' – has delighted many a reader with its comic attack on masculine egotism and intellectual self-inflation. Its end is dark, however, hinting at a scenario in which the wife will wreak a final, awful revenge:

> I gave him a fable one night
> about a little cock that wouldn't crow, a razor-sharp axe
> with a heart blacker than the pot that called the kettle.
> *I'll cut off your tail, all right,* I said, to *save my face.*
> That shut him up. I laughed last, longest.
>
> (*TWW*, p. 19)

Mrs Aesop might not have a room of her own but she does have a dis-enchanted mind of her own. Aesopus was, according to *Lemprière's Classical Dictionary*, a Phrygian philosopher who dedicated his fables to his patron Croesus and whose biographer, Maximus Planudes, asserted that he was 'short and deformed';[22] hence 'He was small, / didn't prepossess'. This is our cue for how to read the volume as a whole: men have, historically speaking, had the last word as well as the power and the wealth. But this does not, and never has, stopped women challenging their world view – and this is precisely what *The World's Wife* does. It does so through humorous debunking, with a wonderful brio and feisty zest that is far more effective than sober-sided feminist criticism. It has its own emotional chronology, too, which moves us from the experience of the adolescent girl losing her virginity to an older man in the first poem, through various chartings of disillusion and disenchantment with heterosexual experience and marriage, alongside a gradual and joyous affirmation of women's desire for each other, to the final poem which celebrates the love of a mother for her daughter (and, by implication, bonds between women). The analogies with Duffy's own life are clear: lover of the much older Adrian Henri whilst still an adolescent; intellectual devel-opment as a student of philosophy; maturation into poet, lesbian and mother of a daughter in adulthood. Thus in one sense, the volume is deeply personal and autobiographical. Indeed, Duffy has commented in interview: 'Each poem had to be personally honest, and have some kind of autobiographical element in it, whether it had happened to me or whether it was an emotional or intellectual truth.'[23]

However, *The World's Wife* also very clearly presents itself as engaging with a tradition of women's writing and thought. Not sur-prisingly, then, running through the volume there is a heavy emphasis on speech, silence and finding one's voice as a woman. In this, and in its overall structure, it resembles Plath's volume of poetry *Ariel* which, in its original configuration, worked its way out of anger to end on a note of hope: 'The bees are flying. They taste the spring' ('Wintering').[24] Indeed, *Ariel* concluded originally with the famous 'Bee Sequence' poems (of which 'Wintering' is the last) and which extol the forging of a separate female identity in the powerful figure of the Queen Bee within a community that has exorcised the male ('They have got rid of the men, / The blunt, clumsy stumblers, the boors. / Winter is for women').[25] Similarly, Duffy's volume moves towards regeneration of the self through the creation of a strong female identity. This identity is a complex one. It is founded not only on a witty irreverence for the masquerade of masculinity, as voiced by the many long-suffering wives of 'great men', but also on a reaffirmation of tenderness, imagination, emotional warmth, physical sensuousness and creativity. These qualities, portrayed as positive and life-enhancing, are not confined only to women although they are often pitted against 'masculine' self-aggrandisement and selfishness; furthermore, they are also occasionally combined with other qualities traditionally perceived as 'masculine', such as boldness, strength and single-mindedness. Thus, Duffy's portrayal of such characteristics does not represent merely a nostalgic return to a 1970s feminist essentialist agenda. Rather, it celebrates a sort of emotional pluralism. In so doing, it seeks to challenge the conventional gendering of feeling and to focus on the redemptive power of what Alison M. Jaggar has defined as 'outlaw' emotions – emotions that are politically (because epistemologically) subversive:

> Outlaw emotions are distinguished by their incompatibility with the dominant perceptions and values, and some, though certainly not all, of these outlaw emotions are potentially or actually feminist emotions. Emotions become feminist when they incorporate feminist perceptions and values, just as emotions are sexist or racist when they incorporate sexist or racist perceptions and values . . . Outlaw emotions stand in a dialectical relation to critical social theory: at least some are necessary to developing a critical perspective on the world, but they also presuppose at least the beginnings of such a perspective. Feminists need to be aware of how we can draw on some of our outlaw emotions in constructing feminist theory and also of how the increasing sophistication of feminist theory can contribute to the reeducation, refinement, and eventual reconstruction of our emotional constitution.[26]

Hence Duffy's irreverence for tradition and the individual great man, whose weaknesses and faults are comically exaggerated so as to reduce him to a figure of ridicule, no matter what his role in history. We see here not the heroism or importance of men as documented in the archives or in myth or in the Bible, but the human impact and cost of their choices and their lives on others. We see them not in high and public profile but through the eyes of their wives within the perspective offered by the bedroom and the kitchen. In fact, we see them horrid and at home. Thus we are made fully aware of the true sources of their fame: Midas' greed; Tiresias' vanity and hypochondria; Pilate's fear, insecurity and cruelty; Sisyphus' blind workaholism; Faust's deviousness and lust for power; Samson's emotional aridity; Quasimodo's abusiveness; Perseus' sexual infidelity; the devil's murderousness; Pygmalion's sexual immaturity; Freud's fantasy of penis power; Orpheus's arrogance – all qualities traditionally exonerated within the masculine quest for glory, fortune and power. The binary divide of villain and hero becomes irrelevant since both are seen in this volume to be obsessive, inadequate and insecure; being the wife of a great man can be as emotionally deadening as being the partner of a common murderer.

In celebrating 'outlaw' emotions, the poems in *The World's Wife* perhaps inevitably chart a gradual break away from conventional attitudes to gender and from heterosexuality.[27] They also, however, implicitly document the seductive attractions, for women, of collusion with the patriarchal system – including access to power and wealth (shown, for example, in Mrs Faust's admission that she 'grew to love the lifestyle' (*TWW*, p. 23)). As the volume progresses, this value system is finally displaced by an optimistic trust in change, represented most movingly in the volume's closing poem, 'Demeter'. Here, the narrator's love for and pride in her daughter suggest hope in the intelligence and eloquence of a new generation of women represented by 'the small shy mouth of a new moon' (*TWW*, p. 76). In that sense, the journey between the first and the last poems of *The World's Wife* is a long one that embraces many recognised feminist strategies, including that defined by Alicia Ostriker as 'revisionist mythmaking':

> Whenever a poet employs a figure or story previously accepted and defined by a culture, the poet is using myth, and the potential is always present that the use will be revisionist: that is, the figure or tale will be appropriated for altered ends, the old vessel filled with new wine, initially satisfying the thirst of the individual poet but ultimately making cultural change possible . . . These poems generically

assume the high literary status that myth confers and that women writers have often been denied because they write 'personally' or 'confessionally'. But in them the old stories are changed, changed utterly, by female knowledge of female experience, so that they can no longer stand as foundations of collective male fantasy. Instead . . . they are corrections; they are representations of what women find divine and demonic in themselves; they are retrieved images of what women have collectively and historically suffered; in some cases they are instructions for survival.[28]

Of the volume's thirty poems, twelve revise Greek myths, eight revise portraits of actual men (from Faust[29] and Darwin to Elvis Presley and the Kray Brothers), five revise Biblical stories and three revise fairy or folk tales (the remaining two deal with a cinematic creation, King Kong, and a character from literature, Quasimodo). In so doing, they certainly give us women who are both 'divine and demonic'.

The first three poems form what we might call a doorway to the volume, in this respect, since in turn they re-work a well-known folk tale, a Greek myth and a Biblical story. 'Little Red-Cap' revises 'Little Red Riding Hood' in order to explore a rite of passage through puberty, the seductions of heterosexuality and initiation into the male-dominated world of writing.[30] Here, the wolf is transformed into a pseudo-sophisticated and self-centred poet, 'reading his verse out loud / in his wolfy drawl, a paperback in his hairy paw, / red wine staining his bearded jaw' (*TWW*, p. 3). As in Angela Carter's 'The Bloody Chamber' (itself a revision of the Bluebeard folk tale), the heroine's apparent collusion with this display of male vanity is made clear: 'I made quite sure he spotted me, / sweet sixteen, never been, babe, waif, and bought me a drink, / my first' (*TWW*, p. 3). The echo here of the mid-twentieth-century popular song line 'sweet sixteen and never been kissed' indicates a certain naivety but this is quickly undercut by Little Red-Cap's confession of her motives for collusion: 'You might ask why. Here's why. Poetry. / The wolf, I knew, would lead me deep into the woods, / away from home, to a dark tangled thorny place / lit by the eyes of owls'. In this encounter, she plays along with the game of seduction and loses her virginity ('scraps of red'). However, through this loss she gains not only sexual knowledge but also knowledge of what will happen to her own poetic talent if she allows herself to become enmeshed in a relationship with a male writer – he will simply devour her 'white dove' of language. So she takes what she wants:

in a poetic apprenticeship of ten years, she devours his books and finds a more sustaining excitement in the 'words, words' of his lair. Then comes the moment of truth: that if she stays with him her own talent will never find expression : 'it took ten years / in the woods to tell that a mushroom stoppers the mouth of a buried corpse' (*TWW*, p. 4). So she takes the axe of understanding to the world around her and, in dispatching the wolf, releases the power of a matrilineal legacy as well as her own energy, power and talent: 'I took an axe to the wolf / as he slept, one chop, scrotum to throat, and saw / the glistening, virgin white of my grandmother's bones. / I filled his old belly with stones. I stitched him up. / Out of the forest I come with my flowers, singing, all alone.' The opposition between silence and language which has structured the poem – with the wolf appropriating sound – is here resolved. The 'silent railway line' and the stoppered mouth, the wolf's drawl and tedious howl, give way to her own use of language which is expressed metaphorically through references to birds and music: 'in search of a living bird – white dove -'; 'Words . . . warm, beating, frantic, winged'; 'birds are the uttered thoughts of trees'; 'I come . . . singing, all alone'. Here, then, is her manifesto: she will be the poet; she will become Orpheus; she will liberate herself. Any self-aggrandisement associated with this is, however, undercut by the poem's humour which resides partly in the deliberate reworking of clichés: 'clapped eyes on'; 'ripped to shreds', 'same rhyme, same reason', 'I stitched him up'. In an interview given in 1988, Duffy stated – in commenting on her deliberate use of cliché – 'I like to use simple words but in a complicated way so that you can see the lies and truths within the poem.'[31] This, then, is a writer who intends to work with the language of the people, rinsing and restoring cliché in order to make her readers perceive hidden narratives. Moreover, this narrator does not look to her own fame, but sees her task as that of finding an individual poetic voice within a female tradition. In retrieving the 'virgin white' of her grandmother's bones, she is re-enacting both Virginia Woolf's retrieval of Judith Shakespeare ('But she lives; for great poets do not die; they are continuing presences; they need only the opportunity to walk among us in the flesh')[32] and Sylvia Plath's determined fight against overwhelming engulfment by the Colossus, the male world of poetry.[33] Yet the last optimistic line, in which the narrator chooses aloneness but carrying flowers and 'singing', looks not back, but forward to the future and to the final poem of the volume. In 'Demeter', the daughter will bring 'all spring's flowers / to her mother's house' and we shall meet a girl whose warmth and shy but articulate confidence will continue this agenda of 'thinking back through one's mothers' (*TWW*, p. 76).

If 'Little Red-Cap' rejects heterosexuality in pursuit of poetic female integrity, 'Thetis' revises the Greek myth by lending the sea deity the powers of transformation that are accorded to Peleus, her lover, in the original version. In the Greek tale, Thetis's refusal of Peleus is thwarted by his trapping her when she is asleep and preventing her escape by assuming different forms. She then bears him several children, one of whom (Achilles) is destined to become greater than his father. In Duffy's version, Thetis resists diminishment by the more powerful male, and it is she who enacts a series of metamorphoses, through animal and element, until the final transformation into fire itself:

> Then my tongue was flame
> and my kisses burned,
> but the groom wore asbestos.
> So I changed, I learned,
> turned inside out – or that's
> how it felt when the child burst out.
> (*TWW*, p. 6)

Echoing Plath's poem of resurrection, 'Lady Lazarus' (which concludes, 'Beware / Beware. / Out of the ash / I rise with red hair / And I eat men like air'),[34] the lines suggest, in addition, a retrieved and almost pentecostal ability to utter ('Then my tongue was flame'). The final words celebrate a fundamental difference between the sexes: only woman can give birth – although 'the child' here is perhaps also the inner expressive self of Thetis with which she has had to struggle, through so many transformations, to set free.

'Queen Herod' revises the biblical stories of Herod, the three wise men and the birth of Jesus in a conflated narrative which offers an alternative, female, logic for Herod's murder of all male children under the age of two in Judea. In Duffy's version the three wise men are replaced by three exotic and glamorous Queens ('dressed in furs, accented' *TWW*, p. 7) who are also clearly related to the fairy godmothers at Snow White's cradle and who offer a more benign version of the 'three ladies' as portrayed in Plath's 'The Disquieting Muses'.

Powerful, they are also benevolent (wishing grace, strength and hap-
piness for the Queen's child) and wise. Irreverently and daringly, one
of them – the lesbian black Queen – stares at Herod's wife 'with inso-
lent lust', bending to scoop out her breast so that the baby might feed.
This moment, which is nurturing as well as erotic, marks both the
beginning and end of a matriarchy: the beginning, in that the poem
contains its own optimism and confidence in modern women's ability
to protect each other from masculine exploitation and abuse ('No man,
I swore, will make her shed one tear'); the end, in that – in historical
retrospect – the reader knows that the birth of the Messiah will usher
in a long era of Pauline Christian thought antipathetic to women's bodies and minds. It is the black Queen's warning of this new era that
prompts Queen Herod to give the order 'Take men and horses / knives,
swords, cutlasses. / Ride East from here / and kill each mother's son.
/ Do it. Spare not one' (*TWW*, p. 9). The poem's conclusion, which celebrates both women's ability to nurture tenderly and their murderous
strength, draws on images of the Apocalypse for its effects:

> We wade through blood
> for our sleeping girls.
> We have daggers for eyes.
>
> Behind our lullabies,
> the hooves of terrible horses
> thunder and drum.
> (*TWW*, p. 10)

These first three poems, then, set up a series of transitions which
will structure and inform the whole volume: they offer women readers movement from listening to speaking; from silence to eloquence,
from weakness to strength, from marginal to central, from passivity to
action. As the volume proceeds, such confidence is buttressed by an
implied affirmation of 'outlaw emotions' despite the plights of individual women. Mrs Midas' capacity for tenderness, sensuality and intimacy ('I miss most, even now, his hands, his warm hands on my skin,
his touch' (*TWW*, p. 13)) is rendered redundant by her husband's
imprudence, greed and vanity. Pilate's wife's generous recognition of
Christ's extraordinary charismatic presence (whether or not he was
divine) is eclipsed, historically, by her husband's anxious fears and
insecurity, which result in the cruelty of crucifixion. Mrs Sisyphus' ability to enjoy the ordinary things of life – a walk in the park or a drink

of wine – is negated by her husband's workaholic obsession with task performance. Pygmalion's desire to possess his bride as an object, made manifest in his infantilisation of her and his obsession with her physical presence, are challenged, finally, by her expression of an adult, sexual passion. Mrs Rip Van Winkle's delight in finding time and space for herself in 'late middle age', which she spends painting and travelling, is comically but bleakly threatened by her husband's desperate chemical retrieval of his virility – a tension neatly captured in the rhyming of 'Niagara' (the subject of her latest pastel) with 'Viagra' (*TWW*, p. 53). Frau Freud, in her wonderful list of euphemisms for the penis, undermines the supposed objectivity of psychoanalytic discourse through hinting at vaginal envy as the source of her husband's obsession with the phallic ('the squint of its envious solitary eye' (*TWW*, p. 55)). And so on, and so on.

There are also, though, poems which recount the destructive effects of the husband's egotism and cruelty on the female mind such that the wife herself becomes an apprentice in aggression, cruelty and self-destruction: Mrs Quasimodo is driven, by her husband's verbal abuse of her, to minor acts of vandalism; Medusa's terrifying demeanour is seen as a metaphorical representation of 'Love gone bad' – the depression that set in when her husband turned to younger women; 'The Devil's Wife' gives us a character, perhaps based on the Moors murderer Myra Hindley, whose worst acts were prompted by her infatuation with a diabolic male partner. Yet other poems show us women who have moved beyond heterosexual relationships into a cynical self-sufficiency: in 'Circe', for example, we see the disillusionment of the mature woman. Men are, for her, no longer heroes or even desirable; instead, they have their uses – in this context, as food for thought in more ways than one. For, in a parody of a television cookery programme, Circe's talents and powers are domesticated into culinary skills. Here, 'the skills of the tongue' have become paramount and men are reduced to mere recipe ingredients: 'Now, let us baste that sizzling pig on the spit once again' (*TWW*, p. 48). To offset these blackly comic elements of the volume, however, we are presented with delicate moments in which the sexes move towards each other and in which the rigidities of masculinity and femininity are loosened. 'Delilah' shows us the warrior seeking the gift of intimacy, 'Anne Hathaway' recalls moments of heterosexual erotic tenderness and imagination in Shakespeare's famous second-best bed and 'Queen Kong' gives us an inverted world in which the man is allowed to be nervous, dreamy and delicate whilst the woman is strong, excessive, determined and passionate. For, if the collection's energy derives partly from its strong reaction to the aggressive materialism and power-seeking evident in a capitalist patriarchal society, it also derives a serene strength from its celebration of 'outlaw' qualities such as tenderness, sensuality, imagination, intimacy, generosity, creativity and love. Whilst Duffy occasionally links these qualities to men in *The World's Wife* (thus avoiding essentialism), on the whole they are associated mainly with female characters, knowledge and value systems.[35]

In my initial remarks on *The World's Wife*, I suggested that the three opening poems set the volume's agenda. I want to conclude my discussion of this work by drawing attention to three other poems, all of which rework Greek myths. They are, I suggest, important both in encapsulating Duffy's celebration of 'outlaw' values and in leading up to the volume's conclusion. In 'Eurydice', we see a revision of the Greek myth that develops the themes set up in 'Little Red-Cap'. Other poets, including D.H. Lawrence and H.D., have adapted the tale of Orpheus and Eurydice in order to explore the dynamics of creativity; Duffy does so with a candid irreverence for both the individual and tradition, with a special swipe (again) at the conceit of the male poet. 'Deadness' for the female narrator consists in being 'out of this world', down in the shades of Hades, no longer available as Muse to the pest of a man 'who follows her round writing poems' and who 'once sulked for a night and a day because she remarked on his weakness for abstract nouns' (*TWW*, p. 58). A writer herself, she nevertheless did all his typing for him and knows that the blurb on the back of Big O's books – which soars into the realms of hyperbole – is 'Bollocks'. Placing herself in a long tradition of talented women who helped male partners or relatives in their work – from Milton's daughters to Dorothy Wordsworth to Plath (who typed out Hughes's poems for him) – she signals disaffection from such exploitation. Her retreat to Hades, it is implied, had nothing to do with Pluto and everything to do with wishing to escape both Big O's appropriation of her as Muse and typist and the male chauvinist world of publishing:

> And given my time all over again,
> rest assured that I'd rather speak for myself
> than be Dearest, Beloved, Dark Lady, White Goddess, etc., etc.
> In fact, girls, I'd rather be dead.

But the Gods are like publishers,
usually male,
and what you doubtless know of my tale
is the deal.

(*TWW*, p. 59)

The famous 'deal' here, however, is changed completely by Eurydice's
determination to remain severed from her husband and to stay free of
being 'trapped in his images, metaphors, similes, octaves and sextets,
quatrains and couplets, elegies, limericks, villanelles, histories, myths
. . .' (*TWW*, p. 60). She is finding her way from being seen as an object
to becoming a subject. She does so, finally, by a trick that is dependent
on Big O's arrogance for its success: he turns round the moment she
says, 'Orpheus your poem's a masterpiece. / I'd love to hear it again'
(*TWW*, p. 61). He thus loses her for ever and at the same moment
unwittingly releases her from psychological imprisonment:

> The dead are so talented.
> The living walk by the edge of a vast lake
> near the wise, drowned silence of the dead.
>
> (*TWW*, p. 62)

Here, then, to be 'dead' to the male world of writing is to become alive
as a female subject and author: the connection with Plath's realisation
of authentic subjectivity through suicide is perilously seductive but
perhaps not to be pursued too closely. In Duffy's poem, unlike Plath's
'Edge', the sombre alternatives of death in life or life in death are offset by a jaunty conspiracy between the narrator and the 'girls', the
implied readers who are invited to ditch one dominant cultural narrative in favour of another that challenges the *grand récit* of gender difference as expressed in high art: 'Girls, forget what you've read. It
happened like this –'. This is girl power with a vengeance and it recalls
Duffy's statement that her poems look 'for the missing truth, rather
than accepting the way we've been taught'.[36]

Duffy's revision of the Greek tale of Penelope gives us another
'missing truth': that women can destroy themselves and their creative
abilities by colluding with the patriarchal notion that a woman is
incomplete without a male partner.[37] The dominant version of the
myth shows us Penelope as the faithful wife of Ulysses who left to fight
in the Trojan War but who did not return until after a ten-year
absence. Suitors clustered round her, persuading her that he must be

dead. Dependent on these suitors for support, yet not wishing to marry any of them, Penelope foiled their persistence by declaring that she would make a choice of one of them as soon as she had finished a piece of tapestry on which she was employed. At night, however, she undid the work she had done in the daytime. This continued until Ulysses finally returned home. In Duffy's poem, however, Penelope's tapestry has a subject: her own life. In the record of this life we see first the careless freedoms of a happy young girl whose joy is associated with nature and growth ('an acorn / pushing up through umber soil' (*TWW*, p. 70)). This sure and free identity disappears completely 'in a wild embroidery of love, lust, loss, lessons learnt' when, as a young woman, she falls in love with Ulysses. During his long absence, however, she finds a surer, more peaceful sense of self that requires neither self-sacrifice nor completion by another:

> I was picking out
> the smile of a woman at the centre
> of this world, self-contained, absorbed, content,
> most certainly not waiting

(TWW, p. 71)

His return is therefore neither long-awaited nor particularly welcome since it disrupts this female serenity of self. The poem's conclusion suggests not only the resumption of the sexual act but also anger at this unwanted violation of a mature female identity: 'I licked my scarlet thread / and aimed it surely at the middle of the needle's eye once more.'[38]

It is, then, no surprise to find that the final poem, 'Demeter', celebrates the mother–daughter bond and, by implication, a community of women. Here, though, it is Demeter, rather than Persephone, who is held in winter's icy grip – metaphorically a spiritual and emotional wasteland. Duffy inverts the Greek myth so that, rather than the mother seeking to rescue the daughter from Pluto's cold clutches, it is the daughter who rescues the mother and who heals her broken heart:

> She came from a long, long way,
> but I saw her at last, walking,
> my daughter, my girl, across the fields,
>
> in bare feet, bringing all spring's flowers
> to her mother's house. I swear
> the air softened and warmed as she moved,

the blue sky smiling, none too soon,
with the small shy mouth of a new moon.
(*TWW*, p. 76)

The contrast between this emotional redemption and the frozen ambiguity of Penelope's response at the return of Ulysses is stark. Again, though, the volume's closing poem does not have to be read as condoning either essentialism or separatism, although it can profitably be related to both Jaggar's delineation of 'outlaw' emotions and Woolf's concept of women as constituting an Outsiders' Society.[39] However, it certainly offers emotional or spiritual relations between women as a counter to that aspect of western ideology that has traditionally reduced woman to animality, intellectual infancy and dependency within the languages of philosophy and religion. Both discourses offer a purely male genealogy which have erased relations between mothers and daughters. Read philosophically, then, 'Demeter' can be seen as figuratively expressing the intellectual agenda of Luce Irigaray: that 'the only way in which the status of women could be altered fundamentally is by the creation of a powerful female symbolic to represent the *other* term of sexual difference'.[40] Only this will enable woman to find her own separate being: otherwise, she will always be there for men, available for their transcendence but cut off from her own. As Margaret Whitford points out, for Irigaray, 'western culture is not founded on parricide (as Freud hypothesized in *Totem and Taboo*), but on matricide'.[41] In so wittily giving a voice to the world's wife, Duffy amuses and entertains but she also alerts us to the cultural and social implications of a philosophical legacy that has helped privilege the narrative of the world's husband for far too long.

## Notes

1 Mary Midgley and Judith Hughes: 'When women read philosophy they tend to fall into an embarrassed habit of thinking that they ought not to criticize the ludicrous views which result, that it is unfair and anachronistic to think that people of this calibre ought to be able to avoid going into print with this sort of stuff' (*Women's Choices* (London: Weidenfeld and Nicolson, 1983, p. 45)) as cited in Ellen Kennedy and Susan Medus (eds), *Women in Western Political Philosophy: Kant to Nietzsche* (Brighton: Wheatsheaf Books, 1987), p. 21.

2 See, in particular, Jane E. Thomas, '"The intolerable wrestle with words": the Poetry of Carol Ann Duffy', *Bête Noire* 6 (winter 1988), pp. 78–88, and Linda

Kinnahan, '"Looking for the Doing Words": Carol Ann Duffy and Questions of Convention' in James Acheson and Romana Huk (eds), *Contemporary British Poetry: Essays in Theory and Criticism* (Albany: State University of New York Press, 1996), pp. 245–68.

3  Carol Ann Duffy, *Mean Time* (London: Anvil, 1993), p. 25.

4  William Shakespeare, *Hamlet*, III.i.79–80.

5  Ibid., III.ii. 358–80.

6  Deryn Rees-Jones also draws attention to what she describes as the poem's 'parodic echoes of the gravediggers' scene in *Hamlet*', *Carol Ann Duffy* (Plymouth: Northcote House, 1999), p. 19.

7  Elisabeth Bronfen, *Over Her Dead Body: Death, Femininity and the Aesthetic* (Manchester: Manchester University Press, 1992).

8  I owe this observation to Geoffrey Harris of the European Studies Research Institute, University of Salford. Reproductions of the two works referred to here can be found in Mary Ann Caws, *The Surrealist Look: An Erotics of Encounter* (Cambridge, M: MIT Press, 1997), pp. 70, 276.

9  Alison M. Jaggar, 'Love and Knowledge: Emotion in Feminist Epistemology' in Ann Garry and Marilyn Pearsall (eds), *Women, Knowledge and Reality: Explorations in Feminist Philosophy* (London and New York: Routledge, 1996), p. 166.

10  For other critics' comments on Duffy's use of the ventriloquist's dummy as subject matter see Thomas, p. 27; Rees-Jones, pp. 18–20, and Neil Roberts, *Narrative and Voice in Postwar Poetry* (London: Longman, 1999), pp. 189–90.

11  'The Dummy', *Selling Manhatten* (London: Anvil Press, 1987), p. 20.

12  The chosen authors were Plato, Kant, Darwin, Aristotle (2 works), Descartes, Wittgenstein, Hume, Nietzsche and Thomas Aquinas. Reported in *The Guardian*, September 2001.

13  See, for example, Hélène Cixous, 'Sorties: Out and Out: Attacks/Ways Out/Forays' in Elaine Marks and Isabelle de Courtivron (eds), *New French Feminisms: An Anthology* (Brighton: Harvester Press, 1981), and Margaret Whitford (ed.), *The Irigaray Reader* (Oxford: Blackwell Publishers, 1991).

14  The syllabus for the Honours degree in Philosophy at Liverpool University, as well as including options entitled 'Kant and After', 'Plotinus', 'Bradley's Metaphysics', now includes one entitled 'Feminist Philosophies'.

15  Kennedy and Mendus (eds), *Women in Western Political Philosophy*, pp. 3–4.

16  Cixous, 'Sorties', p. 90.

17  Andrea Nye, 'The Voice of the Serpent: French Feminism and Philosophy of Language', in Garry and Pearsall (eds), *Women, Knowledge and Reality*, p. 327.

18  See, in particular, Luce Irigaray, 'Women-mothers, the Silent Substratum of the Social Order' and 'The Power of Discourse and the Subordination of the Feminine', in Margaret Whitford (ed.), *The Irigaray Reader* (Oxford: Blackwell, 1991), pp. 47–52 and pp. 118–32, and also Margaret Whitford, *Luce Irigaray: Philosophy in the Feminine* (London and New York: Routledge, 1991).

19  Judith Butler, *Bodies that Matter: On the Discursive Limits of 'Sex'* (London and New York: Routledge, 1993), p. 37.

20  Linda Kinnahan, 'Carol Ann Duffy and Questions of Convention', in James Acheson and Romana Huk (eds), *Contemporary British Poetry: Essays in Theory and Criticism* (State University of New York Press, 1996), p. 248.

21  Virginia Woolf: 'For we think back through our mothers if we are women', *A Room of One's Own* (Harmondsworth: Penguin Books, 1972 [1929]), p. 76.

22  *Lemprière's Classical Dictionary Writ Large* (3rd edn) (London: Routledge and Kegal Paul, 1984), p. 20.

23  'Metre Maid', *Guardian*, 25 September 1999.

24  Ted Hughes's complete reorganisation of the volume's contents before its publication, however, means that most readers are more familiar with the order as it now appears in the Faber imprint of *Ariel*. See Marjorie Perloff, 'The Two Ariels: The (Re)Making of the Sylvia Plath Canon' in her *Poetic Licence: Essays on Modernist and Postmodernist Lyrics* (Evanston: Northwestern University Press, 1990), pp. 175–97, for a thorough and illuminating analysis of the differences between the two versions.

25  Sylvia Plath, 'Wintering', *Ariel* (London: Faber and Faber, 1965), p. 69.

26  Alison M. Jaggar, 'Love and Knowledge: Emotion in Feminist Epistemology' in Garry and Pearsall (eds), *Women, Knowledge and Reality*, pp. 180–1.

27  See Antony Rowland, 'Love and Masculinity in the Poetry of Carol Ann Duffy', *English*, 50:198 (autumn 2001), pp. 199–218 for an illuminating essay on Duffy's more recent poems as 'refreshing in their total rejection of the heterosexual male' (p. 214).

28  Alicia Ostriker, 'The Thieves of Language; Women Poets and Revisionist Mythmaking', in Elaine Showalter (ed.), *The New Feminist Criticism: Essays on Women, Literature and Theory* (London: Virago Press, 1986), pp. 315–16.

29  The figure of Faustus, who appears in many literary texts, including Marlowe's *Tragical History of Dr Faustus* and Goethe's *Faust,* is founded on Dr Johann Faust, or Faustus, a magician and astrologer, who was born in Württemberg and who died about 1538. See J.C. Cooper (ed.), *Brewer's Myth and Legend* (London: Cassell, 1992), pp. 93–4.

30  Its title, however, is clearly a re-working of the Grimm Brothers' version of the Little Red Riding Hood story which is entitled 'Little Red Cape'.

31  Carol Ann Duffy, interview with Andrew McAllister, *Bête Noire*, 6 (winter 1988), p. 75. See also Deryn Rees-Jones on Duffy's use of cliché in *Carol Ann Duffy* (1999), pp. 12–14.

32  Woolf, *A Room of One's Own*, p. 112.

33  For an interesting reading of this aspect of Plath's poetry see Steven Gould Axelrod, *Sylvia Plath: The Wound and the Cure of Words* (Baltimore: Johns Hopkins University Press, 1990).

34  Sylvia Plath, *Ariel* (London: Faber, 1965), p. 19.

35  Duffy's representation of gender and emotions seems to place her between second-wave feminism and a more radical or sceptical approach to the construction of femininity and masculinity such as can be found in Judith Halberstam's *Female Masculinity* (Durham and London: Duke University

Press, 1998). For more on this see Antony Rowland, 'Patriarchy, Male Power and the Psychopath in the Poetry of Carol Ann Duffy', in Daniel Lea and Bethold Schoene-Harwood (eds), *Male Order* (Amsterdam: Rodopi, 2003).

36 'Metre Maid'.

37 As Hilde Hein notes in her essay 'Liberating Philosophy: An End to the Dichotomy of Spirit and Matter' (Garry and Pearsall (eds), *Women, Knowledge and Reality*, pp. 437–53), the origin of this belief lies in the Aristotelian notion that women are merely passive receptacles who nurture the life implanted in them by the male principle, the active agency. As she points out, the idea of 'renting' a womb for the purposes of artificial insemination is validated, to a certain extent, by the Aristotelian tradition (p. 439).

38 There is perhaps also an echo here of the end of Plath's 'Ariel': 'And I / Am the arrow, / The dew that flies / Suicidal, at one with the drive / Into the red / Eye, the cauldron of morning' (*Ariel*, p. 37).

39 See Virginia Woolf, *Three Guineas* (London: The Hogarth Press, 1986 [1938]), p. 122.

40 Whitford, *Luce Irigaray: Philosophy in the Feminine*, p. 22.

41 Ibid., p. 25.

# 6

## 'The chant of magic words repeatedly': gender as linguistic act in the poetry of Carol Ann Duffy

### JANE THOMAS

> In this sense, gender is in no way a stable identity or locus of agency from which various acts proceed; rather, it is an identity tenuously constituted in time – an identity instituted through a *stylized repetition of acts*.[1]

IT IS GENERALLY accepted by commentators on her work that Carol Ann Duffy's poetry is concerned with the nature of human identity and its construction in, and by, language.[2] Feminist critics have been particularly drawn to Duffy's interrogation of the way language 'speaks' the individual and the implications of this process for women whose subjectivity and social existence is negatively constructed in this way.[3] What is still under discussion is the degree to which her work posits the existence of an 'I' that pre-exists signification and is for ever alienated by the signifying practices that give it a voice and an identity.[4] It is clear that certain early poems, particularly those in *Standing Female Nude* and *Selling Manhattan,* express nostalgia for a core individual essence that is ungendered and culturally 'innocent'. This notion of the frustrated, pre-linguistic self gives rise to metaphors of lost childhood, alienation, foreignness, homesickness, psychosis and love:

> The words you have for things die,
> in your heart, but grasses are plainsong,
> patiently chanting the circles you cannot repeat
> or understand. This is your homeland,
> Lost One, Stranger who speaks with tears.[5]

However, this concern with the 'transcendental signified', the inarticulate and unnameable repressed that is outside and beyond language but from which language originates, creates a fundamental contradiction in her work. If language is a system of signs for what is not there, a substitute or consolation for 'pure' unmediated experience, attempts to communicate or communicate with that experience through language, in this case through speaking or writing, are bound to be partial, approximate and frustrated:

> We scratch in dust with sticks,
> dying of homesickness
> for when, where, what.
>
> (*SM*, p. 19)

At the same time, as Judith Butler suggests, the assertion of an 'I' (or 'we') that writes or speaks of a lost realm outside language can be accomplished only through the linguistic signifying process itself: 'the rules that regulate the legitimate and illegitimate invocation of that pronoun, the practices that establish the terms of intelligibility by which that pronoun can circulate'.[6] In other words it is language, and the rules that govern its structure and usage, that allow us to formulate and articulate a sense of selfhood in speech or writing, and we do so by invoking the linguistic sign for the self – 'I'. It is impossible to conceive of a self outside of language. Consequently, the intelligible or acceptable invocation of identity is the product of certain rule-governed discourses including gender, which converge to produce the 'I' that speaks or writes of itself and others. These rule-bound discourses pre-exist us and establish the patterns we are shaped by. The issue therefore, for a feminist and a poet, is how to take part in the symbolic order but at the same time question its values and meanings.

Judith Butler's theory of the 'performativity' of gender builds on Michel Foucault's claim that identities are *produced* rather than *represented* by discourses, and Derrida's statement that every time we use a discursive term we are engaged in a citational act. In other words we repeat it echoing or quoting its previous usages. Derrida uses the term 'iterability' to refer to this repeatability of language.[7] For Derrida, therefore, identities are constructed 'iteratively', through a complex set of citational processes that are positioned within, and determined by, discourse and which in turn determine and shape behaviour.[8] The compulsive repeating of signifying processes over time builds up what

Butler calls the 'sedimented' identity or subjectivity of an individual, and the possibilities of change or the subversion of dominant forms of subjectivity reside in this process:

> In a sense, all signification takes place within the orbit of the compulsion to repeat ; 'agency,' then, is to be located within the possibility of a variation on that repetition. If the rules governing signification not only restrict, but enable the assertion of alternative domains of cultural intelligibility, i.e., new possibilities for gender that contest the rigid codes of hierarchical binarisms, then it is only *within* the practices of repetitive signifying that a subversion of identity becomes possible ... There is no self that is prior to the convergence or who maintains 'integrity' prior to its entrance into this conflicted cultural field. There is only a taking up of the tools where they lie, where the very 'taking up' is enabled by the tool lying there.[9]

In this context language is only one of a range of signifying practices that determine what it is to be male or female, but it is a powerful one. As Kristeva states, language is 'the materiality of that which society regards as a means of contact and understanding'.[10]

The act of gender requires a performance that is repeated. This repetition is at once a re-enactment and re-experiencing of a set of meanings already socially established, many of them represented in, and by, linguistic terms.[11] In this respect words can be seen as 'magic' in that they have the power to produce effects through constant reiteration. For Butler, however, the very instability of the norm, and the terms that claim to signify it, creates the potential for new, socially problematic identities that may eventually usurp the prevailing ones. Rather than looking for agency in a notion of an 'I' that pre-exists signification, Judith Butler's performativity theory of gender suggests ways in which prevailing constructions of identity – particularly gendered constructions – can be subverted and altered through the very processes that bring them into being.

Butler argues against the essentialist idea that gender differences reside in our biological or psychic natures and claims instead that they are produced by contingent social practices. Our subjectivity, or sense of self, is constructed out of various social practices and discourses, many of which conflict and compete with one another. To illustrate this Alsop, Fitzsimons and Lennon cite the injunction to women to be 'proper mothers' and 'competent' members of the workplace where that competence is measured on a male-defined model of long hours, diminishing leisure time and one hundred per cent commitment.[12] Our inability, as individuals, to fulfil the demands of all these injunctions successfully leads to compromise and variation, which in turn helps to destabilise and resignify the various ways in which we express our identities. In addition we might add that the meanings that inhere in the terms that help to structure our sense of self are themselves unstable. They change in different social contexts and in different periods of time. In this way gendering can be seen as a 'process' rather than a fixed, and wholly determining, category.

In this chapter I want to discuss the extent to which Duffy's poetry examines the 'magic' power of words and the way they work through complex iterative processes. Citation and iterability in the form of lists, chants, mantras and 'litanies' is a strong feature of her work, and her deployment of both draws attention to the way linguistic acts work as part of the signifying process through which identity is constituted. This notion of the performativity of language is in dialogue in Duffy's work with a nostalgia for a sense of agency outside linguistic systems, and a desire to use language to postulate, paradoxically, the existence of a realm outside and beyond signification.

In an early poem, 'The Dolphins',[13] the creatures seem for ever alienated by language, in particular by the way it simultaneously enables and limits the possible ways of articulating subjectivity. This is metaphorically suggested by the pool in which the captive animals exist: 'We are in our element but we are not free. / Outside this world you cannot breathe for long.' The double meaning of the term 'in our element' suggests that, although the dolphins require water to survive, the pool in which they find themselves is circumscribed, limited, and shallow and as such represents a disturbingly alien environment. The trainer's whistle periodically hails them from its limits to repeat a series of tricks. The dolphin's survival is consequent upon the faultless and repeated performance of these tricks, for they can never return to where they originated, and failure will result in rejection and possible extermination. Whether the dolphins were born into captivity or captured as adults is unspecified. What is certain is that they have been 'translated' from one watery element to another. In the process they have lost the 'blessing' of the endless, unformed possibilities that preceded their entry into the pool. This sense of limitless depths and expanses could signify either the ocean which they have been separated from or the libidinal chaos and multiplicity that precedes the subject's entry into language, which Kristeva terms the 'chora'. Chris Weedon defines Kristeva's chora as 'the site of those meanings and modes of signification which cannot be reduced to the symbolic order and which exceed rational conscious subjectivity'.[14]

The water of the pool may make possible the survival of the dolphins and bring about a consciousness of their condition but it provides neither 'truth' nor 'explanations'. Their performance is a direct result of the training process of language, and each act inscribes them ever more firmly in their new condition, structuring what was once inchoate and without direction into 'well-worn grooves / of water on a single note'. Performance brings recognition, marked by approbation and reward, but the sense of something lost persists in the silver flash of their companion's skin 'like memory of somewhere else'. In this respect the title of the poem is ironic, drawing attention to the slipperiness of the signification of the generic term. The meaning of the word 'Dolphins' changes with its context. The values ascribed to the ocean-living animal differ when that animal is in captivity and exploited for commercial gain. This poem is dominated by a sense of loss and nostalgia, and language is portrayed as reductive and deadly:

> There is no hope. We sink
> to the limits of this pool until the whistle blows.
> There is a man and our mind knows we will die here.

In 'I Remember Me' (*SFN*), a commuter describes the peculiar effect of looking out of the lighted Tube train at the waiting passengers on the crowded, darker platform. The doubly reinforced plate glass of the window reflects the speaker's face momentarily superimposed on the body of someone else outside the train. This commonplace situation is defamiliarised in the poem and open to a plurality of different readings. Among these is the notion of emergent subjectivity and its struggle to recognise, and embrace, itself in language as distinct and unified. The dolphins carry a faint memory of a time when they did not feel alienated from the forms they have been forced to adopt in relation to 'the man'. This memory is stirred when each dolphin sees itself reflected in the shape of its companion and hears the 'music of loss forever / from the other's heart'. This 'recognition' of self in the other is idealised and romanticised in the poem as being like love, 'The other knows / and out of love reflects me for myself'. It contrasts strongly with the alienating signifying processes of the dolphinarium activated by the interpellating whistle of 'the man'.

In 'I Remember Me' the connection, or 'recognition', between 'self' and 'other' is blurred, leading to an insecurity in the speaker's self-registration. The two rarely coalesce: 'Despair stares out from tube-trains at itself / running on the platform for the closing door' (*SFN*, p. 16). The poem seems to suggest that a successful fusion between the self and its linguistic embodiment is not possible. 'Barefaced truths', in the dictionary sense of 'blatant' or 'undisguised', are 'wordless' and the speaking subject experiences only non-recognition or, at best, mis-recognition in the available linguistic terms. The situation is likened to failing to elicit a response from the lover you are expecting to meet: 'Mostly your lover passes / in the rain and does not know you when you speak'. 'True' recognition, the poem suggests, can only happen if the subject can see reflected, or 'know' again, in the other what it has lost. In this respect, 'true' recognition is impossible for we can never return to a pre-linguistic state and still retain an acceptable and persuasive identity. Regression to a 'lost' pre-linguistic innocence carries with it the risk of psychosis manifested by the unravelling of, or deconstruction of, identity. Again the title can be read ironically in that the 'I' of the poem singularly fails to 're-member' itself in that it cannot recall or recognise in language the fragmented memory of the time before language. In the title of the poem the speaker shifts between an 'I' that orders and acknowledges and a 'me' that experiences. The body of the poem rejects both however, in favour of the more impersonal third-person 'you'. In this way it enacts the very alienation from the perceived forms of self-expression that it seeks to explore. The speaker remains trapped outside social recognition, constantly fragmented and in danger of dis-memberment.

In 'Dies Natalis' (*SM*) Duffy describes this sense of alienation in terms that suggest it is universal to all living things. A being comes to consciousness in different forms – cat, bird, man and finally newborn child. As each existence is articulated in language the speaker communicates a sense of isolation from those around it. In the final section of the poem the baby describes the process whereby language brings it into being out of the undifferentiated chaos of experience. From talking to itself 'in shapes' the baby begins to recognise how language rearranges and orders its experience into faces, tastes, sounds, taking it further away from the semiotic realm. Language effects the baby's gradual entry into gendered consciousness: 'They are trying to label me, / translate me into the right word' (*SM*, p. 12). Its identity is built up gradually through a process of iteration: 'These strangers own me, / pass me between them chanting my new name' (*SM*, p. 13). However, the acquisition of a sense of self is at the cost of direct access to the sensual realm of experience that language cannot recreate, but the process is viewed less negatively than in 'The Dolphins'. The 'well-worn grooves of water / on a single note' become 'Mantras of consolation':

> I will lose my memory, learn words
> which barely stretch to cover what remains unsaid.
> Mantras of consolation come from those who keep
> my portrait in their eyes. And when they disappear,
> I cry.
>
> (SM, p. 13)

The new metaphor suggests that language effects a change of consciousness in the subject that calms and compensates it for its loss. The word 'mantra' gives the sense that through its iterative power language leads subjects to become, in Butler's words, 'entranced by their own fictions'.[15]

Several of Duffy's poems support the assertion that alienation from the training processes of language brings with it the risk of psychosis entailed in the loss of identity. This is particularly the case where the speaking subject is female and unable to find positive meaning in the signifying processes that work to shape her subjectivity in rigid and fossilised forms: 'wife', 'mother', 'whore' etc. In 'The Dolphins' and 'I Remember Me' the speakers are ungendered. In 'Woman Seated in the Underground, 1941' (*SFN*), Duffy constructs the dramatic monologue of the female figure in Henry Moore's drawing by the same title. In the poem the speaker is suffering from amnesia brought on by the shock and chaos of the air raid and is sheltering with a crowd of unfamiliar people in the Tube station. Again the poem foregrounds the notion of 'recognition' in the sense of identifying those around her as known before, as well as being identified or 'validated' by them. As people they are unable to tell her who she is, and as possible modes of being they offer her no positive ways out of her psychosis: 'I forget. I have looked at the other faces and found / no memory, no love' (*SFN*, p. 50). The comment 'Christ, she's a rum one' could be interpreted as describing the speaker's eccentric appearance or her sexual behaviour.

The speaker's assertion of her pregnancy situates her in the discourse of gender and heterosexuality. However she does not know her 'name'. In this context her 'proper name' is both her own personal name and the term that fixes her signified identity. She knows she is a woman but with nothing to 'fix' her further – 'no wedding ring, no handbag, nothing' – she is open to the charge of 'looseness'. The term 'loose woman' signifies unregulated sexual behaviour and an unstable identity, where unstable further signifies 'unspecified' and psychotic. Again the idea of 'love' is used to suggest secure self-definition. The woman cites it in order to ward off the problematic 'looseness' that threatens to dislocate her: 'No. Someone has loved me. Someone / is looking for me even now. I live somewhere.'

Like the speaker of 'I Remember Me' she is denied any form of recognition – particularly from the 'Other' she addresses using the discourse of love: 'I sing the word *darling* and it yields nothing.' The words in italics in stanza two of the poem come from the popular Second World War song 'Lili Marlene' in which a camp follower is deserted by her soldier lover, who may have been killed in action. Without him to validate her identity she reverts to the status of prostitute. The song functions as a comment on the speaker's situation revealing the contingent nature of her subjectivity. Her status as lost wife or loose woman cannot be determined by an act of will on her part. It is dependent on a defining male presence. Although she has been trained in the acts of femininity, and can automatically perform them – 'My hands mime the memory of knitting' – they fail to channel the self into its appropriate grooves. The pregnancy 'doesn't show yet', it has yet to exert a plastic force on her body and her sense of self and, deprived of the stabilising effects of a coherent subjectivity and a position from which to articulate herself, she begins to unravel into psychosis:

> my mind
> has unravelled into thin threads that lead nowhere.
> In a moment, I shall stand up and scream until
> somebody helps me. The skies were filled with sirens, planes
> fire, bombs, and I lost my self in the crowd.

In this poem the idea of subjectivity shifts uncertainly between a reflective and a constructive model. The speaker fails to recognise herself in the cultural and linguistic mirrors that surround her whilst at the same time discovering that the powerful defining terms that she cites compulsively – 'darling', 'baby' – have lost their shaping power and fail to signify any longer.

The form of Duffy's dramatic monologues draws attention to the fictive, inadequate and yet inescapable process by which the self is composed and articulated. The dramatic monologue is the ultimate performative gesture in which the subject constitutes itself in language believing, like with the speaker of Robert Browning's 'My Last Duchess', that it is in control of the means of expression and can deploy it in order to make itself clear. Duffy's dramatic monologues dramatise the process whereby the subject is brought into being, con-cretised, through the linguistic act. However, under interrogation, or the act of close reading, words admit ambiguity, contradiction and irony. Gaps open up in the unified surface of the self as language takes over and the illusion of agency dissipates. The very act of 'self-staging' is fraught with compromise. The linguistic terms we deploy to bring ourselves into being, and the meanings that inhere in those terms, pre-exist us and preordain what it is possible to say and the ways in which it is possible to say it. Sometimes the speakers powerfully register the extent to which representation constrains, constructs and frustrates in the very process of bringing them into being. This is particularly the case when they are female. Others embrace the symbolic contract without equivocation. These speakers are more often specifically gen-dered as male. This reluctance to query the signifying processes and the linguistic forms that shape the subject leads, as we shall see, to its own form of psychosis.

The quotation that forms the title of this chapter is taken from 'Whoever She Was' (*SFN*) in which the speaker whose subjectivity has been formed in relation to the cultural and linguistic signifiers of motherhood confronts the loss of that which validated her identity. Possibly her children have grown up and left home, and without them the various citations of femininity that have cohered to form the illu-sion of a unified identity have broken down into images and phrases that no longer have the power to articulate who she now is. It could be that the subject of the poem has never been 'properly' trained by the powerful iconic images of motherhood. They have become increas-ingly indistinct, unstable and inadequate, and their contradictions more clearly exposed. The comforting movie cliché of the perfect mother contrasts strongly with the inadequacy implied by the burning apples. At the same time, the veiled reference to the myth of Daphne – 'My hands, / still wet, sprout wooden pegs' – suggests the extent to which the subject is enmired and restricted by the forms that shape her subjectivity (*SFN*, p. 35).[16] The voices that confirmed and reflected back her identity, constantly reiterating the name 'Mummy', are reduced to 'the ghosts of children on the telephone', indistinct and without substance. The identity of the 'they' in the poem is unclear, suggesting both the absent children and also some sinister, threatening association of forces with the power to police the norm and punish any deviation from it: 'Making masks from turnips in the candlelight. In case they come.'

Further clichéd maternal gestures are introduced in stanza two as the images of nurse and mother collide in the intriguing ambiguity of the line 'cleaning wounds / or boiling eggs for soldiers' where 'soldiers' signifies members of an army as well as strips of bread and butter. The phrase 'The chant / of magic words repeatedly' is positioned in stanza two so that it comments on these images as well as on the placatory sayings used on fractious and demanding children that follow: 'I do not know. / Perhaps tomorrow. / If we're very good.' These soothing, insincere platitudes suggest the ways in which the subject is induced to see successful sublimation in validated gender roles as its own reward, or else to accept the uncertainty and endless deferral of gratification that linguistic forms offer. The maternal role itself, like the films in which it features and the rows of identical paper cut-out dolls which are its metaphorical equivalents, is endlessly reiterated echoing the hoops and the 'well-worn grooves of water' in 'The Dolphins', until its gestures appear instinctive.

However, like the dolphins, the subject of 'Whoever She Was' has retained a growing sense of herself as positioned outside the loop but the poem gives no sense of the creative potential of this imperfect performance. 'Mummy's never wrong': again, this phrase suggests both the platitude as well as the validated subject position, and implies the death of the subject. However, an unqualified acceptance of its terms which leads the subject to identify itself in its linguistic reflection has similar deadly consequences: '*You open your dead eyes to look in the mirror / which they are holding to your mouth.*' As in 'Woman Seated in the Underground, 1941', the subject of 'Whoever She Was' is forced into psychosis by the failure of prevailing gendered forms of subjectivity to call her into being. The act of self-expression – the soundless, wordless 'outbreath' that could occlude the reflected image – never happens. The breakdown of the maternal 'form', and the ensuing breakdown of the subject, is mirrored in the breaking down of the ordered structures of the poem itself. The alternating six- and eight-line units of stanzas one and two and the rhyming couplet 'night/tight' at the end of stanza two suggest the sonnet form which becomes barely detectable in stanzas three and four.

The poem 'You Jane' (*SFN*) is strategically placed on the page facing 'Whoever She Was' and is an example of Duffy's deliberate and telling structuring of her collections. In 'You Jane', Duffy constructs the dramatic monologue of a subject who unconditionally accepts the signifying processes that rigidly demarcate gender roles. The title of the poem is a partial quotation of Johnny Weissmuller's description of his role in the 1932 film *Tarzan – Ape Man* for *Photoplay* magazine: 'Me Tarzan. You Jane' which, like so many often-quoted movie lines, never appeared in any of the *Tarzan* films.[17] However it remains the definitive and most economical invocation of the nature and interdependence of heterosexual gender roles. The male speaker of the poem cites a number of clichés in validation of his masculinity. The process is circular and self-perpetuating in that the terms he uses to articulate his sense of himself simultaneously construct what they appear to describe, and present an impregnable front: 'You can punch / my gut and wait forever till I flinch. Try it' (*SFN*, p. 34). What these terms signify is already socially established and presents a set of well-worn grooves, repeatable acts and gestures, which have trained and shaped this masculine self. Their meanings are validated by 'the wife's' uncomplaining acquiescence in her own monologic feminine interpellation as sex object, servant and mother of his children. She is cast in the 'supporting' role. The 'feminine' against which our speaker defines himself ('At night I fart a guinness smell against the wife') is constructed as an undifferentiated 'Other' that incorporates all possible variations on the feminine theme. In fact the distinction between 'the wife' and 'the mother-in-law' is so fine that the speaker's sexual aggression appears directed against both:

> Although she's run a bit to fat
> she still bends over of a weekend in suspenders.

> This is the life. Australia next year and bugger
> the mother-in-law.

There is a hint, at the end of the poem, that 'the wife' still retains some sense of a realm outside signification which she has access to through dreams. This is a familiar metaphor in Duffy's work, as in 'I Remember Me': 'It must be dreams that make us different, must be / private cells inside a common skull' (*SFN*, p. 16). However, unlike 'the wife' and the female speaker of 'Whoever She Was', the male speaker of 'You Jane' acknowledges no gap between language and experience:

> She says Did you dream, love? I never
> dream . . .
> > . . . When I feel, I feel here
> where the purple vein in my neck throbs.

'Psychopath' (*SM*) takes the rigid demarcation of gender roles reiterated in 'You, Jane' to its logical and violent extreme. Like the female subject of 'Whoever She Was', the psychopath's identity is deeply indebted to frequently reiterated, one-dimensional images from the cinema and other areas of popular culture: 'Jimmy Dean', 'Johnny, Remember Me', 'Brando'. 'Elvis', 'Jack the Lad', 'Ladies' Man' even Humphrey Bogart's Rick Blaine ('Here's / looking at you') that, like Johnny Weissmuller's 'Tarzan', carry with them certain connotations of masculinity (*SM*, pp. 28–9). Our psychopath cites these terms and coheres around the composite image they produce: 'I run my metal comb through the D.A. and pose / my reflection between dummies in the window at Burton's' (*SM*, p. 28). However, unlike the female subjects of 'Woman Seated in the Underground, 1941' and 'Whoever She Was', he embraces the potential of signification, and the apparent permission granted by his reiterated terms for acts of violent sexual aggression against women. The cultural stereotypes mould the form of his masculinity like the 'new skin' of his leather trousers:

> When I zip up the leather, I'm in a new skin, I touch it
> and love myself, sighing Some little lady's going to get lucky
> tonight.

His irony is chilling. The psychopath's conclusion 'Easier to say Yes' refers to his sexually reluctant female victim as well as to his own acquiescence to the negative and violent modes of self-articulation offered to him (*SM*, p. 29). Like the speaker of 'You Jane', he has no sense of an alternative either inside or outside language: 'Tomorrow / will find me elsewhere, with a loss of memory'.

In the same way, the psychopath's obsession with his masculine identity necessitates the domination, violation and obliteration of its perceived and threatening feminine opposite. Again different versions of the 'feminine' are compounded into a construct of the 'Other' that does not discriminate between 'the girl', 'Dirty Alice' and 'Mama'. In stanza four the retelling of his humiliating sexual initiation blends into his description of 'the girl's' abduction so that the reader is momentarily confused as to which one it was who 'told me her name on the towpath' (*SM*, p. 28). In addition the placing of the refrain 'She is in the canal', in stanzas one and six, suggests that the murder of the girl is a direct consequence of the mother's perceived sexual betrayal. It could also signify the murder of the mother: 'My sandwiches were near her thigh, then the Rent Man / lit her cigarette and I ran, ran . . . She is in the canal.'

The psychopath is caught up in an endlessly reiterated act of self-love that leaves no space for alternative modes of being: 'These streets are quiet, as if the town has held its breath / to watch the Wheel go round above the dreary homes' (*SM*, p. 29). Like Narcissus, his self-obsessed mythical counterpart, he desires his own image. The momentary obliteration of self in the wordless 'outbreath' ('my breath wipes me from the looking-glass') is replaced by his seamless identification with rigid, monologic definitions of a particular type of masculinity ('My reflection sucks a sour Woodbine and buys me a drink. / Here's / looking at you'). Here, the Bogart quote could also constitute a direct threat to the reader. It also functions as an address which may impel the reader to examine his or her own gendered subjectivity. For the psychopath, the image is the reality and he can see neither outside nor beyond it.

If the male speakers of 'Psychopath' and 'You Jane' represent versions of Narcissus, then the female speakers of 'Woman Seated on the Underground, 1941' and 'Whoever She Was' represent Echo who, in Ovid's myth, has no personal investment in the meaning of the terms she is condemned endlessly to repeat.[18] The link with Echo is suggested in stanza three of 'Whoever She Was':

> A scrap of echo clings
> to the bramble bush. My maiden name

> sounds wrong. This was the playroom.
> I turn it over on a clumsy tongue. Again.
>
> (*SFN*, p. 35)

The psychopath is identified with the carousel and the big wheel that, like the hoops, loops, grooves and circles of other poems examined here, are metaphors for the complex iterative process through which the self is formed and performed. This process endlessly perpetuates the rigid gender roles that offer themselves as modes of articulation for the self. To stand outside the process and refuse its terms is to be condemned to the realm of the inarticulate and the absence of even the illusory sense of unity that permits one to make an intervention, however prescribed, in the symbolic order. However, to embrace its terms literally and without question is to risk a different form of psychosis that reveals itself in the subject's inscription in rigid, violent or self-destructive modes of being.

Images of breath, fog and smoke occur frequently in Duffy's poems as metaphors for what cannot be expressed in verbal or written language: 'The dreams we have / no phrases for slip through our fingers into smoke' ('Saying Something' *SFN*, p. 18). Duffy frequently uses the metaphor of 'talent' to describe this untapped, sometimes negative and destructive potential in the subject. In 'Education for Leisure' (*SFN*, p. 15) a violently psychotic subject tries to obliterate the prevailing forms of subjectivity the world offers by inscribing another one across his or her reflection: 'I breathe out talent on the glass to write my name.' The effect of the gesture is transitory and ephemeral receiving no recognition from those who deploy the processes that help to determine his sense of self: 'Once a fortnight, I walk the two miles into town / for signing on. They don't appreciate my autograph'. The speaker seeks a more lasting 'translation' of meaning through small repeated acts of murder ('now the fly is in another language') that culminate in another direct address or threat to the reader: 'I get out our bread-knife and go out. / The pavements glitter suddenly. I touch your arm.' Here the deadly implications of the negative construction of subjectivity extend beyond the speaker to affect others. Frustration with prevailing forms leads to wordless, direct action. For the female subject of 'Woman Seated in the Underground, 1941' it was the scream that registered a protest against the obliteration of the self; for the male subject of 'Education For Leisure' it is violence and possibly the obliteration of another.

Post-structuralist theories of the linguistic construction of subjectivity claim that there is no realm beyond the signifying process from which to mount a challenge to it. All notions of identity and experience outside language are delusory. The linguistic categories that construct subjectivity are what make subjectivity possible. For Judith Butler words, particularly those that constitute gendered identities, have a symbolic power in that they produce or accomplish what they name. To pronounce a new-born baby 'a girl' is to initiate the process whereby the child strives to become the successful embodiment of the feminine norm. Although she never entirely succeeds in this endeavour the girl is compelled to 'cite' the norm repeatedly in order to qualify and remain a viable subject.[19] However, as suggested earlier, Butler also claims that the possibility of destabilising and resignifying our gendered identities lies in the 'inadequacy' of the performance which brings into being new, compromised alternative subject positions which are equally unstable. At the same time, if language is the medium through which meaning is communicated, then the chance to resignify and reconstitute the meanings that inhere in the terms it offers us lies in their very instability and slipperiness. As a poet Duffy is committed to exposing and exploiting the creative potential of language. Her work suggests that because poetry derives its force from ambiguity, association and multiplicity of meaning, in addition to its defamiliarising potential, it has the power to reconstitute the world in differently meaningful ways.

In 'Sit at Peace'[20] a child's revolt against the training processes of gender is diffused by the repeated exhortation '*Sit at peace, sit at peace, all summer*'. The suggestion that the child is being trained in femininity is reinforced by the small domestic task of shelling peas. Again the image of occluding and overwriting a socially validated image – this time that of the quiescent female child – is introduced through the metaphor of condensation: 'You would rather stand with your nose to the window, clouding / the strange blue view with your restless breath.' However, here the child has nothing to write or draw over the view and remains in an inarticulate state of limbo between conflicting modes of self-articulation. Climbing the 'Parachute Tree' – a gesture of tomboyish freedom from the behavioural restraints that girls are subject to – results in a symbolic fall, after which the child is content to acquiesce: 'A long still afternoon, dreamlike. / A voice saying *peace, sit at peace, sit at peace*.' The poem demonstrates, among other things,

how 'femininity is . . . not the product of a choice, but the forcible citation of a norm, one whose complex historicity is indissociable from
relations of discipline, regulation, punishment'.[21]

In Duffy's poem 'Litany'[22], however, the child makes a linguistic
intervention that can be read as an unconscious rejection of the citational processes that have constituted the gendered identities of her
mother's peers. As Sean O'Brien suggests:

> The poem presents rigidity bordering on paralysis, Women who have
> become almost Jonsonian embodiments of their own inhibitions,
> occupying a bored, inarticulate hell of middle-age, into which mar-
> riage and childbirth have automatically and immediately consigned
> them. The poem is a bleakly comic examination of 'women's tribal
> fear of invoking something by naming it'.[23]

In this way it could be read as an investigation of the 'performativity'
of words. The self-entrancing reiterations of middle-class domesticated and domesticating femininity of forty years ago: *candlewick /
bedspread, three piece suite display cabinet . . . Pyrex* are rigidly
inscribed in a home shopping 'catalogue', constituting an endless and
constantly repeated list or 'litany'. The 'magic' of threatening or disruptive terms is diffused by spelling them out: 'An embarrassing word,
broken / to bits, which tensed the air like an accident'. This is the arena
in which the child's gendered identity is formed, and the process is
likened to learning to speak a special language consisting of terms
whose meanings are totally arbitrary:

> This was the code I learnt at my mother's knee, pretending
> to read, where no one had cancer, or sex, or debts,
> and certainly not leukaemia, which no one could spell.

The child's alienation from the process is suggested by the term 'pretending to read' which refers both to the book, with which she amuses
herself, and also perhaps to the 'code' itself, of which she is sceptical.
Other modes of self-articulation are suggested in the line 'a butterfly
stammered itself in my curious hands' but they remain, as yet,
unformed. A 'Litany' in liturgical terms is a 'series of petitions, humble
requests, supplications for use in church services or processions recited
by clergy and responded to usually in recurring formulas by the
people'.[24] It forms a soothing, formulaic chant that pretends to bring
about communion with God – the ultimate guarantor of truth. In this

poem the petitions are met with a wholly inappropriate response from the young girl that breaks the spell and is read by the 'congregation' as a direct attack on their value system:

> A boy in the playground, I said, told me
> to fuck off; and a thrilled, malicious pause
> salted my tongue like an imminent storm. Then
> uproar.

The child is disciplined through the iterative process of apology: 'I'm sorry, Mrs Barr, Mrs Hunt, Mrs Emery, / sorry, Mrs Raine' and punished by having her mouth washed out with soap. Although she can still 'summon' their names and the taste of the soap, she can also recall her rebellious interjection and the brief piquancy it added to the sound-track.

Duffy's later work is increasingly equivocal as to the potential of or even the existence of an undifferentiated realm outside significa-tion. In 'Originally' the speaker asks:

> Do I only think
> I lost a river, culture, speech, sense of first space
> and the right place? Now, Where do you come from?
> strangers ask. Originally? And I hesitate.
>
> (TOC, p. 7)

On one level the hesitation could be read as the result of 'the emigra-tion of childhood' that functions as a metaphor for the loss of the semi-otic 'homeland' effected by the increasing inscription of the subject into language. It also describes the literal childhood relocation from one country to another. As the child becomes competent in whatever medium of communication is available to it, it experiences an increased alienation from 'our own country' until 'you forget, or don't recall, or change'. As in 'Dies Natalis' language has displaced the pre-linguistic realm and so the child cannot respond immediately to the question of origins. However, language has also displaced and replaced 'the other country' in that it is impossible to talk about a pre-linguistic condition without using language and thereby bringing about the very process the subject is trying to circumvent. The closing lines of 'Originally' also raise the possibility that the semiotic realm might not even exist. These lines contrast strongly with the opening of

'Homesick' (*SM*, p. 19), in which the speaker suggests that all attempts to differentiate our experience through language is merely the attempt to reach back to the pure, unmediated drives of the semiotic:

> When we rearrange
> the rooms we end up living in, we are looking
> for first light, the arrangement of light,
> that time, before we knew to call it light.

As we saw in 'The Dolphins', the 'other country', or first place of origin, is often imagined in Duffy's work as an undifferentiated watery realm: a sea or river. Images of rivers in later collections suggest the mythical River Meander of Phrygia that winds in and out in no particular direction, eventually turning back to its source. The river of pre-linguistic experience is closed in on itself and without direction. The River Lethe also springs to mind: the river of the Underworld (or Underground) where souls gather to drink and forget their past life prior to being reborn. To aspire to return, or remain, there is to forfeit the possibility of self-articulation and communication, the rebirth into language. The poem 'River' (*TOC*) strives to articulate the unalloyed pleasure of unmediated experience, the moment before it is translated into words that will remain preserved in a book like a pressed red flower. However the momentum of the poem is away from singing 'loudly in nonsense' and forwards into language. It ends on a question:

> If you were really there what would you write on a postcard,
> Or on the sand, near where the river runs into the sea?
> 
> (*TOC*, p. 53)

In 'In Your Mind' (*TOC*, p. 55 ) the speaker asks, 'The other country, is it anticipated or half-remembered?', raising the possibility that the knowing and skilful use of language, such as that employed by the poet, can anticipate or even help to bring a different realm of meaning into being.

Duffy's work is strongly committed to the 'act' of poetry as a means not only of revealing the performative 'magic' of words but also of utilising that magic to reformulate and reconstitute the world around us. At its best and most affective, poetry foregrounds the creatively polysemic nature of words, their tendency to shift and diffract under interrogation, opening up the sense of possibility that the linguistic process appears to close down. In a recent interview Duffy describes the begin-

ning of a poem as 'a moment of tiny revelation . . . a new way of seeing something, which almost simultaneously attracts language to it –
and then the impulse is to catch that with a pen and paper'.[25] For her,
the process usually takes a few days 'until the poem seems to have
assumed the same shape as the original revelation'. 'M-M-Memory'
(*TOC*) describes the struggle inherent in the process of writing a poem.
It considers the relationship between language and what it apparently
displaces whilst speculating on the process of recalling, in the sense of
summoning back and remembering (or reconstituting) the lost
experience:

> and you sit, exhaling grey smoke
> into a purpling, religious light
> trying to remember everything
>
> perfectly
> in time and space
> where you cannot.
>
> (*TOC*, p. 36)

The spilt oil and everything it signifies ('Names, ghosts, m-memory') is
no longer accessible as experience but the speaker settles for its imperfect, but nevertheless meaningful reconstitution in language. The use
of synaesthesia communicates the alchemy of language – the process
of recall ('forgotten, half-forgotten, half-recalled') – that transforms a
word from something preserved and dead, its meanings impacted and
inert, to something that excites, or 'salts', the tongue (the organ of
taste as well as language itself) and stimulates the senses. Seemingly
petrified words can be worked on, their subtle meanings extracted like
flavour from a slowly dissolving sweet.

> Kneel there,
> words like fossils
> trapped in the roof of the mouth,
> forgotten, half-forgotten, half-
> recalled, the tongue dreaming
> it can trace their shape

The staccato initial letters of the poem's title, echoed in the refrain,
mime the struggle to articulate both the unspeakable and the anticipated sensory pleasure of taste as the petrified words soften and
release their potential.

Each successive volume of poetry from *Standing Female Nude* to *Meantime* re-examines the relationship between language, experience and the act of poetry. In her later collections Duffy becomes increasingly sceptical of a notion of truth existing outside, beyond or before language. Instead her work revels in the power of language to constitute the reality we experience and the ways in which we experience it. Duffy's poems highlight the responsibility of the poet to work with and on words, dissolving the layers of sedimented meaning that leave them ossified and dead in order to liberate their polysemic energy. 'Away and See' (*MT* p. 32) could stand as a poet's manifesto with its invocation to 'Test words / wherever they live; listen and touch, smell, believe. / Spell them with love'. Here 'spell' suggests the breaking down of words into their constitutive letters to see how they work, and also the 'magic' of words, the way they can be used in a charm or incantation to make surprising things happen.

The poem 'Plainsong', with which this chapter opened, has strong connections with the equally sensual and evocative 'Prayer' which concludes the collection *Mean Time* published six years later. Both describe the epiphanic moment stimulated by the sight of sunlight shining through the leaves on a tree; both are saturated with the sense of alienation, the yearning for 'home' and nostalgia for another mode of being metaphorically conceived as childhood. Both titles invoke the religious discourse of communion through the highly ritualised and repetitive acts of prayer and chanting. In both poems, the startlingly secular use of these specifically religious terms suggests the idea of a metaphysical or 'divine' 'truth' that can be accessed through language whilst also satisfying the atheist with their persuasive demonstrations of how language gives both form and substance to that 'truth'. In 'Plainsong' not only is experience freshly realised using language, it communicates itself linguistically: light constitutes itself in 'phrases', trees 'sing', tears 'speak' and the tolling of the evening bell translates itself into the incantation 'Home, Home, / Home'. Whilst the speaker in 'Plainsong' appears arrested, lost and also 'absolved' in the 'almost impossible' pre-linguistic realm, she or he is also situated in a kind of liminal zone between this and a kind of rebirth into language. The 'circles' the speaker cannot 'repeat / or understand' could represent the new, and as yet unrealised, modes of repetitive signifying including the endless unformed possibilities that reside in language itself. As each possibility becomes discursively realised, it offers a mode of being that simultaneously liberates and constrains.

In 'Plainsong' the speaker is 'no-one's child', the 'Lost One', the Stranger. In 'Prayer', the child is called into being out of the dusk and into the home: 'Then dusk, and someone calls / a child's name as though they named their loss' (*MT*, p. 52). Here the act of calling a child in from play, with the implication that that child will manifest itself eventually, symbolises the idea of language as invocation. At the same time, the poem actively constructs the speaker's and the reader's childhood with its citation of those rituals that formed its sedimented layers – 'the distant Latin chanting of a train', 'Grade I piano scales' and finally the litany of the shipping forecast – that rhythmical and soothing reiteration of familiar, meaningless names such as 'Rockall. Malin. Dogger. Finisterre' that evokes a particular response in those born in Britain in and around the 1950s.[26]

The metaphors of prayer and plainsong connect with other religious terms including chant, mantra and litany that are utilised in Duffy's work to specifically secular ends. Like the circles, wheels and grooves which also feature strongly, they are all linguistic manifestations of Butler's notion of the 'stylized repetition of acts'[27] which contribute to the embodiment of the self and the reality that the self experiences. Duffy's poetry suggests that the potential for the disruption and destabilisation of the dominant norms (including the norms of gendered behaviour) lies in the polysemic nature of the words and terms that seek to fix those norms. Indeed poetry can be seen to embody this process of destabilisation with techniques such as personification, metaphor, metonymy and synaesthesia that re-write the prescriptive rules of linguistic discourse. As a poet Duffy is committed to exposing and exploiting the 'magic' of words, suggesting ways in which slight, sometimes barely perceptible variations in the chant can bring about new ways of seeing and being seen. In many ways her work embodies Butler's notion of 'the possibility of a different sort of repeating … the breaking or subversive repetition'[28] of those styles that form our subjectivity, and as a woman poet the discourse of gender is firmly at the forefront of her concerns.

## Notes

1 Judith Butler, 'Performative Acts and Gender Constitution: An Essay in Phenomenology and Feminist Theory', in Katie Conboy, Nadia Medina and Sarah Stanbury (eds), *Writing on the Body: Female Embodiment and Feminist Theory* (New York: Columbia University Press, 1997), pp. 401–17, p. 402.

2   See David Kennedy, *New Relations: The Refashioning of British Poetry 1980–94* (Bridgend: Seren, 1996), and Neil Roberts, in *Narrative and Voice in Postwar Poetry* (London and New York: Longman, 1999), pp. 189–95.

3   See Danette Dimarco, 'Exposing Nude Art: Carol Ann Duffy's Response to Robert Browning', *Mosaic: A Journal for the Interdisciplinary Study of Literature*, 31:3 (1998), pp. 25–39, and Alan Robinson, *Instabilities in Contemporary British Poetry* (London: Macmillan 1988), pp. 194–201.

4   Roberts suggests that 'It would be drastically misleading to represent Duffy's poetry in terms of a post-structuralist freedom from the nostalgia for origins and presence' (*Narrative and Voice*, p. 192).

5   Carol Ann Duffy, *Selling Manhattan* (London: Anvil Poetry Press, 1987), p. 60.

6   Judith Butler, *Gender Trouble: Feminism and the Subversion of Identity* (London and New York: Routledge, 1990), p. 143.

7   See Rachel Alsop, Annette Fitzsimons and Kathleen Lennon (eds), *Theorizing Gender* (Oxford: Polity Press, 2002), p. 134.

8   See Andrew Parker and Eve Kosofsky Sedgwick (eds), *Performativity and Performance* (New York and London: Routledge, 1995), pp. 1–18.

9   Butler, *Gender Trouble*, p. 145.

10  Toril Moi (ed.), *The Kristeva Reader* (Oxford: Blackwell, 1986), p. 3.

11  Butler, *Gender Trouble*, p. 140.

12  See Alsop, Fitzsimons and Lennon, Chapter 4.

13  Carol Ann Duffy, *Standing Female Nude* (London: Anvil, 1985), p. 58.

14  Chris Weedon, *Feminist Practice and Poststructuralist Theory* (Oxford: Blackwell, 1987), p. 89.

15  Butler, 'Performative Acts', p. 405.

16  Daphne was saved from violation by Apollo by being transformed into a laurel tree. See Mary Innes, trans., *The Metamorphoses of Ovid* (London and New York: Penguin, 1977), Book 1, pp. 482–591, 43.

17  I am grateful to Neil Sinyard, Senior Lecturer in Film Studies at the University of Hull, for this information.

18  See *The Metamorphoses of Ovid*, Book III, 334–517 in Innes, pp. 83–7.

19  Judith Butler, 'Critically Queer', *GLQ*, 1:1 (1993), pp. 17–32, p. 23.

20  Carol Ann Duffy, *The Other Country* (London: Anvil Poetry Press Ltd, 1990), p. 9.

21  Butler, 'Critically Queer', p. 23.

22  Carol Ann Duffy, *Mean Time* (London: Anvil, 1993), p. 9.

23  Sean O'Brien, 'Carol Ann Duffy: *A Stranger Here Myself*', in *The Deregulated Muse* (Newcastle: Bloodaxe, 1998), p. 165.

24  *OED*, 2nd edn.

25  Independent interview www.independent.co.uk/story.jsp?story=45475.

26  The most evocative sea area, Finisterre, was abandoned by the Meteorological Office and replaced by Fitzroy. It no longer features in the UK shipping forecast.

27  Butler, 'Performative Acts', p. 402.

28  Ibid.

# 7

## 'What like is it?': Duffy's *différance*

STAN SMITH

### Something in between

CAROL ANN DUFFY's poem 'Away and See'[1] commands the addressee to 'Away and see the things that words give a name to'. This might seem to echo William Carlos Williams's mantra, 'No ideas but in things'.[2] But the contrariness of 'things' – the word, the concept, that is – is that it lacks all 'thingyness'. It is not one of those thickly onomatopoeic, 'interesting words', full of pretensions to engage with the substance and solidity of the world, which Duffy casts aside in an interview:

> I'm not interested in words like 'plash', you know, Seamus Heaney words, interesting words. I don't like them. I like to use simple words but in a complicated way so that you can see the lies and truths within the poem . . . You can put little spotlights on phrases, like clichés, that will show how although they look like a plastic rose in fact they've got roots underneath. They have meaning.[3]

This deceptively modest manifesto for a linguistically based poetics, for a conceptual poetry not afraid of abstractions, generalisations, discursive statement, goes against the grain of a tradition of sensuous poetic immediacy that has been constructed, retrospectively, to run from Shakespeare and Donne, through Hopkins and Hughes, to Heaney himself.

There is in fact a peculiar generalised abstractedness, a discursive transparency, to the very 'idea' ('the very idea!') of 'things'. For all its alleged inclusiveness, the word swivels on a central indeterminacy, for it speaks always of things in general, but not of any specific 'thing', in a way which evacuates such 'things' of their particularity. The *Ding-an-sich* of philosophy is itself an abstract concept. There are shoes, and ships, and sealing wax, but no such thing as the 'thing in itself', for to speak of such is to enter a level of abstraction in which presence, substance and the *quidditas*, or 'whatness', of an entity have already evaporated. What remains is a set of arbitrary signifiers which in no way correspond to the tangible, material objects they give a name to.

'Nothing's the same as anything else', 'Away and See' goes on to say, playing with paradox, as the words fall apart into their component morphemes. For if 'no thing' resembles 'any thing else', then the very act of generalising them as 'things that words give a name to' is suspect, self-subverting, radically disputing the capacity of language to capture the reality of the 'real' (a word derived from the Latin, *res*, a thing). This structural indisposition of language, its inability to do more than gesture, point ineffectually towards and at things, accounts for Duffy's stress in this interview on language not as flamboyant original utterance, cutting through in its vivacity to some intrinsic ground of being, but on its ordinary everyday usage, the small change of social intercourse: 'I would often put a cliché in italics, or a fragment of speech that seems very ordinary, next to something else in the hope that it would nudge the reader into seeing it the way I do.' Indeed, her own attempt to explain what she is doing with language turns here into a wrestle with inarticulacy and, in a final fumbling, an admission of failure:

> When I'm writing a poem, when any poet is, what we are often trying to do is get the sound of a non-linguistic sort of music. I can have the rhythm or a whole sound in my head and no words. And it isn't music, it isn't language, it's something in between. It has a colour, almost a shape. So I'm not aware that I'm doing that in a poem on a hyper-conscious level; that is partly the way I speak anyway and it will just translate into the poem like that, whatever it is I have to say, and how I say it, that is how it's coming out. It isn't a technique and because it isn't a technique I can't describe it.[4]

Duffy's 'things that words give a name to' does not, that is, presume a naive philosophical realism, predicated on the direct correspondence of word and thing. The ubiquity of translation in all language acts is a central preoccupation of her work, as is that fretting over the non- or pre-linguistic, which can only be gestured towards in the inadequate metaphors of an 'almost' music, an 'almost' shape, which is really 'something in between'.

'Away and See' constantly defers to the processes of signification, through the 'translations' of metaphor (the sun as a boiled sweet), by the appeal 'Write to me soon', translating the addressee into an imputed writing subject, by the way in which it moves surreptitiously from 'real' fruit in a 'real' market, via the metaphor of a record's 'flip-side', to the 'market of language', that is, a system of abstract exchanges, negotiated meanings. If words refer to an exterior objective world, they do so only narcissistically, self-absorbed and self-admiring at the very moment that they announce their objects. If they tell us, like Milton, that the world is all before us, they also speak of a paradise perpetually lost, one where words and things may once have co-existed in perfect union, but do so no longer. They exemplify accurately, that is, Derrida's idea of meaning constructed in '*différance*', in the play of difference which is also an endless deferral down the chain of signifiers. For, in reality, words are inadequate, treacherous. They slip and slide with imprecision, have perpetually to be 'tested' and 'spelt' (or, like magic, 'spelled') before they can be believed.

Significantly, the 'things' the poem lists, unlike Hopkins's inventories of 'dappled things', seem on the verge of abandoning their status as nouns naming objects to become verbs of process and action, stretched, as syllables take flight, into something more transitive and gerundival:

> Away and see the things that words give a name to, the flight
> of syllables, wingspan stretching a noun. Test words
> wherever they live; listen and touch, smell, believe.
> Spell them with love.

Finding it impossible to say just what she meant in another interview, Duffy offered instead what she there spoke of as a previously unpublished poem by way of explanation. 'The Professor of Philosophy Attempts Prayer' contains an epistemological variation on the metaphor of bird flight:

> I see that feathered things are made to fly
> But are they *really there*? What I perceive
> To be ain't necessarily so. I'll die
> Well off, but with nothing of value to leave.[5]

The poem itself begins with the abstract, algebraic chain of signifiers of formal Logic, before immediately deconstructing it with the slanted syllogisms of human encounter: 'If a then b, if me then Thee'. Wittily, the phrase 'feathered things', recalling the periphrases of eighteenth-century poetic diction, subordinates the quiddity of 'birds' (itself a generalisation which refuses to specify any particular species, even of the most commonplace, garden variety) to a sub-category of the genre 'things', in a way which parodies the philosopher's preoccupation with ever larger categories of the generic and universal. In this same interview, Duffy spoke of coming 'from a working-class background which, in many areas, was inarticulate', where 'language was often perceived as embarrassing, or dangerous', and added:

> I'm aware of the limits of language, how it barely stretches to hold whatever one wants to say, unless it's only 'pass the salt'. If there's a tension between any alleged fluency and this awareness, then good. Life's like that. Language is.[6]

That last syntactic juxtaposition suggests both a paralleling and an identification of 'language' and 'life'. But it also contains an almost certainly unintended but nevertheless significant double entendre. For if life is 'like that' (that is, exists in the dimension of simile and similitude, not identity), in the end, language, though it is also 'like that', also just simply 'is'.[7] This 'something' may be 'nothing of value', but it also reminds us, in the colloquial phrasing of a once-popular song, that 'What I perceive / To be ain't necessarily so'.

An intercalated 'otherwhere', not simply the Scotland which she had to leave as a child to live in an alien England, is the true location of Duffy's 1990 collection, *The Other Country*.[8] 'Words, Wide Night' in this volume (*TOC*, p. 47) establishes both an approximation and a distance between the two concepts juxtaposed in its title, to make in its closing two lines a similar play with the fraught relation between similitude and identity. It is a poem specifically concerned with the simultaneous inadequacy and ineluctability of language, a gratuitousness which allows the writer in the poem to cross out the word 'pleasurable' and replace it with the word 'sad' without in any way falsifying the experience she is attempting to define, 'For I am in love with you and this // is what it is like or what it is like in words.' The three-way play between 'is', 'is like', and 'is like in words' points towards Duffy's reflections on the mother-tongue, exemplified by the similarity and difference of her mother's Glaswegian idiom, in the penultimate poem of the volume (*TOC*, p. 54), 'The Way My Mother Speaks'. The poem addresses the crucial difference between '*saying* things' and 'saying *things*', reflecting on language's peculiar ability to say what Swift's equine logicians called 'the thing which is not':

> For miles I have been saying
> *What like is it*
> the way I say things when I think.
> Nothing is silent. Nothing is not silent.
> *What like is it.*

The way someone says things and the things they say, and what they say or fail to say about the place they occupy, or fail to occupy, are intimately linked, for one sensitised by linguistic deracination and working-class inarticulacy to the dangerous and embarrassing artifice of language. This is why, I think, Duffy places this poem immediately before the last poem in the book, 'In Your Mind', which provides in its opening words the title for the whole volume: 'The other country, is it anticipated or half-remembered?' This is a country whose 'language is muffled by the rain which falls all afternoon'. Within such muffled discourses one changes places as one exchanges words, or as one may 'swap a coin for a fish on the way home'. Language can say one thing and its opposite simultaneously, for, amidst 'the certainty of place' the subject is perpetually 'lost but not lost'. That certainty is itself shaky, however, the ground of being unreliable, as is demonstrated by the way the shift of a simple preposition can convert (turn) the verb 'turns', in a symptomatic dislocation and dis-locution, into something altogether shiftier, so that all that is solid melts into air: 'The certainty of place turns on the lights / all over town, turns up the scent on the air.' If the lights all over town are turned on by the certainty of place, then it is also the case that such certainty turns, hinges, depends on, all those lights, as the volume of scent is turned up, increased, but is also a turn-up for the books. Such verbal destabilisation dissolves the certainties of place in order to instate a different kind of certainty, a momentary access, 'In Your Mind', to that other country, the Otherwhere upon which Here and Now depend, and to which language, fluent in the negotiation of absences, provides an access:

> For a moment
> You are there, in the other country, knowing its name.
> And then a desk. A newspaper. A window. English rain.
> (*TOC*, p. 55)

## Something happening

The opening poem of *Standing Female Nude*,[9] 'Girl Talking', starts with a troubling indeterminacy:

> On our Eid day my cousin was sent to
> the village. Something happened. We think it was pain.

It is an indeterminacy from which much follows. Pain does not usually happen: it is suffered or inflicted. What does happen here, in the reporting, is a kind of deadening of subjectivity, both in the girl spoken of and in the speaker, which also suppresses interpretation. 'Something' is not an evasion. It is just not specifiable. That is its horror. The uncertainty of 'We think it was' then relates not to something unspeakable but to something it seems hard, even impossible, to identify. There is a discrepancy between event and interpretation, a discrepancy for which we have been prepared by the distance, in the opening phrase, between our probable ignorance as readers of what an 'Eid day' is (the festal day celebrating the end of Ramadan) and the speaker's taking it for granted. The next stanza also deploys a problematic word, or rather one we know which here has a totally different meaning, 'coy', but then attempts to define it, not in terms of what it 'is', but what it 'is like': 'It's like / a field.'

'Afterwards it did not hurt', the poem says, objectifying the pain (or possibly its cause) as 'it', giving it the unquestionable certainty with which one observes that 'It rains'. The subject of this pain begins to be specified, given a name, Tasleen, addressed by others as a real person, a companion. But that 'something', contrariwise, stubbornly refuses definition, though it finally kills: 'She thought something / was burning her stomach . . . // After an hour she died.' 'From that day we were warned not to do this', the speaker reports. But what is 'this'? The narrative invites us to imagine her stomach pain as pregnancy, or abortion, or some other consequence of the (possible) trading of sex for flour at the start. But the last line of the poem, closing a sequence of terse, strangely 'objective' sentences, observes, at first it would seem inconsequentially: 'Baarh is a small red fruit. We guard our hearts.' This is the same kind of rhetorical effect as 'Life's like that. Language is', paratactically juxtaposing two discrete statements in a way which implies their relation, but not specifying what that relation is, leaving the reader to supply the links. The poem, like many of Duffy's, almost taunts its readers with their exclusion from the inner significance of that which it narrates, leaving them fumbling in the gaps of its parataxes.

Each of this poem's four stanzas contains an unfamiliar concept (in stanza three it is the children's game called, without explanation, 'Jack-with-Five-Stones'). In each case enough information is supplied to allow us to imagine a context, but not enough to share in their inner significations, within the speaker's discursive community. 'Baarh' is, then, 'a small red fruit', which can be inferred to be in some way related to what happened to Tasleen, but how and why remains perpetually withheld. There is 'something' here at the core of the poem that the reader doesn't know, and is not being told. This reticence, or withholding, is a key trope of Duffy's poetry, which regularly appears to mediate events, stories, experiences it refuses fully to translate, make transparent, withholding the total interpretative context. Even when its exotic words are explained, their foreignness remains as an indecipherable otherness at the heart of what simultaneously seems to invite to a shared humanity. What persists is an indeterminable 'something', apparently moving from generality to specificity in that shift from 'something happened' to 'something was burning', but ultimately indecipherable. And this is only a second-hand story, after all: only a 'Girl Talking', a story, doubly mediated in a sequence of incomplete 'translations', in which intimacy is denied as readerly anxiety increases, in a strange tension between a universalising empathy and a deadpan narration which will not open to the reader. The girl who talks is also, it would appear, estranged from the events of which she talks, herself not knowing what those 'somethings' are.

Variations on the phrase 'something happened' recur in Duffy's work. The oddity of this usage was perhaps suggested by Joseph Heller's novel of that name, published in 1974. Heller's *Something Happened* perpetually defers telling us what it was that happened, in a repressive movement which cannot confront the enormity of that event, throughout the text working endless changes on pronouns or adverbs formed out of the permutations of 'some-', 'no-', 'any-', 'every-', on the one hand and '-body', '-one', '-thing', '-where', etc. on the other. Its narrator's whole account is premised on the proposition in a one-sentence second paragraph: 'Something must have happened to me sometime', to explain the anxiety, 'dread' and the 'smell of disaster mounting invisibly and flooding out toward me' which is his perpetual

state of mind, a conviction that 'Something did happen to me somewhere that robbed me of confidence and courage and left me with a
fear of discovery and change and a positive dread of everything
unknown that may occur'.[10]

It is just such a tension, between a cold, 'professional' indifference
to events and their real enormity, which characterises the 'War Photographer', 'Home again / to ordinary pain', developing his still images
of ongoing atrocity (*SFN*, p. 51):

> Something is happening. A stranger's features
> Faintly start to twist before his eyes,
> A half-formed ghost . . . .

What is twisting here is the flat surface of the negative as the image
emerges in the dark-room. But as the stanza itself develops we learn
that the image is of a real man twisting as he dies, killed by soldiers in
some foreign street. The photographer's 'spools of suffering set out in
ordered rows' speak of a traumatised reality, their arbitrary 'order' a
sign of moral exhaustion, images of 'A hundred agonies in black-and-
white / from which his editor will pick out five or six / for Sunday's
supplement', meretriciously making the hypocrite 'reader's eyes prick
/ with tears between the bath and pre-lunch beers'. If 'solutions slop in
trays', these are only developing solutions, not solutions (answers) to
the many catastrophes of Belfast, Beirut, Phnom Penh.

A variant on the phrase occurs just before this in the same volume.
'Ink on Paper' (*SFN*, p. 49) presents three 'Compositions', all of which
pun on the ideas of composing, compositor, and (moral or physical)
composure, the latter itself seen as always some form of deliberate
'composition':

> On the table, apples imitate an old motif . . .
> . . . Something has happened. Clouds
> move away, superior and bored. A cigarette
> fumes in a brown clay ashtray, ignored.

The poem speaks of the indifference of things, but also of our own
reciprocal indifference towards them until we suddenly concentrate,
as in a painting, on their autonomous quiddity. These are 'still life'
compositions, but their stillness and silence speak of all the activity
that has happened, and is now ended, or is going on elsewhere, or
remains latent in their 'composition'. The latter word applies to three

stages in the creation of these scenes. The ink sketches are compositions picturing a room with objects. But a prior act of composing
occurred in the careful and deliberate arrangement of the scene,
setting it up theatrically to make it the object of the compositions. For
this is not a pristine world, innocent of human intent. Those apples
'imitate an old motif': they are apples acting the part of apples, performing themselves. The imitation is not just in the sketching, but in
the act of composing them in the first instance to become objects for
the artist to sketch. The ambiguity of the title involves too, the poems
which report them, mediated by the compositor's inky lines on the
page ('composition' is the word by which school essays used to be designated). There are, then, three levels to this composing: the poem
composes in words the pictures drawn in ink; those compositions in
turn record the scenes composed by some prior and absent hand to
construct just this artful sense of the unpremeditated spontaneity of a
world of objects.

For all the absence of people from these scenes, the poem begins
with an experiencing subject, 'The heart is placid', and the absences
depicted everywhere implicate the subjects who are absent, the dark
red armchair 'with no one in it' waiting patiently for someone, the
empty wet wellingtons warming 'ghost-legs at the fire'. The drawings
evoke things they cannot possibly depict, the smell of onions frying,
the noise of crying, off, which can only be imagined, invented, by a
spectator. If 'This bowl of fruit obstinately refuses / to speak the language', the speaker here, recalling perhaps David Hume's philosophical dismissal of colour as a secondary, merely subjective attribute of
matter, insists on the importance of the observing subject, for 'The
grapefruit / will only be yellow as long as anyone looks'. Things may
refuse to participate in human experiences, as the peaches remain
'aloof', but, even within the inky compositions, a human subject finally
manifests itself in the last 'composition':

> Unwatched, the man watches the cat, watching.
> An orange is more still than the near-silence.

This is paradoxical, since although the generic 'man' is not watched in
the picture (the generic 'cat' would appear to be watching something
else), the describer is watching him, the artist will have watched him,
and the reader is now caught up in the mediated illusion of watching
him, by courtesy of the textual account. But 'watch', in its three varia-

tions, is an odd verb to use, rather than the more customary 'look at', since it suggests a continuous act with a duration in time, not the kind of instantaneous perception a picture seems to require. The poem, that is, both invokes and dismisses the reader in the act of perception, or, as it seems to imply, voyeurism. The recession of unreciprocated watchings is posited, it seems, on the absent person ('no one') who may recently have sat in that dark red armchair, who *may* be that woman alleged to be 'crying / on the other side of the door' amidst 'the smell / of onions frying'. The scarcely noticed internal rhyme of 'frying' and 'crying' adds to our unease, insinuating links beneath the surface of appearances, leading us to speculate on the cause of her tears: is it the onions, or some great emotional scene that took place in this room a moment ago? And these questions of emotional content distract us from the disturbing practical questions of representation: how can a *picture* propose the *sound* of crying or the *smell* of onions from a (non-existent) room 'on the other side of the door' which is only lines of ink on paper? Adding to our unsettlement in this painterly scene is the tantalising hint of T.S. Eliot's equally paradoxical account, in 'The Metaphysical Poets' (1921), of modernist composition in a mind which is 'constantly amalgamating disparate experience', so that falling in love and reading Spinoza are constantly 'forming new wholes' with 'the noise of the typewriter or the smell of cooking'.[11]

The voyeurism of such an aesthetic epistemology is spelt out in 'A Provincial Party, 1956' (*SFN*, p. 40), in which a reluctant housewife, dragged by her husband to some suburban would-be orgy to watch a blue movie, registers both the squeamishness and the titillation of watching the 'things going on / on the screen which would turn your Mam to salt', until 'You daren't look, but something is happening / on the Cyril Lord'. The phrasing is deliberately unclear whether that something is happening on a carpet in the film or in the room where it is being shown. In the same way, 'daren't look' suggests the prurient self-contradictoriness of the observer, since without looking, albeit surreptitiously, she could not report what is happening, while the reader, reading between the lines of her oblique reporting, shares in her voyeuristic complicity by reconstructing in imagination what that hinted 'something' must be.

As the poem 'Beachcomber' (*MT*, p. 20) advises, contemplating what seems to be a photograph from the poet's childhood, 'This is what happens', in narratives of which one observes that 'This is about something', without ever fully fathoming what that 'something' is. 'But', as the poem goes on to say, 'this is as close as you get. / Nearly there.' The speaker seems to be for ever excluded from the inner significance of the event caught by the camera. But so does the reader, struggling to decrypt a something that remains stubbornly between the lines. We infer that 'something happened', something horrific perhaps involving the 'Beachcomber' of the poem's title – a violation, possibly, of the child the speaker was. But that child could be herself the beachcomber, innocently collecting starfish, seaweed, crabs, a conch shell. For the poem goes on to envisage the possibility of an intervention in the event (whatever it is that 'happened') by the grown-up that child has become, only to conclude that nothing could have been said, or altered: 'and what / what would you have to say, / of all people, / to her / given the chance? / Exactly.' That last word, with which the poem finishes, suggests that, whatever it was, it had to happen, was always going to happen, and could never be averted, no matter how much or little was said. But in its play between indeterminacy ('chance') and precision ('Exactly') it refuses to tell us what that something was. Instead, its indeterminacies echo in the poem's shell like the sound of the sea in a conch, infinitely suggestive, never specified.

## Saying something

'Something' is a word which recurs with remarkable frequency in Duffy's poetry. It communicates a particular kind of indeterminacy to her texts, representing a refusal to come straight out and say just what she means, whether from fear, anxiety, discretion, reticence, or, most usually, because that meaning is undefined, not known. Sometimes it is the very figure of desire, that unidentified thing which cannot be specified because the power of desire lies in its indeterminacy, in one's not knowing what it is one wants, as voiced by Moll in 'A Clear Note' (*SFN*, p. 27): 'There's something out there / that's passing me by.' But that unknown, desired and dreaded 'something out there' matches a corresponding indeterminacy within, as in 'Till Our Face' (*SFN*, p. 22): 'Something inside me / steps on a highwire.' That this is a love poem, and indeed that 'something' possibly the moment of orgasmic climax, indicates just how complexly evasive is Duffy's use of the word, summed up in that other, consummate love poem that hesitates to be a love poem, 'Saying Something' (*SFN*, p. 18). The poem says something, but never says the words it wants to say, 'I love you', able only, searching in a dream of being in a foreign city, 'for a word to make them you', to approximate to the declaration with the trivialising diminuendo of 'Sweetheart'.

The poem struggles to reject the idea that anything constructed within discourse is by definition an imposture. If 'Things assume your shape' – discarded clothes in the bathroom, for example – 'This is not a fiction' but (with a play on 'material') 'the plain and warm material of love' which, in its turn, 'My heart assumes'. But that reciprocity of outer and inner in a shared 'assumption' (there are theological implications to the word, for someone raised a Catholic), is more apparent than real. If 'Our private language starts the day', that language runs away from meaning, unable to catch 'the dreams we have no phrases for', which 'slip through our fingers into smoke'. The speaker is restricted to 'Pedestrian daylight terms' which, in a dissonant note, merely 'scratch / darker surfaces', invoking absences which leave her with only 'the ghost / of love'. However, the poem concludes on an upbeat note, with that recurrent image of Duffy's of someone, in this case her lover, 'turning on the lights', so that in the end simply giving a name to the person (though that name is not in fact given to the reader) is enough to say something:

> I come in
> From outside, calling your name, saying something.

Love is 'Hard to Say', as the poem of that name (*TOC*, p. 45) admits, its normal currency 'tired clichés', words like 'grubby confetti, faded, tacky, blown far // from the wedding feast'. The poem had begun with an indeterminacy and the demand for something concrete and precise:

> I asked him to give me an image for Love, something I could see,
> or imagine seeing, or something that, because of the word
> for its smell, would make me remember, something possible
> to hear. *Don't just say love*, I said, *love, love, I love you.*

But those immediate qualifyings and alternatives ('see' becoming 'imagine seeing', seeing slipping into smelling and hearing), that reduplicated denial of language in language ('*Don't just say* . . . I said') demarcates the impossibility of reuniting words and things, of saying exactly 'What like is it'. Instead, a sunburst of similes expresses what it is 'like' to 'want . . . you', an experience which will remain forever beyond language.

More often, Duffy's characters feel anger and frustration at their inarticulacy, like Bernadette in 'A Clear Note' (*SFN*, pp. 30–1), aware of 'Listening / as language barely stretched to cover / what remained unsaid', which is nevertheless 'the things that seem natural to us'. All language is in this sense 'Weasel Words', as described in the epigraph to the poem of that name (*TOC*, p. 14): '"words empty of meaning, like an egg which has had its contents sucked out by a weasel"'. And yet, 'When the words have gone away / there is nothing left to say', says 'Alphabet for Auden' (*SFN*, p. 10) – which is not as simple as it sounds, since it could mean that there is nothing left to be said, but also that nothing – no self – is left behind to say it. For, as the next sentence makes clear, consciousness cannot be disentangled from the language in which it finds itself, a foundling none the less lost for being self-made: 'Unformed thought can never be, / what you feel is what you see. / Write it down and set it free / on printed pages, © Me.' In formulating itself, that 'Me' becomes the lord and owner of its copyright, constituted as the legal subject of tort and contract. Conjugating the verb, translating 'amo, amas, amat' into an English construal of self-hood at the centre of a grammar of relations, 'I love, you love, so does he', the wayward self immediately loses itself in playing at not being itself, which only exposes that we are, in reality, not quite ourselves, picking up Auden's reference to himself in the third person as 'Mother': 'I'll be Mother, who'll be me?'[12]

'Free Will' (*SFN*, p. 25) expresses the alienation and non-involvement of the speaker in what is happening to her in terms of an almost pathological linguistic incompetence:

> The country in her heart babbled a language
> she couldn't explain. When she had found the money
> she paid them to take something away from her.
> whatever it was she did not permit it a name.

We presume that this is an abortion, but since it is here a thing that words are not permitted to give a name to, we do not and cannot know for sure, so that that nameless 'something' ('Whatever it was') rapidly becomes a mere 'nothing', but a 'nothing' which in the very repetition of its nullity becomes a cause for grief: 'It was nothing yet she found herself grieving nothing.' The mind seeks to numb itself, but it has, so to speak, a mind of its own, so that 'Things she did not like / to think about persisted in being thought'. The romanticised real 'country in the heart', which babbles in a language she cannot explain (not cannot understand, but cannot communicate to others, translate), is, in reality, an alien terrain within the self – the discourse of another which may be more one's self than the conscious, wilful subject who refuses to name that something/nothing.

If the overly articulate 'Head of English' patronisingly challenges the visiting poet to 'Convince us that there's something we don't know' in the poem of that name (*SFN*, p. 12), it is clear that her very self-assurance guarantees her exclusion from what she calls 'an insight to an outside view'. Another 'school' poem just before this, 'Comprehensive' (*SFN*, p. 8), plays on the wider meaning of a word used to describe a system of schooling which, intended to break down class divisions in education, now has to cope with the complexities of a multicultural Britain. The poem, however, refuses the wishful ideology of inclusiveness (comprehensiveness) of the educational theorists. Each stanza presents the experience of a pupil from a different indigenous or immigrant culture, without suggesting that they have any community of values and assumptions that can include (comprehend) them all. The poem opens with the hopefully helpful translation offered by an African child for whom Duffy's special use of the phrase 'is like' seems to promise a perception of similarity within difference: 'Tutumantu is like hopscotch, Kwani-kwani is like hide-and-seek.'

But even between the girl and her sister language divides as well as connects. Her sister came back to Africa, she recalls, speaking only English, so that 'we fought in bed because she didn't know / what I was saying'. In English exile, they talk now about 'the things we used to do / in Africa and then we are happy'. Africa, the other country, is here more important than those indeterminate and unspecified 'things' they talk about, for such things exist primarily as metonymies of desire, figures for a lost home, a lost continent. In the third stanza, an Asian immigrant child recalls that 'People wrote to us / that everything was easy here'. But 'everything' is as empty a signifier as that 'nothing' which in the next stanza the English Michelle's mum 'won't / let me do', the double negative paradoxically giving substantive status to the pronoun. While the English boy fantasises about the army or emigration to Australia as a way out of his alienation, the Muslim boy who speaks in the last stanza is, he says, hopeful and ambitious, and his 'everything' ironically takes on a positive aspect not apparent in the others, though it speaks at the same time of the problematic relation between consciousness and its objects: 'At first I felt as if I was dreaming, but I wasn't. / Everything I saw was true.'

That last, all-inclusive but unspecific pronoun retains at its core a real and subversive 'nothing'. It is not possible to provide a 'comprehensive' narrative of these different and discrete lives and heritages, yoked fortuitously by the school which is their only point of convergence. The school itself, as the product of a conflicted history of educational reforms, is not the impartial, all-embracing space where all these narratives meet but a politically disputed arena, a place of division and unreconciled multiplicity where, it may be, *every* thing is 'true' because *no* thing in particular is. The reader is implicated in the act of seeing without understanding, listening in to all the parallel but untranslated narratives which the poem endeavours to 'comprehend', that is, to hold together, within a liberal ecumenical conception of childhood which may itself be delusory. Perhaps the only way each child 'is like' the others lies in his or her subjection to the specific and different cultures that have made them what they are. Certainly, in 'Ash Wednesday 1984' (*SFN*, p. 14), the sectarian Roman Catholic education in which Duffy was reared is seen as a form of child abuse, constructing a cultural prison-house where 'Dead language rises up and does them harm', offering only 'accents of ignorance' and the 'bigot's thumbprint', and, through the institution of the confessional, a perversion of story-telling in the 'weekly invention of venial sin / in a dusty box'.

'Lizzie, Six', the plangent, Lorcaesque song interposed between 'Head of English' and 'Ash Wednesday' (*SFN*, p. 13), casts a beaten and abused 6-year-old as the image of what that acculturation can mean. The poem that follows 'Ash Wednesday', 'Education for Leisure' (*SFN*, p. 15), offers a disturbing insight into the discursive universe of one of those abused children, when he grows up, someone who may be an actual or potential serial killer: 'Today I am going to kill something. Anything.' The indiscriminate nature of this hatred against the world that appears, collectively, to have wronged him, is realised in that easy shift from 'something' to 'anything', transfixed in paratactic isolation. Disturbingly, such murderous intentions seem like a perversion of the writer's urge to transform and translate. *King Lear*'s image of the crushed fly ('As flies to wanton boys, are we to the gods; / They kill us

for their sport'), which he recalls from school, 'was in / another language and now the fly is in another language'. The self is infinitely
translatable, at least in fantasy, and it has the power to translate others, to convert 'something' (fly, cat, goldfish, budgie) into 'nothing',
until 'There is nothing left to kill':

> I am a genius. I could be anything at all, with half
> the chance. But today I am going to change the world.
> Something's world.

Chance again interposes itself between the 'anything' one could be and
the 'something' one is, and in this world of particular somethings, one
of those somethings is going to have its world changed, translated
from being a live subject to being a dead thing, by the godlike act of
the killer. As the poem closes, the speaker draws a knife, to pronounce,
chillingly, as if picking out the reader, 'I touch your arm.'

### Fretting for something else

'Another language' is as much a key to Duffy's work as the idea of 'the
other country', since, whether actual or metaphoric, each is experienced as an aspect of the other. 'River', which comes between a poem
called 'The Literature Act' and 'The Way My Mother Speaks' at the end
of *The Other Country* (*TOC*, p. 53), presents this at first in the most literal terms:

> At the turn of the river the language changes,
> a different babble, even a different name
> for the same river. Water crosses the border,
> translates itself, but words stumble, fall back.

But the poem rapidly turns into an epistemological enquiry about the
nature of meaning, asking rhetorically, 'What would it mean to you if
you could be' with the woman seen on a path in that other country,
where the birds have different names and

> blue and silver fish dart away over stone
> stoon, stein, like the meanings of things, vanish?

The speaker speculates that this woman 'feels she is somewhere else
. . . simply because / of words'. But of course there is no way of knowing this other than by attributing to her, in her foreignness, the same
kind of reactions the speaker would have herself. Clearly the woman

'sings loudly in nonsense' only for the speaker, who equally clearly cannot hear her, for the different babbles of the opening stanza are each of them meaningful, not babble at all, to their native speakers. 'Babble' is a product of linguistic difference, but the word 'like', that quiet little 'quasi-preposition or conjunction' (even the *Oxford English Dictionary* is uncertain of its true grammatical status), reminds of likeness even as it constitutes difference. Simply because of language we are all equally 'somewhere else'. At some point in the past, 'stone', 'stoon' and 'stein' were the same word, sent on their different ways by some secondary fall of Babel, but retaining still the likeness within difference which implies, beyond division, a shared reality in the world of things. The speaker can infer with some confidence that that woman in another country will be feeling similar things to her observer, crooning songs about similar things, looking in a similar way at those 'feathered things' whose flight takes them across linguistic boundaries, or the fish which, 'like the meanings of things', dart away, vanish, only to reappear.

Translation, for Duffy, is at the heart of the human, the guarantee perhaps of a common humanity at the very moment that it testifies to human divisions. The poem 'Translation'[13] may take as its epigraph a dismissive *obiter dictum* from Artaud that '*All writing is garbage*' but what it enacts is the centrality of translation to being human, so that, in a poem whose language translates a number of ordinary events into enigmatic narratives, 'strange half-truths', sexual intercourse becomes an 'invented' act with a fantasised other, not the man actually 'push[ing] into her' – becomes, that is, a translation. Etymologically, according to the *OED*, translation is 'Transference; removal or conveyance from one person, place, or condition to another'. It is thus, for Duffy, the human condition itself, as indicated by a poem such as 'Dies Natalis' (*SM*, pp. 10–13), where play with the idea of metempsychosis becomes a metaphor for the way the subject is socially constructed as a changing yet curiously constant being. The newborn baby learns to become itself by giving fixity and form to that initially indeterminate 'something' which 'is constantly changing / the world, rearranging the face which stares at mine' – that is, its mother. In the process of learning to name a world, the self is also named, nominated to an identity, a process which the poem sees as the primal act of translation: 'They are trying to label me, // translate me into the right word.' 'Model Village' (*SM*, pp. 21–2) rehearses the catechisms by which the child is interpellated to such a specific linguistic identity ('See the cows . . . Cows say *Moo* . . .', etc), creating a 'model' reality in the head which then shapes all the self's negotiations with the 'real'.

Duffy speaks in interview of her fascination with her own childhood, as she gets older: 'The way things branded the senses; which now they don't do . . .'[14] This is immediately given a linguistic inflection, for that oddly brutal metaphor of violation and enslavement is also a process of translation which constructs the self within a realm of artifice, estranging the real as it gives it names: 'The way language itself seemed new and odd, artificial or censoring. I think perhaps childhood events shape everything that follows.' That last, truistic observation assumes here the nature of a quasi-Lacanian ontology in which the child finds and loses itself in the translation, which is also a fall, from the Imaginary into the Symbolic order. Such a construction of the subject occurs not once and for all but is perpetually reprised. In 'We Remember Your Childhood Well' (*TOC*, p. 24) parents retrospectively strive to rewrite the narrative of their grown-up daughter's past:

> Nobody hurt you. Nobody turned off the light and argued
> with somebody all night. . . . nobody locked the doors.

But in a sense, these real 'nobodies' and 'somebodies' have a point. If 'The secret police of your childhood were older and wiser than you, bigger', they were also there first, for they constituted the very ground of being and language, on which the child first came to consciousness. At the core of the self there is another. For Duffy this otherness can sometimes be figured as the truly authentic, that reality which was forfeit when the self was uprooted from its true home, in the other country of the Imaginary, and translated, which is to say displaced, into the particular places, things, words of one's actual, contingent identity. It is just such a recognition that lies at the heart of that remarkable poem of demographic, linguistic and cultural relocation, 'Translating the English, 1989' (*TOC*, p. 11), where 'the English' refers simultaneously to a people and to an alien yet familiar language.

Viewed in this wider sense, translation is an ubiquitous phenomenon. The act at the centre of *Selling Manhattan*, focused in its title poem, is the 'purchase' (literally, a seizing hold) of Manhattan island from the '*Injun*' for twenty-four dollars' worth of glass beads. This transfer of ownership ('*I got myself a bargain . . . / Now get your red ass out of here*') is a genuine act of translation in several senses, for with the new owners come a new language and a new set of cultural (mal)practices, 'drown[ing] out / the world's slow truth with rapid lies' (*SM*, p. 34). The native American who speaks here is the very figure of displacement, living in the ghost of grasshopper and buffalo, vanishing like the salmon going mysteriously out to sea. But there are other ways of being a displaced person, as for example the immigrant or euphemistically named *Gastarbeiter* of that remarkable poem, 'Foreign' (*SM*, p. 47). The poem opens by inviting imaginative sympathy with a condition that, by the end of the poem, has become through imagination the reader's own, as if we have in turn been taken over, translated into the strangeness of exile, learnt to 'think / in a language of your own and talk in theirs'. The most significant transaction of the poem, however, is its surreptitious elision of language and money, implicating that universal solvent in the processes which displace 'economic migrants' from one end of the earth to another, just as it once turned the American Indian off his native soil:

> And in the delicatessen, from time to time, the coins
> in your palm will not translate. Inarticulate,
> because this is not home, you point at fruit. Imagine
> that one of you say *Me not know what these people mean.*
> *It like they only go to bed and dream.* Imagine that.

The pidgin English, like the repeated call to 'imagine' with which the poem ends, effects a translation even as it seems to deny its possibility. For these sentences *are* meaningful, indeed share with the inarticulate working classes of whom Duffy spoke in her interview, and with the maternal voice of 'The Way My Mother Speaks', a crucial conviction of similarity, and therefore possible solidarity, within difference: '*It like* . . .' There are many ways in which 'the coins . . . will not translate', the money economy interposing itself between the people it simultaneously binds together in a global system of exchange. But that last call invites to a self-displacement which would also be a significant act of trans-cultural empathy.

The condition of the self is to be perpetually, as the title of one poem puts it, 'Away from Home' (*TOC*, p. 49), merely 'lodging' in an unfamiliar place identified only as 'somewhere', its inhabitants a series of indeterminate 'someones':

> Someone somewhere will always be leaving open
> a curtain, as you pass up the dark mild street,
> uncertain, on your way to the lodgings.

Though the poem ostensibly concerns a particular trip away, the onto-logical anxiety it evokes becomes an analogy for the whole way of being-in-the-world of an 'uncertain' subject beset by 'a blurred longing' for obscure objects of desire. The distress felt in this 'Anonymous night' where there is 'Something wrong' seems to be dispelled by the thought that 'Tomorrow you return', and by the call home which brings the reassurance, in the last line of the poem, that 'The telephone is ringing in your house'. But the feeling remains that the experience to which the self has here awoken is the metonymy of a metaphysical condition. The poem does not, after all, complete that journey home, nor is the receiver lifted in the empty house. As much as the waiting at the cross-roads for Godot in Beckett's play, the conviction that this home exists, with a phone ringing in it, is an act of faith which sustains the anxious self standing in a urinous public phonebox 'at the edge of a demolition site'. This is recognisably the same place of transit, at the intersection of past, present and future, as that described in 'Hometown' in the same volume (*TOC*, p. 10), a world 'you can't find anymore', for

> Wherever I went then, I was
> still there; fretting for something else, someone else,
> somewhere else. Or else, I thought, I shall die.
>
> And so I shall.

Translation, the *OED* reminds us, can also mean, in Catholic theology, 'removal from earth to heaven'.

## Something he could not have

'Someone' and 'somewhere', like 'something', recur in Duffy's work, and are yoked more than once, in a conjunction which seems to have some private resonance. In 'Somewhere Someone's Eyes' (*TOC*, p. 27), the incoherent, reported fumblings of its last stanza ('*Somewhere* . . . he said, but we'd had enough . . . / . . . *Somewhere someone's...*') are taken up by the voice of the poem in its conclusion: 'Across the white fields somewhere / someone's eyes blazed as they burned words in their mouth.' 'Woman Seated in the Underground, 1941' (*SFN*, p. 50), based on a Henry Moore drawing, invents a monologue in which the woman proclaims, 'Someone has loved me. Someone / is looking for me even now. I live somewhere.' However, she 'sing[s] the word *darling* and it yields nothing' for, as she says, 'I lost myself in the crowd.' A similar losing of the self seems to lie at the heart of 'Dreaming of Somewhere Else' (*SFN*, p. 37), set in a Liverpool which the god of mercantile capital has abandoned, a place where now 'nothing will happen . . . ever'. In a bleak final image, the poem casts that 'somewhere else' not as a lost, possibly recoverable home but as a long-extinguished galaxy whose light is only now reaching us, too late to matter, a bleakness underlined by the final demotic put-down from some unidentified and last-minute interlocutor: 'Somewhere else another universe takes light years / to be seen even though it went out already. *You wha'?*'

That homesickness is an ontological and not contingent condition in Duffy's poetry is confirmed explicitly in 'Homesick' (*SM*, p. 19), with its opening confession:

> When we love, when we tell ourselves we do,
> we are pining for first love, somewhen,
> before we thought of wanting it.

This nostalgia, amidst 'the rooms we end up living in', in a world where love is always imperfect, music only an echo of itself, is for a fullness of self-presence in which sign and referent, language and things, are one – something we cannot have. Such a lost order of things, felicitously summed up by the neologism 'somewhen', is associated with 'first light', 'that time, before we knew to call it light', and with 'first sound, what we heard once, / then, in lost chords, wordless languages'. In a world of simulacra, copies, echoes, we are 'dying of homesickness / for when, where, what', for a lost unity of being in which the self comes home to an unmediated time and place where all beyonds are incorporated in the instant, without any waste sad time stretching before and after. It is in fact a yearning straight from the mainstream of the Christian mystical tradition.

Fretting after that 'something else' left out, left over in any particular formulation accounts for Duffy's sense that it is what words do not say, the 'something in between' the thing and its saying, which is the true home of language and self alike. But this is a home from which both are for ever excluded, as if from Eden or a Manhattan sold irredeemably to the dispossessor.[15] The subject lives thus in perpetual debt, but, as the poem 'Debt' (*SFN*, p. 33) indicates, without ever really knowing to what, or how to become solvent:

> He bargained with something he could not believe in
> for something he could not have . . .
> There was nothing he would not do. There was
> nothing to do but run the mind's mad films.

The play between those two nothings goes straight to the empty heart of the dilemma. As with Don Paterson's jokily football-laddish title for his first volume, *Nil Nil* (1993), Duffy sees the human condition as a 'no win' situation. The casino gamblers in 'Oslo' (*MT*, p. 32), are optimistic in their belief that 'This life you win some, lose some'. 'Losers' (*TOC*, p. 35) is more realistic:

> Each day
> is a new game, sucker, with mornings and midnights
> raked in by the dealer. Did you think you could keep those cards?

In this universal casino, 'clocks shuffle the hours slowly' and all the self can do is nostalgically remember 'the hands you were dealt, the full-house of love, / the ace-high you bluffed on'. 'Mostly we do not notice our latest loss / under the rigged clocks', but 'The times / it hurts are when we grab the moment for ourselves, nearly . . . // and the bankrupt feeling we have as it disappears.'

## Something you're sure you knew

In Duffy's poetry, gambling – in particular card games, and, even more particularly, the shuffling and dealing of a hand – is a recurrent metaphor for existence. 'Poker in the Falklands with Henry & Jim' (*SFN*, p. 54) is explicit enough: 'We three play poker whilst outside *the real world* / shrinks to a joker. So. Someone / deals me a queen.' That playfully italicised cliché of philosophy and everyday life, '*the real world*' is the place where soldiers of the Queen die in earnest, as the speaker realises, observing that 'Perhaps any moment my full house might explode' though he will never know he has been dealt – another cliché – '*the final card*'.

The image can be found in most of her volumes, never simply literal, sometimes with an unusual twist. 'Away From Home' (*TOC*, p. 49), for example, speaks of a town approached by train, where 'the first houses / deal you their bright cards', including a kitchen Queen of Hearts and 'a suburban king counting his money'. 'Never Go Back' (*MT*, p. 30) speaks of 'Anecdotes shuffled and dealt / from a well-thumbed pack', while 'The Cliché Kid' (*MT*, p. 18) inverts the parental stereotypes as justification for his mental disturbance by speaking of a transvestite father and 'the sound of Ma / and her pals up late, boozing, dealing the cards'. 'An Old Atheist Places His Last Bet' (*SM*, p. 16), facing a declining life, makes the allegory clear, insisting to a non-existent God, 'Deal the cards. I wait / for a king as shadows lengthen.' Opposite him however he sees only 'the dealer's vacant place, piled high with chips'. Uncaring whether he wins or loses (he can only lose), in the last line of the poem, confronting his destiny, he turns the card, but also turns his poker face. Even in *The World's Wife* 'Mrs Beast' recalls in detail 'my Poker nights' with other mythical females, watching 'those wonderful women shuffle and deal / . . . bet and raise and call'.[16]

This is not for Duffy just a traditional metaphor for fate – the hand one is dealt by life. It goes deeper than this, and links with, for example, the motif of the transmigration of souls in 'Dies Natalis'. This is why it is the shuffling and dealing which dominate in her use of the metaphor. The card game, to adapt Lacan, is structured like a language. Like language, like life, it endlessly recycles a finite number of signifiers, roles, stereotypes. All lives are in this sense clichés, as 'The Cliché Kid' rightly recognises. But in any one deal it is not simply the particular configuration of the cards, but also the skill with which they are played which counts: a good hand can be thrown away by incompetence or a bad one bluffed into success. What is equally important for Duffy's metaphor is that these are games in which money is won or lost, changes hands, slips through the hands: circulates. The poem 'Money Talks' (*SM*, p. 33) gives the cliché of its title an original twist by likening discourse and cash. What money says, when it talks, is 'I am the authentic language of suffering'. Nothing in itself, it is the measure and master of all things. It speaks through the whore who asks, 'Mister, you want nice time? No problem', and the gigolo who enquires, 'Do you fancy me, lady? Really?' It can pass through the eye of a needle, and underwrite its own convertibility: 'I got any currency / you want.'

In a money economy, the same fungibility obtains for human beings as for things. 'Someone Else's Daughter' (*SFN*, p. 59) presents this insight in the most harrowing terms, foreseeing that a woman's heroin-addicted daughter, dying, 'will shrink to a childhood snapshot / as someone else's daughter moves into the squat'. The world is full of someone else's daughters: the room will always find a new occupant. The pathos of the poem lies in the bitter tension between the idea of a unique, unrepeatable individual on the one hand and the easy replaceability of the generic being on the other. 'Queen Herod' (*TWW*, p. 8) speaks of her daughter as 'my little child, / silver and gold, / the loose change of herself, / glowed in the soft bowl of herself'. But to see the self as mere 'loose change' is to see how easily exchangeable it is, running away like money or water.

The figure of Midas, who converted all things to gold with his touch, occurs directly or obliquely in several of Duffy's poems. The hunchback gambling on the fruit machine in 'Translation' (*SM*, p. 39), fixated on 'bright uneatable fruit', is one of his manifestations. But he figures most prominently in 'Mrs Midas' (*TWW*, p. 12), where he is indicted by an indignant wife for his futile and destructive fetishisation of a commodity that 'feeds no one . . . slakes / no thirst'. Midas is a paradoxical figure, embodying the irony of commodities, for if gold is the universal solvent, in that everything can be changed into it and it can be changed into everything, what Midas does by turning everything into gold is to reify, commodify them, make them *merely* things. If gold, in being the measure of everything, becomes also its terminus and only destination, then the world congeals to a halt. In this, it is only another figure for death. In 'Plainsong' (*SM*, p. 60), 'No Midas touch / has turned the woods to gold', as the self walks amidst the trees' 'phrases of light', 'straining / to remember something you're sure you knew.' It is the indeterminacy of that 'something' which makes it so haunting. But 'The words you have for things die / in your heart', leaving only the grasses 'chanting the circles you cannot repeat / or understand'. And this inarticulacy and incomprehension is the self's true home, 'your homeland, / Lost One, Stranger who speaks with tears'.

If words give a name to things, they also estrange those things, make them strange. To find them truly is to witness the death of words. 'Eurydice' (*TWW*, pp. 58–62) speaks of the Underworld of the dead not as a 'some-' but as a 'nowhen', 'a place where language stopped', 'where words had to come to an end'. It is, in fact, the final silence at the heart of things, their inhuman, speechless 'thingness'.

Summoned back to life by the voice of the searching poet, Eurydice feels only the indignation of brute matter that does not want to be 'trapped in his images, metaphors, similes', his 'histories, myths'. In the end, like Eurydice impatient to return to her death, things will refuse the words that give a human name to them. Those names are a delusive attempt to domesticate, make safe, the difference and the strangeness of things. This is the original and final something that the self strains to remember in 'Plainsong', a lost memory which in its very emptiness is also a premonition, whispering like the grasses' plainsong of first and last things, like the evening bell tolling 'Home, Home, / Home, and the stone in your palm telling the time'. For, as Wittgenstein observed in words Eurydice seems to half recall, death is outside the language, not an event in life:

> The dead are so talented.
> The living walk by the edge of a vast lake,
> near the wise, drowned silence of the dead.

## Notes

1 Carol Ann Duffy, *Mean Time* (London: Anvil, 1993). I have discussed this poem in 'The Things that Words Give a Name to: the "New Generation" Poets and the Politics of the Hyperreal', *Critical Survey*, 8:3 (1996), pp. 306–22.

2 William Carlos Williams, *Paterson, Book One* (New York: New Directions, 1946), 'The Delineaments of the Giants'; this edn, *Paterson* (New York: New Directions, 1958), p. 6, line 14.

3 Carol Ann Duffy, interviewed by Andrew MacAllister, *Bête Noire*, 6 (winter 1988), 75–6.

4 MacAllister, p. 75.

5 Carol Ann Duffy, interviewed by Jane Stabler, *Verse*, 8:2 (summer 1991), pp. 125–7. The poem had in fact been published in *Thrown Voices* (London: Turret) in 1986.

6 Stabler, p. 127.

7 One wonders whether there is here an unconscious echo of Robert Graves's title for a collection of White Goddess poems: *Man Does, Woman Is* (London: Cassell, 1964). The book's title poem uses one of Duffy's favourite metaphors, that of the card game, and concludes by asking, in very Duffyish mode, 'Can a gamester argue with his luck?' Certainly Duffy's casually idiomatic phrasing also hints at that 'something in between' which lies between 'is' and 'is like', of which Graves had written in an earlier poem, that 'extra-territorial' dimension, an 'Otherwhere' neither Here nor There, which is poetry's proper domain. See Robert Graves, 'From the Embassy', *Collected Poems 1975* (London: Cassell, 1975), p. 153:

> 'I, an ambassador of Otherwhere
> To the unfederated states of Here and Thee
> Enjoy (as the phrase is)
> Extra-territorial privileges . . . .

8  Carol Ann Duffy, *The Other Country* (London: Anvil, 1990).

9  Carol Ann Duffy, *Standing Female Nude* (London: Anvil, 1985), p. 7.

10  Joseph Heller, *Something Happened* (London: Jonathan Cape, 1974; this edn, London: Corgi Books, 1975), pp. 9 and 14.

11  T.S. Eliot, 'The Metaphysical Poets', *Selected Essays* (London: Faber, 1972), p. 287.

12  'Talent' (*SFN*, p. 42) takes this linguistic construction of identity to its logical extreme, imagining a tightrope act as a linguistic performance (or vice versa): 'This is the word *tightrope* . . . . // There is no word *net*.' The tightrope walker 'teeters but succeeds', though the spectators clearly want him to fall, and then, the poem concludes, 'The word *applause* is written all over him.' The wit of the poem lies in the total coincidence of text and tightrope act, so that each defines the other. The poem itself, in fact, performs self-referentially a tightrope act between the linguistic order and the realm of things.

13  *Selling Manhattan* (London: Anvil, 1987), p. 39.

14  Stabler, p. 124.

15  Philip Larkin, about whom Duffy has a poem ('An Afternoon with Rhiannon', *TOC*, p. 34), also demonstrates a high frequency of the words 'something' and 'nothing', but the words are deployed less programmatically than in Duffy's verse. On this see my 'Something for Nothing: Late Larkins and Early', *English*, 49:195 (autumn 2000), pp. 255–75.

16  Carol Ann Duffy, *The World's Wife* (London: Macmillan, 1999), pp. 73–5.

# 8

## 'What it is like in words': translation, reflection and refraction in the poetry of Carol Ann Duffy

### MICHAEL WOODS

THIS CHAPTER seeks to offer a view of Duffy's poems that address the idea of translation in a variety of ways. There are poems that deal with the literal translation involved in changing from one language to another, while others address metaphorical translations such as the political transformation of Britain since 1979. Duffy's general interest in the visual arts, and the surrealists in particular, is used to explore the ways in which language itself can be translated into another medium. There are also translations through dramatic monologues where Duffy offers us views of the world through the eyes of other people. It is also important to signal that Duffy has epistemological concerns with regard to language; that is, the nature and scope of knowledge and the ways in which language allows us to explore this. She read philosophy at university so it is unsurprising that Ludwig Wittgenstein's theories about language are germane to the present discussion, along with those of Ferdinand de Saussure, Roland Barthes and Jacques Derrida.

At the heart of Carol Ann Duffy's poetry is a continual acknowledgement and exploration of the limits of language. It is significant that a poet of such felicity with the medium of the art itself should have at the centre of her poetics an acute sense of an ever-present tautology predicated upon what amounts to a post-structuralist awareness of the unstable nature of the sign. So, while Duffy may be a regarded as a live reader of her own work *par excellence*, and is therefore popularly perceived as eminently accessible, there is a very clear sense, when reading poems she rarely chooses to perform, of her recognising the need to mediate between what Roland Barthes refers to as the *lisible* or 'readerly' and *scriptible* or 'writerly'.[1] Also, the tension between the logocentric and phonocentric is crucial when considering the concept of voice in Duffy's poetry, something with which she is especially concerned. In championing difference, she also interrogates *différance*.[2] Duffy is well known for her use of the dramatic monologue, but the multiplicity of voices that also emerge from her first- and third-person lyrics should not be forgotten. Recognising the plurality of meaning possible in both the written and the spoken, she explores the relative valencies of words and voices. In testing words 'wherever they live' she demands that they should earn their keep. There is an explicit engagement with the problems inherent in privileging either logocentricism and phonocentrism, and even with a position that doubts the capacity of words to mean at all, and this is articulated in the early poem, 'Saying Something' in which the persona signals the apparent inability of language to access real meaning: 'The dreams we have / no phrases for slip through the fingers like smoke.'[3] She negotiates this difficulty, in part, by oscillating between poems such as 'The Grammar of Light' that seek to construct, in her own terms, wordless languages, and those such as 'Prayer' which do appear to place more trust in words and their ability to name and console. There is also a stance that falls between these poles where language is presented as a gateway to the possible. At the heart of Duffy's poetic is a striving for truth, clarity and the tuned-into frequency of the voice she presents in any given poem. She is acutely aware, as Raman Selden points out, that: 'Phonocentrism treats writing as a contaminated form of speech. Speech seems nearer to originating thought. When we hear speech we attribute it to a "presence" which we take to be lacking in writing.'[4]

In attempting to confront the absence of presence through her multiple attempts at voicing, Duffy is ultimately bound to the reality that she is repeatedly articulating for, through and to the reader, the presence of absence. This stems from her understanding of, and subscription to, a deconstructive position in which 'speech can be viewed as a species of writing'[5] because those features of speech that tend to occlude pure thought processes and their expression derive from the manner in which, historically, oratory sought greater and greater eloquence at the expense of clarity of communication. In 'Away and See', for example, she eschews the vicarious and presents us with a poetic

Paraclete, an exhortation to trust our own senses, to live experientially.[6] In writing the poem, she celebrates what language is able to do but also draws attention to the way in which a poetic construct as a snapshot of 'reality' undermines itself; the words of which it is made are in an unstable relationship with one another, never mind with a world 'out there' that we might hope they may make sense of. Here is a clear example, then, of the poet's recognition that the artist can only be an interpreter of experience, rather than an unacknowledged legislator, who offers a translation of 'what it is like in words'.[7]

'The Grammar of Light' (*MT*) further explores of the limitations of language. It is perhaps the most strikingly direct of Duffy's poems that seeks to transcend words and does this by using light as an alternative system of signification. Of course, there is an inherent paradox here; Duffy is exceptionally articulate in conveying to the reader the inarticulacy of words. Like the grammar of language, this alternative grammar may be viewed in both prescriptive and descriptive terms. Duffy concentrates on the prescriptive model by musing that there are 'so many mornings to learn' (*MT*, p. 33) and the descriptive through empirically observed detail. The poem begins with the image of a night-time kiss. The 'meaningless O' is the shape of the mouths as they kiss but the light that enabled the lovers to find each other is not meaningless, it 'teaches, spells out'. Already words as a means of exploring the world are being replaced, translated out of themselves. Duffy deliberately applies pronunciation terms to her imaginary grammar of light. Mornings are described as 'fluent' and the stars go 'stuttering on', indicating difficulty in articulation but also reminding us of the way the light we see coming from stars is sometimes perceived as intermittent, and what leads us to claim that they twinkle. Like speech apparatus, light can itself be inarticulate at times. The waiter who 'balances light in his hands' reminds us that we could make such an observation without the light to make sense of the situation. Added to this, we could not say that he has 'silver' coins in his pocket. We need not go much further here but might consider what we *could* say without light. We are told in stanza three that a bell 'shines', a verb enacting its visual being and one that significantly precedes its expected primary sonic function. The fact that it is 'ready to tell' may be ambiguous as it could simply be saying that it is there because we are able to perceive it as such. We think of the 'toll' of a bell so the poet is again drawing a parallel between what we see and what we articulate and how both relate to a decoding process. A saucer 'speaks to the eye', a deft presentation of light as language. The final stanza uses the word 'slurs' to suggest the fluidity of wax as it runs down a candle but also conveys the effect of wine on speech. As a source of light itself, the candle 'flatters', a well-known effect. The 'Shadows' that 'circle the table' are not unexpected in the subdued lighting of a restaurant at midnight but there is quite a sinister sense that darkness threatens. This is certainly borne out in the final image of death in the last line of the poem. The visual effect created by the word 'blur' is, in the grammar of light, equivalent to 'blur' in the grammar of words. This ingenious rhyme draws the reader's attention to the way in which Duffy has been at pains to reinterpret experience through the medium of the visual. Visual images in the poem invite comparisons with the painterly, and this poem might easily be viewed as chiaroscuro in words. The scenes depicted could easily be viewed as a sequence of paintings, ranging from the purely representational to the surreal. This is analogous to a translation from one language medium to another. Perhaps most striking in the poem is the image of trees that 'think in birds, telepathise'. This neatly encapsulates the way Duffy seeks transcendence from language itself and is intimately bound up with relationships between perception, thought and language. Telepathy implies transference of thought from mind to mind but the extent to which this is possible without language is investigated. The way in which light may be viewed as a means of testing experience may be related to Wittgenstein's picture theory of language. In the *Tractatus* he asks questions that clearly preoccupy Duffy. How is language possible? How can anyone, by uttering a sequence of words, say something? And how can another person understand them?

'Translating the English 1989' (*TOC*, p. 11) seizes on the cliché of the English invention of a foreign visitor to Britain labelling its language 'the English' instead of 'English' and uses the term against such people as they are the ones who have become metaphorically translated by the emergence of a xenophobic, individualistic and alarmingly nationalistic society. This form of translation is intimately bound up with an acute sense of the manner in which the language of an age can act as a barometric measure of its values. In this poem, Duffy seeks to find an equivalent in language for the way in which she perceived England to have been debased under the then Tory government. The title does not simply draw attention to the imperfect thinking or refraction of ideas that results from attempting to move from one language to another, an intellectual, abstract process; it emphasises the manner in which the English as a nation have become metaphorically translated. England's cultural axis has changed to the extent that it lauds the novels of Jeffrey Archer – 'Plenty culture you will be / agreeing' – and *Brookside* as worthwhile whilst reducing the arch, anti-metropolitan to 'Daffodils. (Wordsworth. Up North.)'. Here is an England in which the poetry of the Romantic tradition is, as Duffy's epigraph states, 'lost in translation'. The Romantic is typographically, and ideologically, bracketed off in an attitudinal reduction of everything to the status of mere commodity. The voice presented in the persona of this monologue is easily recognisable but we are simultaneously aware of it commuting to that of the tack-spitting poet as the closing repetition of 'Welcome, Welcome, Welcome' is translated in the mind of the reader, who understands the bitter irony of the piece, into a horrible threat; to set foot in England with the memory of something better is to arrive as the inhabitant of the other country of the past, an England where things were done differently. Duffy's choice of the dramatic monologue is a form eminently suited to her purpose since, in this case, she is drawing attention to the manner in which ideas can become refracted. Lyric tension is replaced by the tension between the poet, the chosen speaker and what is spoken. The opacity of translation is used to expose the transparency of selfish individualism fixed in the mean time that marked the end of the first decade of what was to be a seventeen-year Tory administration. Behind the voice of the poem is the poet as interpreter, affined to the earlier poetic voice of Wordsworth who professed to be speaking to ordinary people.

So, language is interrogated not only in an intrinsic sense but in the ways that it is used or abused by others. Duffy critically assesses the manner in which others offer 'translations' of the truth. 'Weasel Words' (*TOC*) satirises the manner in which politicians deliberately seek to defer meaning for nefarious reasons. Its language and technique derives from the verbatim recording of proceedings in Parliament as set down in *Hansard*, while the framing of the poem is within the formal constraint of the sonnet. This is ideally suited to a subject whose locus is essentially that of clearly defined procedure and known structure. The blown egg that is palpably present in the poem symbolises the language of absence in which politicians so frequently acquire fluency. The traditional form of the sonnet is traduced to expose what is said and done purely for form.

Translation as a means of trying to understand otherness rather than to expose societal change is another of Duffy's concerns. 'The Dolphins' (SFN) tries to find a language to give these animals that is reminiscent of the way Les Murray presents a range of creatures in *Translations From the Natural World*.[8] In some measure one might regard it as a poem that tunes in to a frequency normally perceived only by the very creatures that form its subject. The dolphin says of its companion, 'The other's movement / forms my thoughts' (SFN, p. 58). It articulates its gradual acclimatisation to the aquarium in which it finds itself in terms of translation: 'After travelling such space for days we began to translate.' The dolphins' language is form and shape. Beyond the well-known scientific fact that dolphins are sophisticated communicators – they have been observed to 'speak' in what appear to be utterances – Duffy draws attention to a language beyond words, an idea to which she often returns. In the light of this, it seems appropriate that Duffy should give voice to the creature that seems to have a real language, offering her own translation of what its sense of selfhood might be. The dolphin begins by speaking in the second person. This has the effect of creating a sense of familiarity and affinity between the reader and the creature. However, all that it says beyond the third line of the poem is in the first person plural. This is striking because it leaps into the world of dolphins forced to speak from their perspective about the effects of imprisonment by humans. It uses images of what we might perceive as being associated with freedom and joy in 'swim' and 'dance' but this impression is modified and complicated by the fact that the dolphins' 'world' is the pool in which they perform and not the expansive ocean. There is both pathos and dignity detectable in its voice when it speaks of being in its element but 'not free'. This tension introduces a conflict that is articulated in the remainder of the poem, the dolphins' natural affinity with humans and the latter's propensity for causing misery. The 'constant flowing guilt' refers to the necessity in an artificially created aquatic habitat of having water pumped through the pool. Duffy presents it metaphorically as 'guilt' because the system is effectively an admission that the situation is unnatural and otherwise unsustainable.

A dolphin derives an enormous amount of information about its world through its skin, which reacts to minute changes in electromagnetic fields. Its highly developed sonar is well known. In stanza two even this seems unable to offer 'explanations' that might make sense of its new world. In the 'limits of the pool' it finds 'no truth' but only the monotony of 'the same space always'. It has taken 'days' to 'translate' the truth because the dolphin's mind is so used to expanses of free ocean. Far from illustrating mental incapacity, this presentation of the creature serves to stress its ability to fathom new experience. The culpability of humans in the abduction of dolphins is indicated by the continual presence of 'the man' who is 'above' the pool. This reflects his assumed position of superior status. He reduces the dolphins to performing by jumping through hoops or after a 'coloured ball'. The terrible psychological effects of confinement show in 'for the world / will not deepen to dream in.' Recalling the idea of mediation between languages, we might see the dolphin as a translator rendering an unnatural 'world' in terms of its own natural language, something that has been scientifically well documented. The collective voice in 'we' signals a search for truth and an awareness of selfhood that is not selfish. This is made clear in references to the 'other'. Stanza three stresses the mutual understanding between the dolphins, and they define themselves in terms of each other, 'The other knows / and out of love reflects me for myself.' This touching insight into a relationship signals a sense of otherness, respect for independence and mutuality. The dolphin's companion shares its knowledge that life has changed irrevocably and tries to reduce the attendant pain by simply being a sympathetic 'other' of its species. The reflexive pronoun 'myself' clearly indicates that the fact that the dolphin who speaks in the poem is able to maintain its integrity as a result of this mutual understanding. The sense of loss of former freedom is intensified by the visual description, 'We see our silver skin flash by like memory / of somewhere else.' The simile brings together the dolphins' intimate bodily knowledge of each other but simultaneously reminds them of a time when there would be a multitude of such sights. Dolphins are naturally gregarious and often travel in shoals of several hundred. Their real world is now referred to as 'somewhere else'. The dolphins' response to performing tricks with a ball is defined, naturally enough, in terms of the presence or absence of the man. They 'have to balance till the man has disappeared'. This detail is important to consider as it emphasises the human's utter control.

In observing that the 'moon has disappeared' there is a visual association being made between the spheres that are the ball and the moon. An unnatural, man-made object has replaced the natural regulator of the tides; a parodic, garish substitute for the real moon. The final stanza's presentation of the dolphins' predicament is bleak and hopeless. The image of a record being played repeatedly is used as an analogue for the seemingly eternal circuits that the dolphins make in the pool that confines them. The fact they 'circle well-worn grooves / of water on a single note' effectively translates the experience of sound into the terms of the aquatic mammal. The monotony of existence communicated in a 'single note' and its effects is compounded by the dolphin's expression of utter desolation as, in the next sentence, it tells of the effect of its companion's mournful voice. Its eternal 'music of loss', keening over its predicament and impending doom is enough to turn the listening dolphin's heart 'to stone'. It has sympathy for its own kind. The poem closes with reminders of oppression, control and confinement. Possibility that was once limitless for the dolphins now has 'limits' that will become impossible to bear. The final line, with its reference to 'our mind', neatly links the plural possessive pronoun with the singular noun 'mind' indicating a collective voice for a species. The tense change to 'we will' draws attention to the contrast between what the dolphins had, what they have now and can expect in the future. As a result, the dolphins assume an almost mythic status in that they appeal to archetypal impulses in us and in nature; they are not just the creatures that form part of it. 'The Dolphins' may be read just as easily as a poem about human disillusion, betrayal and loss of direction as one about animals. As an interpreter of experience it offers us a new language into which we would do well to translate ourselves.

'River' (*TOC*) uses words as a means of showing the way they reflect, and are rooted in, other countries or cultures. However, 'Water crosses the border, translates itself' in a manner that transcends such restriction, unlike the baby in 'Brothers' whose pre-linguistic, pre-reflective self is 'like a new sound flailing for a shape' (*TOC*, p. 53). 'River' may be regarded as another 'wordless language'. Here, we do not have the world made sense of through a grammar of light but through the medium of water. Although a river may cross physical borders and barriers it is not limited by the constraints of different languages in doing so, it 'translates itself'. In this way it is as self-referential as the poem itself in that it seeks more 'to be' than 'to mean'. In direct contrast to water, 'words stumble', the hard consonant 'b' emphasising the clumsiness that can accompany translation. The bird that the woman tries to name in stanza two is the same, irrespec-

tive of the language of the person naming it. The physical act of pre-
serving the flower, which is pressed 'carefully between the pages of a
book', is an interesting way of showing how a physical action following the purely sensory experience of a 'red flower' can be relived independent of language. The fact that it is pressed between pages of
words is a striking reminder that there is more than one way to pre-
serve memories.

The question posed to the reader at the beginning of stanza three
is, in common with 'Away and See', an invitation to concentrate on the
actual experience of things rather than worrying too much about what
name to give them. We are able to derive 'meaning' from sensory detail
in a much more direct way. Language is, after all, a code we use to
articulate that very experience and, as such, could be seen to have
secondary importance outside the normal need to communicate with
others. There is, though, the residual problem that we think almost
exclusively with reference to linguistic structures. The image of the
'blue and silver fish' that 'dart away over stone, / stoon, stein, like the
meanings of things' returns us to the idea that meaning is elusive, and
language protean. The signifying system we use in one language may
be different in another but they all mean essentially the same thing.
The proximity of spelling in three languages of 'stone' is cleverly presented in the alliterated prefix to emphasise Duffy's point. The concluding lines of the poem challenge the reader with another question.
The idea of writing a postcard is connected with brevity and, often,
writing from a new place or country in a way that tells another person
something about it. The whole problem of the relationship between
experience and articulation is deftly presented in the image of an estu-
ary, a place where a river becomes 'translated' into sea through the
mixing of salt and fresh water in brackishness. As an ultimate symbol
of flux, a river is an ideal metaphor for Duffy's exploration of the way
language changes and the manner in which it relates to landscape.
Duffy is concerned here with reflecting upon language in general and
specifically on the morphology or structure of words and their meaning. Words, the raw material of poetry have the capacity to convey
what the poet intends, as well as their capacity to confound it.

The preoccupation with translating experience through language
as faithfully as possible is sustained in 'Away and See' (*MT*). The child-
ish metaphor of the opening line, 'Away and see an ocean suck at a
boiled sun', is immediately transmuted into a much more adult per-

spective in, 'and say to someone things I'd blush even to dream' (*MT*, p. 23). The second stanza begins to deal explicitly with language in the striking beginning: 'New fruits sing on the flipside of night in a market / of language, light, a tune from the chapel nearby'. There is a reminder for the reader that the visual and aural perceptions are crucial for feeding the creative imagination, the translator. The third stanza is worth quoting in full:

> Away and see the things that words give a name to, the flight
> of syllables, wingspan stretching a noun. Test words
> wherever they live; listen and touch, smell, believe.
> Spell them with love.

Duffy again takes up the relationship between words and what they signify and she personifies words themselves in an impressive reversal since it is usually words that are used to personify things. Having said this, she is left with having to articulate this in words, which leads us to ask the sorts of questions about language raised in 'Words, Wide Night' (*TOC*) and 'The Grammar of Light' (*MT*). The idea of a bird being brought into the mind through words is to be viewed alongside the thing itself and the manner in which the alliterated 'n' sounds in 'wingspan stretching a noun' suggest the tension of wings spread out (*MT*, p. 33). Added to this, the phrase on the page is visually 'stretched'. The sense of lift provided by the amplitude of the long vowel sound in 'flight' consolidates the explicit exploration of the poetic possibilities of words. The exhortation to 'test words wherever they live' is as much a challenge offered to poetry in general as it is an instruction to the self. The idea that words are alive is vital to any poet, however suspect they may be. The physical senses mentioned – hearing, touch and smell – form a bridge between the mind and words; they are the confirmatory providers of empirical data that allow us to 'believe' in the world around us. The last two lines of the stanza employ full rhyme, half-rhyme, alliteration and consonance: 'live' and 'love' are a half-rhyme but there is also alliteration and consonance between them and 'believe'; 'smell' and 'Spell' rhyme perfectly, suggesting that the former helps the poet to order experience. Whilst eschewing the vicarious, the poem can only allow re-cognition for the poet and, at best, recognition for the reader. So, the limits of poetic language have to suffice in the business of exploring the boundless.

Moving on from a consideration of a poet simply finding the right words, Duffy often gives voice, or rather voices, to the desire to transcend language in a way that recalls Seamus Heaney's poem 'Oysters' in which the speaker craves that he 'Might quicken . . . into verb, pure verb'.[9] In 'Homesick' the speaker articulates the desire to escape from the trammels of language, to be rather than to name, wanting 'wordless languages';[10] this idea is revisited in a number of poems but developed most extensively in 'The Grammar of Light'. The homesickness for 'when, where and what' alliteratively ties together a desired singularity rendered explicable through the reality that it was once intuitively understood *before* it was articulated and before a relationship between sign and signifier was established. The same desire is articulated in 'Moments of Grace' (*MT*). The first line, 'I dream through a wordless, familiar place' (*MT*, p. 26), engages, characteristically, with the desire to experience and cherish what Wordsworth called 'spots of time' rather than merely to record them. The voice we hear in the italicised words such as '*Like this*', '*Of course*' and '*Yes*' is that which is spoken aloud to and by the persona presented in the poem. It translates the present self into the earlier self and negotiates the fissure between the variegated experiences of life and love. The concentration upon parts of speech in stanza four employs grammatical terms as metaphors for varying intensities of living: 'These days / we are adjectives, nouns. In moments of grace / we were verbs, the secret of poems, talented.' Just as 'Away and See' is a poem that advocates the need for experiencing life directly, 'Moments of Grace' is concerned with capturing and renovating experience from mean time, the inexorable process that seems intent on robbing us of our being, transmuting us from verbs into adjectives and nouns. Of course, the need to be connected with an extra-linguistic state is framed within the confines of language itself. Duffy recognises this ('A thin skin lies on the language'), something that a poet inevitably finds difficult to live with. This 'thin skin', like the insulation on an electric wire, prevents real energy from being experienced. The insulator in the electrical sense is, though, a lifesaver but in the case of the language of poetry it is a killer.

A preoccupation with the need to find 'wordless language', and order beyond the chaos of words themselves is evident in other poems, too. 'Dies Natalis' (*SM*), for example, is an enigmatic exploration of a newborn consciousness but linked to a pre-conscious sequence of

selves that seek to explore the supra-linguistic realm. These metamor-
phosing, protean personae that none the less have to resort to forms of
language, like the cat's mistress who is described as 'searching / with
long, gold nails for logic in chaos' (*SM*, p. 10), may be viewed as the
part of us all that craves some Platonic certitude of imperishable singularity. This is underlined by the fact that the polyphonic voices in
this poem about the genesis of being chime univocally in its pristine
omega, 'I cry'. The phrase clearly signals the first use of the child's
vocal apparatus and recalls Hopkins's sonnet 'As Kingfishers Catch
Fire', in which each thing 'cries itself, What I do is me, for that I came.'[11]
Outside the simple purity of being, though, is the hermeneutic need to
explain human action. This effectively traps the child within an
abstract matrix that is to be dogged by the obfuscations of language.
Conversely, sense is also sought through a language of forms, meaning being mined by the poet from the ore of what amounts to the lexis
of being or, in the example from Heaney quoted earlier, 'pure verb'.
The sea is 'Muttering in syllables of fish', which again highlights the
abstraction that is language, through surreal dislocation as well as the
freedom from permanent shape that the yet-to-be-determined life
enjoys. The bird persona – surely Coleridge's albatross – says, 'I
warned patiently / in my private language', is unable to communicate
or translate except to itself in its own metamorphosis into what seems
to amount to a reluctant capitulation to the human form. 'I talk to
myself in shapes' and 'They are trying to label me, translate me into
the right word' clearly signal resistance. Further, 'I will lose my memory, learn words / which barely stretch to cover what remains unsaid'
takes us to the quick of what havoc language wreaks on the poetry of
life that can be, as Frost would have it, 'lost in translation'.[12] *Selling
Manhattan* anticipates *Mean Time* in poems that dwell on the nature
of language and its ability to reveal or obfuscate. The title 'Strange
Language in Night Fog' could almost stand alone as an acknowledgement of what a poet faces in attempting to make meaning, while the
detail of the poem can leave the reader in no doubt that the lines 'the
pond / had drowned itself' and 'Even their own hands / waved at their
faces, teasing' (SM, p. 17) draw attention to the reflexivity of poetic
language as being about itself in a way that does not necessarily signify anything beyond itself. Language is a sealed system that can refer
only to its own interiority; unmeaning is only a short distance away
and any certainty in naming is unstable and precarious. Fog is as much

symbolic of the unstable relationship between signifier and signified as it is of a general sense of disorientation: 'they told themselves / there must be a word for home, / if only they knew it'. The 'strange language' is such because expected syntagmatic relationships are entirely effaced by the paradigmatic, and it is the latter's signalling of substitution that Duffy muses upon in images such as 'phrases of light' (*SM*, p. 60) and 'the colour of thought is / before language' (*SM*, p. 61). This is not simply a metaphorical felicity but part of Duffy's interest in the epistemological – the nature and scope of our knowing and the way the poet gives voice to this.

Although Duffy is widely and rightly celebrated as a performer of her own work, the 'utterance' of the poems themselves, as Hopkins would have it, more often than not leads to a dwelling upon the 'prepossession' of the words of which they are made. This might seem self-evident but the connotative and denotative dimensions of words are not simply the archly used staple of Duffy's art but a consciously acknowledged philosophical problem. It should not be forgotten that Duffy read philosophy at university and that Wittgenstein has endured in her thinking. 'Whereof we cannot speak, thereof we must be silent',[13] the final sentence of the *Tractatus*, is important to bear in mind when negotiating, for example, the acknowledgement in 'Words, Wide Night' that poetry, however heightened in its utterance, can only ever approximate to what it is to *be*, in the fully human sense. The dramatic monologue is in itself a translation of the thoughts of an imagined speaker, a refraction of experience fettered to the tyranny of words that endlessly defer and defy any attempt at definition. Deryn Rees-Jones argues that Duffy has a 'distrust of language as mediator between idea and object.' And that:

> for Duffy an exploration of the relationship between
> language and experience always dramatises the gap
> between signifier and signified; between what is about
> to be said, and what is then said; between the possibility
> of what might be said, and what can never be said.
> And this distrust of language leads her to an aesthetic
> that privileges experience over the telling of the experience.[14]

As has been shown, poems such as 'Away and See' and 'The Grammar of Light' are poems that purport to escape the confines of language but succeed in drawing attention to their own reliance upon language as a means of articulating frustration concerning that very reliance. It is here that we must reiterate Duffy's deconstructive awareness that the gap between signifier and signified is a precarious relationship that might best be analogised as the spark that may or may not arc across the void between electrodes. This 'all or nothing' scenario has links, too, with a Catholic tradition (repudiated by Duffy though it may be) in which language is privileged above all else. From the Johannine perspective, the Logos or Word brought all into being. In this sense translation was transcended and rendered redundant because what was *said* came to be in the performative utterance of creation. In other words the gap between signifier and signified was obliterated so that word was sign. This idea is explored in 'Education for Leisure' (*SFN*). The strong narrative impulse in the poem, written in the voice of the boy, is striking. Feeling frustrated and ignored, he resorts to physical violence as a means of exerting power over others. He assumes absolute authority by deciding to 'play God' (*SFN*, p. 15).

He does not understand Shakespeare but claims to be a genius. In this allusion to *King Lear*, arguably Shakespeare's darkest tragedy, we are clearly invited to remember Gloucester's words, 'As flies to wanton boys, are we to the Gods, / they kill us for their sport' (IV.i). In playing God, the boy is actually given some of God's words from Genesis to speak but the tense of the verb changes because what was reported is now direct speech: 'I see that it is good' ironically reverses the import of God's reaction to his own creation by showing us someone who is bent on destruction. Duffy engages here with the idea of the performative utterance in which the spoken sign actually results in the instantaneous and miraculous existence of the signified. The resultant obliteration of aporia is the pitch of language to which Duffy repeatedly reminds us that poetry may only aspire. After the opening stanza's statements of intent – 'I am going to kill something' and 'I am going to play God' – Duffy moves from the future indicative to the simple present: 'I squash', 'I pour', 'I pull' and 'I touch' dramatise precisely that primacy of experience over its reportage that Rees-Jones highlights. The boy becomes translated, if we recall Shakespeare's use of the term in *A Midsummer Night's Dream*, from mortal into immortal.

The splintering of meaning and the killing of love and the poetic by the political forces that work on the language are certainly part of Duffy's concern in *The Other Country* but she returns to the limits of language itself in 'Words, Wide Night'. The impossible tense of 'I singing' reminds us that there are things that are unthinkable, since the limits of language are the limits of thought. Wittgenstein's remark 'Unsayable things do indeed exist' is itself something that, tautologically, cannot be said or thought. The famous finishing statement of the *Tractatus* is intimately linked with the problem Duffy articulates in this poem: 'For I am in love with you and this / is what it is like or what it is like in words.' It is a metaphysical statement that attempts to convey the unsayable, unthinkable contention that there is a dimension about which we can say nothing. It seems, though, that the limits of language are not contingent with the limits of feeling, something that Duffy seeks continually to address, offering a multiplicity of 'translations' that do ultimately speak to us in our own language, whatever that may be.

Beyond the translations offered from the standpoint of interpreter of other selves, there are those from the language of one medium to another. In a generic sense, these may be viewed as part of the grammar of light, since they concentrate on paintings. The painterly, paintings and the surrealist artistic mode feature prominently in Duffy's *oeuvre*. Magritte's painting of a pipe entitled *The Betrayal of Images* articulates his concern with truth and his belief that only words are able to fix reality. The famous caption, *Ceci n'est pas une pipe* clearly demonstrates an anxiety concerning the nature of the sign and the relationship between the signifier and signified. This painting could be seen as the obverse of Duffy's 'what it is like in words', a phrase that clearly signals a mistrust of language which, she avers, can at best can only approximate to real experience. While she seeks to escape language in order to access that which is 'wordless', Magritte's doubting the ability of pictorial art to say anything results in his use of words to draw attention to that perceived inadequacy. 'Poem in Oils', like 'The Grammar of Light', takes refuge in the visual, seeking an alternative codifying framework for existence: 'What I have learnt I have learnt from the air, / from infinite varieties of light' (*SFN*, p. 47).

The persona in the title poem of *Standing Female Nude* acts as a translator or interpreter of experiences that are from the other – female – country. The model is dismissive of 'Georges', the artist who 'possesses' her 'on canvas', referring to him as 'Little man' (*SFN*, p. 46). He is presented as self-obsessed, someone who objectifies women. In giving voice to this woman Duffy subverts the man's appropriation of her as object making her the subject. She has gained control. Her dismissive assessment of the man's painting, 'It does not look like me', and the contemptuous 'They call it art' may be read as manifesto statements signalling the relationship between art, society and sexual politics. The written and visual arts are not suspect simply because of the systems of signification on which they rely but because of the way they are differently translated, reflected or refracted by gender and time. Of course, the painting Duffy has in mind is a cubist work by Georges Braque, an artist who sought truth through a visual translation of his own.

The exploration and translation of female otherness cannot be treated exhaustively here but it is important to remember its crucial significance. Two poems, 'Oppenheim's Cup and Saucer' and 'Alliance', serve as polar opposites in that the former presents complete immersion in, and understanding of, female sexuality through the cataloguing of lesbian experience, while the latter presents us with a French woman who has become translated into a life with an English man who, in turn, has become a 'foreigner / lying beside her' (*SFN*, p. 26). Oppenheim's famous art object also includes a spoon beside the cup and saucer; all three are covered thickly in fur. The Sapphic and phallic images are clearly observable simultaneously but the phallic dimension is absent from the poem. The poet as translator has made a telling editorial decision. The French woman presented in 'Alliance' is 'dreaming in another language with a different name / about a holiday next year'. Her life is so diminished that 'What she has retained of herself is a hidden grip / working her face like a glove-puppet.' Her real voice has become a thrown one. Her life is swamped by an English boor who 'staggers in half-pissed / and plonks his weight down on her life'. The female sense of self has been stifled and marginalised. She wakes in the morning to find that her hoped-for life has been turned into a horrible reality away from France, her own country.

The ways in which Duffy translates experience across the gender boundary are developed in the book-length projects *The World's Wife* and *Feminine Gospels*. In the former a multiplicity of voices is marshalled. We are presented with dramatic monologues that tune into the frequencies of a multitude of women from myth and history. Duffy acts as does a variable transducer in a radio. The latter and newest collection is striking in its pervasive use of the third person. The tone is more public and oratorical than personal in the longer poems, modulating towards the lyrical, interiorised and prayerful in the last poems in the book. *Feminine Gospels* should not be mistakenly read as feminist gospels. Here is a sequence of poems that seeks to explore the truths of experience through the refracting medium of myth and flights of the imagination.

I hope to have shown in this chapter that translation in a number of manifestations offers an insight into Duffy's concerns and techniques. She is a poet acutely aware of political as well as linguistic change and is careful to explore the relationship between these phenomena. Equally, she is at pains to explore that need to be heard, either because the voices she adopts would otherwise be ignored or because we need to be reminded that they sometimes shout too loudly. In resisting the temptation to falsely poeticise these adopted voices, she helps to keep alive in modern, mean times, 'with the muscles of a poem' (*SFN*, p. 38), what – in a Wordsworthian sense – could be called unremembered acts of kindness and of love.

## Notes

1  Roland Barthes, *S/Z*, trans. R. Miller (London: Jonathan Cape, 1975).

2  Jacques Derrida, *Of Grammatology*, trans. G.C. Spivak (Baltimore: Johns Hopkins University Press, 1976).

3  Carol Ann Duffy, *Standing Female Nude* (London: Anvil, 1985), p. 18.

4  Ramen Selden, *A Reader's Guide to Contemporary Literary Theory* (Brighton: Harvester Wheatsheaf, 1985), p. 85.

5  Ibid., p. 85.

6  Carol Ann Duffy, *Mean Time* (London: Anvil, 1993), p. 23.

7  Carol Ann Duffy, *The Other Country* (London: Anvil, 1990), p. 47.

8  Les Murray, *Translations from the Natural World* (Manchester: Carcanet, 1993).

9  Seamus Heaney, *Field Work* (London: Faber, 1979), p. 11.

10  Carol Ann Duffy, *Selling Manhattan* (London: Anvil, 1987), p. 19.

11  Gerard Manley Hopkins, *Poems*, ed. Catherine Phillips (Oxford: Oxford University Press, 1991), p. 129.

12  Louis Untermeyer, *Robert Frost* (Washington, DC: Library of Congress, 1964), p. 18.

13  Ludwig Wittgenstein, *Tractatus Logico-philosophicus*, trans C. K. Ogden (London: Routledge, 1981).

14  Deryn Rees-Jones, *Carol Ann Duffy* (Plymouth: Northcote House, 1999), p. 14.

# 9

## 'Skeleton, Moon, Poet': Carol Ann Duffy's postmodern poetry for children

### EVA MÜLLER-ZETTELMANN

O F ALL the sub-genres subsumed under the term of 'poetry', poems for children are probably the group of texts with the widest reach and the strongest emotional appeal. Even those who become addicted to television in their adult lives encountered (and possibly developed a liking for) the occasional lullaby, limerick and nursery rhyme at some stage in their childhood. As an early imaginative stimulus, poems can provide an important formative influence on young children, promoting their emotional, epistemological and linguistic development. In many cases, the attraction of poems for children does not cease with the reader's coming of age, but merely changes its focus: what started out as an exciting journey into worlds unknown becomes in later life a nostalgic attempt to recover an earlier and ultimately irretrievable stage of the self.

Within academia, however, poetry for children is a marginal (i.e. marginalised) phenomenon. Commonly listed under the 'Miscellaneous' section of a writer's *oeuvre*, texts for children tend to fall under the aegis of literary biographers rather than providing the basis for serious scholarly analysis. If children's poetry is investigated at all, the approach adopted will often comprise a combination of pedagogy and developmental psychology coupled with practical advice as to the 'teachability' of the text in question. This frequent concentration on non-aesthetic parameters is also reflected in the way general anthologies of poetry have dealt with the phenomenon. If one chose to take the *Norton Anthology of Poetry*[1] and the *New Oxford Book of English Verse*[2] as authoritative sources on the state of English poetry, one would certainly get the impression that anglophone versifiers held a bilious aversion to readers below the age of 16. The major attraction that children's poetry has held for literary studies in recent years has been the genre's intimate link with a period's norms: owing to its overtly didactic purpose of 'urg[ing] to the paths of virtue'[3] and of making the child conform to society and its moral precepts, older specimens of children's literature have been regarded as key texts for the changing construction and textualisation of morality, gender and, indeed, childhood.

One important indicator of a text's attractiveness to 'serious' literary studies is the degree to which it is able to incorporate contemporary thought and develop it into a new aesthetics. It is this 'state-of-the-artness' of a text, its deviation from the conventional and long-established, and its ability to mirror the mentalities of contemporary society in a form which in itself provides an artistic statement, that make a text a likely candidate for scholarly investigation. Viewed from this angle, the comparative marginalisation of children's poetry within the field of literary studies becomes a comprehensible phenomenon. Literature for children is subject to a number of limitations conditioned by the special needs of its lively, pleasure-seeking readership, and thus to some scholars may seem incompatible with the formal and intellectual challenges of the postmodern avant-garde.

The specific conditioning framework of children's literature – its objectives edifying, informing and entertaining readers who do not yet command the full cognitive, experiential and linguistic range that an author can reasonably expect from the average adult reader – necessitates certain sacrifices as regards the intellectual and artistic scope of the text. The majority of children's literature is 'closed'[4] and 'readerly',[5] featuring a familiar, teleological plot, an unobtrusive, 'transparent' form, and a clear evaluative impetus.[6] All these elements seem a far cry from the features we have come to identify as typical of the twenty-first century, its literature and its sceptical, self-conscious frame of mind. How, then, does the case stand with an author whose work for adult readers is innovative, confrontational and philosophically demanding, who favours pastiche and collage and self-consciously comments on the mechanics of her craft? Is Carol Ann Duffy's poetry for children a body of texts which somehow stands apart from her other works in that it features inferior aesthetics and a traditional outlook on life? Does the genre of children's poetry actually require an artistic and ideological U-turn from an author otherwise known for her probing scepticism and uncompromising originality? In short, is poetry for children by definition an anti-postmodern genre, or does it simply require an author of Carol Ann Duffy's standing to overcome its generic limitations and create a literature which is as intellectual and contemporary as it is simple to understand and enjoy?

When flicking through the pages of Duffy's two volumes of verse for children, *Meeting Midnight*[7] and *The Oldest Girl in the World*,[8] the reader encounters many of the staple elements commonly expected from a volume devoted to a young readership: there are wayward child protagonists, witches and giants, speaking trees, caramel chocolates, snowballs, freckles, confetti and any number of curious animals. Viewed more closely, though, these items, attractive and familiar to children, are placed in strangely defamiliarising contexts, making up weird little stories which almost invariably read contrary to expectation. One of the most startling examples of an unconventional storyline must certainly be 'The Thief, the Priest and the Golden Coin',[9] a poem whose title, by echoing headings such as *The Lion, the Witch, and the Wardrobe*,[10] promises a story of at least moderate excitement. In fact, the story-level of this text barely deserves the name: what the poem presents is an exposition of preliminaries without ever moving on to anything remotely interesting or action-related. In a sense, 'The Thief, the Priest and the Golden Coin' is a literary hoax; it teases its readers by announcing content-centred interest without delivering it, and breaks off in mid-'story', without having provided anything at least faintly approaching a satisfying conclusion.

> Deep in the woods
> in a hole
> in a tree (a silver birch)
> there's a gold coin
> that was filched
> by a thief from a church
> and hidden there
> as he fled
> from a furious priest.
>
> Wheesht.
>
> All that remains to be said
> is that the thief was no gent,

the priest was no saint,
and the coin of gold
in the hole in the tree in the woods
has not yet been spent.

In its opening section, Duffy's poem evokes a scenario filled with detail ('Deep in the woods', 'in a hole', 'a silver birch', 'a furious priest'), promising action and suggesting a future (possibly moral) conflict. In this, the first stanza features some of the attributes central to the phenomenon of aesthetic illusion. In its inherent philosophical tendency, aesthetic illusion is a traditional tool affirming the dominance of the reader's emotional empathy over his or her rational appreciation, the supremacy of the signified over the body of the sign and the greater importance of the illusionistic 'slice of life' *vis-à-vis* the aesthetic make-up of the text. It is thus not surprising that the time-honoured phenomenon of aesthetic illusion constitutes one of postmodernist literature's central targets. By emphasising the difference between reality and art and laying bare the hidden workings of the text, postmodernist literature strives to expose art's specific ontological status. This is largely brought about by a radical devaluation of the story-level so that – out of confusion or sheer boredom – readers are driven to contemplate a text's discourse-level instead.[11]

At its pro-illusionist outset, Carol Ann Duffy's poem 'The Thief, the Priest and the Golden Coin' cites a literary tradition which it deliberately undermines in the ensuing stanza. The destabilisation is one motivated as much by a humorous disrespect of long-established generic traditions as by an urge to subvert conventional patterns of logic, expectation and linguistic relevance. For the young reader, the mechanisms of anti-illusionism brought about by the poem's extreme 'uneventfulness' and its disregard of the principle of teleology achieve a distinctly defamiliarising, awareness-raising effect. Why, after all, do stories need to exhibit a 'neat ending'? Why does an action necessarily have to 'lead' somewhere? How 'realistic' is it when one incident automatically triggers off further more or less spectacular events? These are meta-textual questions, of course, which, as in any self-reflexive literary text, motivate readers to go beyond a mere involvement in the story-line and make them probe generic conventions and their relation to reality.

Apart from exposing common narrative patterns to examination, the poem's radical devaluation of its story-level automatically directs the reader's attention to the non-semantic, material aspects of the text. Since the poem's plot is devoid of both external action and emotional appeal, the story, which in pro-illusionist, mimetic works makes up a text's dominant level, loses much of its attraction. Instead, readers (or rather, listeners) automatically turn to the poem's discourse for compensatory entertainment. With its alliterations, its [f], [i] and striking [tsh] assonances, its phoneme repetitions, rhythms and rhymes, Duffy's poem provides complex aesthetic structures which make up for the virtual absence of a conventional story-line. Thus, the overall impression when reading 'The Thief, the Priest and the Golden Coin' is one of beginning mental visualisation and its ensuing deconstruction. While the poem clearly frustrates the reader's expectation of a thrilling story, it may initiate certain meta-textual reflections and, what is more important, delight its readers with its intriguing sound.

With Duffy's 'Jemima Riddle',[12] there can be no question as to the role of the discourse-level – it undoubtedly takes the predominant position in a poem whose whimsical content is presented in the form of a rudimentary dialogue:

> A:
> Jemima Riddle
> plays the fiddle,
> hey-diddle-diddle
> d.

> B:
> D'you think the kid'll
> play the middle
> bit of it at
> t?

> A:
> No. Jemima Riddle'
> d rather piddle,
> hey-diddle-diddle-
> d.

> B:
> P?

A:
Oui. But a quid'll
Stop the widdle,
then she'll fiddle –
C?

Clearly, the main 'protagonist' of this poem is not the eponymous Jemima Riddle but the poem's intriguing scheme of composition. Concentrating its creative force on its sub-semantic strata, the text exhibits two independent structural patterns which render the poem appealing to readers and listeners alike. That the English language possesses a sizeable number of [idl] words which can actually be integrated into a single, moderately meaningful poem will be a surprise to many. Indeed, one of the main attractions of 'Jemima Riddle', once its sound pattern has become apparent, is to watch the composition scheme unfold and produce yet another specimen of this truly unusual rhyme.

Especially to older children who have learned to read, the typographic level of Duffy's poem houses a number of 'riddles' which are too simple to present a serious intellectual challenge to grown-ups but which may hold exciting discoveries for children. On a very small scale the techniques used in Duffy's nonsense poem demonstrate and implicitly thematise the arbitrary link between sign and referent. All stanzas in 'Jemima Riddle' end on a single grapheme, which is rather an unusual device in itself. It is then left to the poem's readers to ascertain the graphemes' exact function within the context of the poem. Is the letter <t> valid only in its acoustic, non-semantic dimension, comparable, for instance, to the word-music of 'hey-diddle-diddle' in stanzas one and three, or does it actually refer to something beyond itself? Is the letter <C> a logical sequence to the 'A:' and 'B:' indicating the change of speakers, or is it the sign's acoustic properties rather than its typography that point to its true function? It is this oscillation between form and content, body and function, sound and meaning, which turns Duffy's poem into a stimulating introduction to the mechanisms of language and thought. Even if these 'riddles' are ultimately easy to solve, Duffy cajoles her young readership into making a string of associations which is normally left to the recipients of radical postmodern literary texts. For a brief moment, the link between signifier and signified ceases to be natural and self-evident and reveals itself to be an arbitrary tie based on linguistic convention.

If there is one single technique which characterises postmodern literature more than any other, it must surely be meta-textuality, the intellectual, anti-mimetic device of a text reflecting on itself, its mode of composition and ontological status. Meta-textuality is a pheno-menon spanning all literary genres, with its singular effect deriving from its central thematic concern. By referring to art's fictionality, with its two components of 'made-ness' and 'non-reality', of *'fictio'* and *'fic-tum'*,[13] metatextuality can cause what is very often a disruptive and startlingly defamiliarising reading experience. Since metatextual ele-ments are defined by their (overt or covert) reference to the fictional status of art, they directly counteract the principle of emotional reader involvement which constitutes the prime aim of aesthetic illusion. In fact, aesthetic illusion and meta-textuality can be regarded as strictly antagonistic devices. While the one seeks to relocate the reader within an irresistibly appealing fake world, the other forces the recipient to contemplate print and paper, language and fictionality. Meta-textual-ity, then, does what is strictly forbidden in a mimetically oriented aes-thetic context. It openly addresses the difference between art and life, thematises the mechanisms of textual *tromp-l'oeil* and thereby flaunts the high level of artificiality required to achieve an illusionist effect.

Of course, meta-poetry is not a development of radical postmod-ernism, as any reader of Shakespeare's sonnets, Pope's 'Essay on Crit-icism', Keats's 'Ode on a Grecian Urn' or Auden's 'Musée des Beaux Arts'[14] will know. Poetry has always been a type of discourse especially keen on exploring its own conditions, reflecting on its philosophical value and contemplating its moral and political relevance. In fact, meta-textual elements within the lyric genre have a history which may be said to be as long and impressive as that of its hetero-referential counterpart.[15] The twentieth century, while clearly not responsible for establishing the self-reflexive poem as a lyric form, brought about a shift in the philosophical outlook of meta-poetry, its thematic scope and the range of techniques employed. While traditional meta-poetry tended to level its attacks against stylistic devices which it deemed out-dated, inadequate or simply in poor taste, the groundwork of literature remained largely unaffected. Since the advent of post-structuralism, however, few of the central pillars of Aristotelian aesthetics have remained untouched. For meta-poetic productions of the postmodern era this has meant replacing an affirmative or at least neutral stance towards the poetic enterprise with an all-encompassing scepticism.

Today, neither the link between sign and referent, the dichotomy of real versus fictional, the continuity of space and time, the self-identity of objects, nor the principles of logic and causality are exempt from meta-poetry's ironic attack.

Clearly, such a drastic widening of focus requires new and radically destabilising techniques. While mainstream twentieth-century British 'adult poetry' largely stayed clear of the postmodern paradigm and for the most part abstained from implementing its radical aesthetics,[16] in her children's poetry Carol Ann Duffy does not shy away from post-structuralism's formal challenges, but, on the contrary, seems to relish their liberating potential. In her poem 'The Word',[17] which features as the second of a group of three poems headed 'Gifts', the reader is faced with a collection of innovative metapoetic devices:

> The Word
> A friend gave me the Word,
> said Pass it on.
> But I kept the word to myself for seven days.
> At the end of a week it had grown to the length of a phrase.
>
> A friend gave me a phrase,
> said Spread it about.
> But I kept the phrase at home to watch it lengthen.
> By the end of the week it had stretched to the size of a sentence.
>
> A friend gave me a sentence,
> said Shout it loud.
> But by now I was keeping it in. It lived in the bath.
> By the end of the following week it had swelled to a paragraph.
>
> A friend gave me a paragraph,
> said Set it to music.
> But it had the keys to the house, it had come of age.
> At the end of the week it had spread to the width of a page.
>
> A friend gave me a page,
> said Paint it large.
> But the page was bulging, daily fatter and fatter.
> By the end of that week it had beefed itself up to a chapter.
>
> A friend gave me the word
> said Tell all the World.
> But the word was alive and the word had grown to a book.
> This is it. Look.

What is new in Duffy's meta-poetic poem 'The Word' is not so much the explicit naming of literature's material segments ('word', 'phrase', 'sentence', 'paragraph', 'page', 'chapter', 'book'), although one rarely finds them in such encyclopaedic comprehensiveness. Rather, the major innovation of Duffy's text lies in the mode of discourse chosen to exemplify a central postmodern axiom. Usually, poems with a clear meta-poetic intent favour the argumentative mode, as generalisation and logical deduction fit well with themes of a philosophical kind. Duffy, however, considerate of her young audience's needs, shuns abstract theoretical debate and, instead, presents her meta-poetic concerns in narrative form by turning a basic linguistic unit into the poem's prime protagonist.

Thus, 'the word', which also operates as the poem's most important formal element, acts as any (animal) hero of a conventional children's story would. Indeed, the relationship between speaker and word closely resembles the type of friendship plot well known from countless teenage books, where unhappy boys and girls find solace in the paws of a cuddly quadrupedal friend hidden from the eyes of an unsympathetic parent in a garden shed. In Duffy's poem, the ever-growing word strangely oscillates between beast and man, however, with certain patterns of behaviour being distinctly anthropomorphic and teenage-like ('But it had the keys to the house, it had come of age'). Unquestionably, this poem is a fine lesson in media pragmatics, introducing children to the exact terms for identifying a book's various segments and generally telling its young readers 'how to do things with words'[18] ('Pass it on', 'Spread it about', 'Shout it loud', 'Set it to music', 'Paint it large', 'Tell all the world'). More importantly, though, by featuring the word as a self-sufficient, autonomous and ultimately uncontrollable phenomenon which has a distinct life of its own, Duffy's text manages to address post-structuralism's central tenet in a highly amusing manner, which is more than one can say of most treatises and indeed of many literary texts with a similar concern.

Structurally, the poem is a model of clarity, exhibiting on its phonetic, syntactic and morphological levels Hopkins's[19] (and indeed Jakobson's)[20] principle of poetic parallelism. Indeed, so lucid and instantly comprehensible is the poem's structure that one can well imagine the assignment 'Write your own poem' as a stimulating follow-up exercise in a teaching context.[21] Contained in this neat formal corset, however, is a truly subversive device. On the surface, the poem's plot (the protagonist's growth from single word to mighty book) follows a strictly causal and chronological development. When scrutinised more closely, however, the plot's inherent structure gives rise to a number of (ultimately unanswerable) questions. If the unidentified friend functions as the donor of the initial linguistic present ('A friend gave me the Word'), do the subsequent parallelised statements imply that there are additional friends and hence additional presents ('A friend gave me a phrase', 'A friend gave me a sentence', 'A friend gave me a paragraph')? Does the speaker thus give shelter to a veritable menagerie of anthropomorphised typographical units, or does the word initially presented metamorphose into ever larger units? Ultimately, Duffy's poem defies clear explication, so that 'The Word' remains an open text, caught in an endless fluctuation between mutually exclusive meanings. Since in most readers there is a definite desire for conventional logic and textual closure, the poem's semantic indeterminacy provides a stimulus for continuous speculation and prevents the poem from ever turning stale.

But there is yet another feature which in its genuine strangeness and unconventionality surpasses any of the postmodern devices discussed so far. The greater part of the text concentrates on listing typographic segments, reserving them a prominent part on the poem's story-level. In doing so, Duffy's 'The Word' employs the mechanisms of explicit meta-poetry, which makes open reference to issues of an aesthetic kind. Although in theory an overt allusion to the technical scaffolding of a literary text constitutes a serious breach with the central pro-illusionist tenet of concealing the textual artifice, by using universal, non-specific categories such as 'word', 'phrase', 'sentence' and 'paragraph', the text still mainly points outside itself, while its own ontological status of quasi-realness remains largely unaffected. In the poem's very last line, however, there is a sudden shift from the external to the internal, as imperative and emphatic deixis are used to end the poem with a bang: 'But the word was alive and the word had grown to a book. / This is it. Look.'

Suddenly, with the 'textual finger' turning inwards to highlight the writing on the page, the eponymous 'word' of Duffy's poem ceases to be an unspecified unit and turns into the very story of which it is an essential part. This explosive meta-poetic device triggers off a subversive chain reaction which violently disrupts the logic of the text and forces the reader mentally to rearrange all prior information. Now that 'the word' is no longer an object exterior to the language material used to describe it, readers, in their search for semantic closure, are sent to stumble along one of those endless textual loops that have their origin in post-structuralist theory and have been employed by postmodern literature to perplex its readers. In the case of Duffy's poem 'The Word', as indeed in most other instances of textual short-circuits[22] of a similar kind, readers are manoeuvred into a situation where the very basis of their usual mode of thinking is shown to be wholly inadequate. Forced to replace the commonsensical 'if a contains b, then b cannot contain a' by the logically impossible 'a contains b, and b contains a', readers are faced with a conundrum. A word, which in the moment of its utterance speaks of itself, a poem which recounts the 'life-story' of a word, which in the end turns out to have grown into that very poem, a word which has developed into a volume of poetry containing the initial word and an account of its metamorphosis, all this is an exact rendering in literary terms of Hofstadter's famous 'tangled hierar-chies',[23] which he saw characterised by an endless oscillation between signifier and signified, between referential and meta-language:

> Between the operator and the operand, the program and the data, the cause and the effect, the metalanguage and the language, there is a continuous reversal of levels, a frenzied oscillation, in which each in turn sits on the higher level, then on the lower, and so on, not unlike two rivals, each of whom briefly gains the upper hand without ever completely defeating each other.[24]

In providing her young readers with a concrete textual version of Hofstadter's paradoxical figure, Duffy chips away at the foundations of logic and can thus draw on the effects commonly associated with rad-ical subversion and the carnivalesque.[25] Attacking one of the mainstays of western thought, subverting the Aristotelian norm of transparent discourse and breaking with the rules of aesthetic illusion are such serious violations of common epistemology, reader expectation and traditional aesthetics that, in accordance with Bakhtin's theories, Duffy's poem 'The Word' becomes a ludic celebration of what is excluded, marginalised or repressed from rational discourse. Hence, despite its unsettling character, the poem's immediate effect will be the kind of amusement and liberating laughter commonly associated with the carnivalesque.

There is nothing even faintly comic in Duffy's 'Whirlpool',[26] a poem of a decidedly nightmarish quality: no happy, conciliatory ending, no soothing authorial remarks which would mark the scenes described as an insubstantial gothic fancy, not even a short side-glance at objects of a lighter kind to alleviate the oppressive atmosphere of the poem. 'Whirlpool' confronts its readers with one of their acutest fears: the dissolution of the self.

> Whirlpool
> I saw two hands in the whirlpool
> clutching at air,
> but when I knelt by the swirling edge
> nothing was there.
> Behind me, twelve tall green-black trees shook
> and scattered their rooks.
> I turned to the spinning waters again
> and looked.
>
> I saw two legs in the whirlpool
> dancing deep.
>
> I see that horrible choreography still
> in my turning sleep.
> Then I heard the dog from Field o' Blood Farm
> howl on its chain;
> and gargling out from the whirlpool came the watery sound
> of a name.
>
> I bent my head to the whirlpool,
> I saw a face,
> Then I knew that I should run for my life
> away from that place.
> But my eyes and mouth were opening wide, far below
> as I drowned.
> And the words I tell were silver fish
> the day I was found.

In this remarkable poem, items dark and grim are accumulated to produce an effect of intense anxiety. It is as if this one text were made to contain all the horrors of childhood, so that they could be dealt with collectively. Indeed, so enormous is the number of blood-curdling objects and incidents and so relentless is the poem in following them up to their inevitable fatal conclusion ('But my eyes and mouth were opening wide, far below / as I drowned') that it is exactly in this unlikely conglomeration of horrors that readers may find some consolation.

Adult readers familiar with postmodern theories on the construction of the subject will identify the nightmarish incidents at the whirlpool as a fatally botched version of the Lacanian mirror stage.[27] According to Lacan, the newborn baby is a mass of needs and desires which know no sense of self or otherness. In what Lacan considered a decisive step in ontogenetic development, the infant, when first encountering its own image in a mirror, will for the first time experience itself as a unique entity set apart from the objects of its environment. Simultaneous with this decisive realisation of the infant's own image as an ideal, organic and perfect whole, a split between real and imaginary self, between the subject and its mirrored image takes place. Since what the child sees in the mirror is an ultimately unattainable illusion of autonomy and wholeness, the mirror stage predisposes the ego to fiction and delusion. The rift between the I which perceives and the I which is perceived remains one of the driving forces of human life, inciting us to adopt and discard masks provided by cultural discourse on our futile quest to halt the endless deferral of self-identity and meaning.

In introducing the *doppelgänger* motif, Duffy's poem harks back to an earlier, nineteenth-century device of rendering the theme of the subject in crisis, but as usual with Carol Ann Duffy the traditional element is transformed to suit her own ends. This time, the two versions of the self are not shown to be independent entities slowly drifting apart. In what is perhaps an even more frightening variation on the theme, the speaker and his or her liquid 'other' merge, causing the annihilation of lyric speaker and mirrored image alike. Death, the loss of identity, the inescapability of fate, all these are primordial fears which modern society tends either to belittle, to neglect or to suppress. Unless it is for the shocking incursions of terror(ism) into our everyday lives, the western world for the past fifty years has more or less managed to contain humanitarian catastrophes and has placed the paraphernalia of death under strict taboos. Fears, however, remain, and they will surface periodically especially with children, as young people are not yet used to resorting to compensatory mental strategies in the face of problems which ultimately cannot be solved. In her poem 'Whirlpool', Duffy does the only thing possible without belittling what is too serious to be simplified by a trite solution: she describes the horror in all its grim particulars and thus exorcises it – if only for a while.

Now that some of Carol Ann Duffy's poetry for children has been looked at in some detail, it will become clear that what is often considered as the impeding disadvantages of children's literature – the genre's limitations as to the experiential and thematic scope of the material presented, the maxim of quick and easy reading and the genre's clear bias in favour of external action – may actually be applied to create very special textual worlds that meet all the demands of formal and conceptual contemporaneity, while at the same time catering for the young readers' desire for fun and entertainment. Of course, one will search in vain for elaborate philosophical probings into the fictitious character of human life and the instability of the postmodern subject; likewise, there is no subtle exploitation of complex emotions or adult sexual drives, nor is there the kind of formal experiment which might attempt to be so radical as to discard reference and meaning altogether. What is there, though, is an earnest endeavour not to trade simplicity for formal and ideological traditionalism, to take young readers seriously, and to free the genre of children's poetry from a stigma it has not deserved. 'Skeleton, Moon, Poet' – words chosen from the title of one of the poems in *The Oldest Girl in the World* –[28] may thus be taken to stand for the three ingredients that make Carol Ann Duffy's poetry for children so successful: exuberant imagination, playful formal experiment and the poet's uncompromising pledge to render faithfully the grim facts of life.

Carol Ann Duffy's two volumes of verse for young readers, *Meeting Midnight* and *The Oldest Girl in the World*, have all the intellectual vigour and poetic exuberance of her adult poetry and certainly deserve critical attention. Contrary to the initial assumption that owing to its unique conditions, children's literature might by definition be an anti-postmodern genre, Duffy's poetry for children can actually be considered a perfect example of postmodern literature. Meta-textuality, plot-centred illogicality, carnivalesque subversiveness and the deliberately ambiguous rendering of the characters' ontological status are only some of the more striking features of Duffy's idiosyncratic aesthetics, which are employed in her children's poetry to take young readers on an unlimited flight of the imagination.

# Notes

1  Margaret Ferguson et al. (eds), *The Norton Anthology of Poetry* (New York: Norton, 1996).

2  Helen Gardner (ed.), *The New Oxford Book of English Verse 1250–1950* (Oxford: Oxford University Press, 1972).

3  Isaac Watts, *Divine Songs Attempted in Easy Language for the Use of Children*, ed. J. H. Pafford (Oxford: Oxford University Press, 1971 [1715]).

4  Umberto Eco, *The Role of the Reader: Explorations in the Semiotics of Texts* (London: Hutchinson, 1981), p. 8.

5  Roland Barthes, *S / Z*, trans. Richard Miller (Oxford: Blackwell, 1990), p. 5.

6  See Perry Nodelman, 'Interpretation and the Apparent Sameness of Children's Novels', *Studies in the Literary Imagination*, 18:2 (1985), pp. 5–20.

7  Carol Ann Duffy, *Meeting Midnight* (London: Faber, 1999). *Meeting Midnight* was shortlisted for the 1999 Whitbread Children's Book of the Year.

8  Carol Ann Duffy, *The Oldest Girl in the World* (London: Faber, 2000).

9  Ibid., p. 16.

10  Clive Staples Lewis, *The Lion, the Witch, and the Wardrobe: A Story for Children* (London: Bles, 1950).

11  See Eva Mueller-Zettelmann, 'Deconstructing the Self? – Late Twentieth-century British Poetry and the Fiction of Authenticity', *European Journal of English Studies*, 6:1 (2002), pp. 69–84.

12  Duffy, *Meeting Midnight*, p. 27.

13  Werner Wolf, *Ästhetische Illusion und Illusionsdurchbrechung in der Erzählkunst: Theorie und Geschichte mit Schwerpunkt auf englischem illusionsstörendem Erzählen* (Tübingen: Niemeyer, 1993), pp. 38–9.

14  Any reference to the other arts within the framework of a lyric text may also be considered to belong within the range of meta-poetic techniques, since the reference to any type of artistic fictionality will invariably highlight the text's own ontological status.

15  See Eva Müller-Zettelmann, *Lyrik und Metalyrik. Theorie einer Gattung und ihrer Selbstbespiegelung anhand von Beispielen aus der englisch-und deutschsprachigen Dichtkunst* (Heidelberg: Winter, 2000), p. 8.

16  See Jürgen Schlaeger, 'Postmodern British Poetry: Stalking a Phantom?', in Hans-Ulrich Seeber and Walter Gröbel (eds), *Anglistentag 1992 Stuttgart: Proceedings* (Tübingen: Niemeyer, 1993), pp. 33–45; Eva Müller-Zettelmann, 'Deconstructing the Self?', pp. 82–4, and Antony Easthope, *Englishness and National Culture* (London: Routledge, 1999), pp. 177–99.

17  Duffy, *The Oldest Girl in the World*, p. 63.

18  John L. Austen, *How to Do Things with Words: The William James Lectures Delivered at Harvard University in 1955* (Oxford: Oxford University Press, 1989).

19  Gerard Manley Hopkins, 'Poetic Diction', in John Pick (ed.), *A Hopkins Reader* (Oxford: Oxford University Press, 1953 [1865]), pp. 79–81, pp. 80–1.

20  Roman Jakobson, 'Closing Statement: Linguistics and Poetics', in Thomas A. Sebeok (ed.), *Style in Language* (Cambridge MA: MIT Press, 1960), pp. 350–77, 43549, p. 358.

21 In British secondary schools, Duffy's poems have become part of the A-level syllabus.

22 Gérard Genette describes this phenomenon, which he terms 'metalepsis', for the genre of narrative fiction and defines it as the transgression of narrative levels, a device which harbours a strong comic and illusion-destroying potential. See Gérard Genette, *Narrative Discourse: An Essay in Method*, trans. Jane E. Lewin (Oxford: Blackwell, 1980), p. 234.

23 Douglas R. Hofstadter, *Goedel, Escher, Bach: An Eternal Golden Braid* (Hassocks: Harvester, 1979).

24 Jean-Pierre Dupuy, 'Tangled Hierarchies: Self-reference in Philosophy, Anthropology and Critical Theory', trans. Mark Anspach, *Comparative Criticism: A Yearbook*, 12 (1990), pp. 105–23, p. 106.

25 Michail Bakhtin, *Rabelais and His World*, trans. Helene Iswolsky (London: MIT Press, 1968), p. 4 and passim.

26 Duffy, *Meeting Midnight*, p. 36.

27 See Jacques Lacan, *Écrits: A Selection*, trans. Alan Sheridan (London: Tavistock, 1977), p. 1 and passim.

28 Duffy, *The Oldest Girl in the World*, pp. 44–5.

# Select bibliography

## Primary sources

Duffy, Carol Ann, *Fleshweathercock and Other Poems* (Walton-on-Thames: Outposts, 1973)

—and Henri, Adrian, *Beauty and the Beast* (Liverpool, c.1977).

—*Fifth Last Song* (West Kirby: Headland, 1982)

—*Standing Female Nude* (London: Anvil, 1985)

—*Thrown Voices* (London: Turret, 1986)

—*Selling Manhattan* (London: Anvil, 1987)

—*The Other Country* (London: Anvil, 1990)

—*William and the Ex-Prime Minister* (London: Anvil, 1992)

—*Mean Time* (London: Anvil, 1993)

—*Selected Poems* (London: Penguin, 1994)

—(ed.), *Anvil New Poets 2* (London: Anvil, 1994)

—(ed.), *Penguin Modern Poets Vol. 2* (London: Penguin, 1994)

—*Grimm Tales* (London: Faber, 1996)

—(ed.), *Stopping for Death: Poems of Death and Loss* (London: Penguin, 1996)

—*Salmon Carol Ann Duffy: Selected Poems* (Salmon Poetry, 1996)

—*More Grimm Tales* (London: Faber, 1997)

—(ed.), *I Wouldn't Thank You for a Valentine: Poems for Young Feminists* (London: Penguin, 1997)

—*The Pamphlet* (London: Anvil, 1998)

—*Meeting Midnight* (London: Faber, 1999)

—*Five Finger-piglets* (London: Macmillan, 1999)

—*'Rumpelstiltskin' and Other Grimm Tales* (London: Faber, 1999)

—*The World's Wife* (London: Picador, 1999)

—*The Oldest Girl in the World* (London: Faber, 2000)

—*Feminine Gospels* (London: Picador, 2002)


## Secondary sources

Brittan, Simon, 'Language and Structure in the Poetry of Carol Ann Duffy', *Thumbscrew*, 1:1 (winter 1994–95), pp. 58–64

Crawford, Robert, *Identifying Poets: Self and Territory in Twentieth-century Poetry* (Edinburgh: Edinburgh University Press, 1993)

Day, Gary and Docherty, Brian, *British Poetry from the 1950's to the 1990's: Politics and Art* (London: Macmillan, 1997)

Dimarco, Danette, 'Exposing Nude Art: Carol Ann Duffy's Response to Robert Browning', *Mosaic: A Journal for the Interdisciplinary Study of Literature*, 31:3 (1998), pp. 25–39

Gregson, Ian, *Contemporary Poetry & Postmodernism: Dialogue & Estrangement* (London: Macmillan, 1996)

Kennedy, David, *New Relations: The Refashioning of British Poetry 1980–94* (Bridgend: Seren, 1996)

Kinnahan, Linda, '"Look for the Doing Words": Carol Ann Duffy and Questions of Convention', in James Acheson and Romana Huk (eds), *Contemporary English Poetry* (New York: State University of New York Press, 1996), pp. 245–68

Michelis, Angelica, 'The Pleasure of Saying It: Images of Sexuality and Desire in Contemporary Women's Poetry' in Detlev Gohrbandt and Bruno von Lutz *Seeing and Saying: Self-referentiality in British and American Literature* (eds), (Frankfurt: Peter Lang, 1998), pp. 59–72

—'A Country of One's Own: Gender and National Identity in Contemporary Women's Poetry', *European Journal of English Studies*, 6:1 (2002), 61–9

O'Brien, Sean, 'Carol Ann Duffy: A Stranger Here Myself', in *The Deregulated Muse* (Newcastle: Bloodaxe, 1998), pp. 160–70

Radstone, Susannah, 'Remembering Medea: The Uses of Nostalgia', *Critical Quarterly*, 35:3 (1993), 54–63

Rees-Jones, Deryn, *Carol Ann Duffy* (Plymouth: Northcote House, 1999)

Reid, Mark, 'Near Misses Are Best', *Magma*, 2 (June 1994), 34–8

Roberts, Neil, *Narrative Voice in Postwar Poetry* (Harlow: Longman, 1999)

Robinson, Alan, *Instabilities in Contemporary British Poetry* (London: Macmillan, 1988)

Rowland, Antony, 'Love and Masculinity in the Poetry of Carol Ann Duffy', *English*, 50:198 (autumn 2001), 199–218

—'Patriarchy, Male Power and the Psychopath in the Poetry of Carol Ann Duffy', in Daniel Lea and Berthold Schoene-Harwood (eds), *Male Order* (Amsterdam: Rodopi, 2003)

Thomas, Jane, '"The Intolerable Wrestle with Words": The Poetry of Carol Ann Duffy', *Bête Noire*, 6 (1988), 78–88

Woods, Michael J., *Carol Ann Duffy: Selected Poems* (London: York Press, 2001)

## Electronic sources

www.eskimo.com/-kirsten/duffy.htr

www.eskimo.com/-kirsten/duffy1.htr

www.eskimo.com/-kirsten/duffy6.htr

www.sbu.ac.uk/stafflag/carolannduffy.htr

www.english.colchsfc.ac.uk/cad10.htm

www.schools.channel4.com/online_resources/netnotes/epp/text/eppnn2.htm

www.bris.ac.uk/Depts/English/journals/thumbscr

## Interviews

Bentley, Vicci, Interview with Carol Ann Duffy, *Magma*, 3 (winter 1994), 17–24

Forbes, Peter, 'Profile: Carol Ann Duffy', *The Guardian Review*, 31 August 2002, 20–3

McAllister, Andrew, 'Carol Ann Duffy Interview', *Bête Noire*, 6 (winter 1988), 69–77

'Metre Maid', *The Guardian Weekend*, 25 September 1999, 20–6

Stabler, Jane, Interview with Carol Ann Duffy, *Verse*, 8:2 (summer 1991), 124–8

# Index of works by Carol Ann Duffy

Note: 'n' after a page reference indicates a note number on that page.

'$' 39, 40

'Adultery' 3, 42, 43, 44, 59, 69, 70
'Afternoon with Rhiannon, An' 168n
'Alliance' 9, 65, 184
'Alphabet for Auden' 155
'And How Are We Today' 10
'Anne Hathaway' 113
'Army' 6
'Ash Wednesday 1984' 3, 157
'As I Quench' 6
'Away and See' 140, 143–6, 170–1, 177–8, 179, 181
'Away from Home' 18, 161–2, 164–5

'Back Desk' 10
'Beachcomber' 152–3
*Beauty and the Beast* 6–8
'Before you were mine' 22
'Biographer, The' 22
'Brink of Shrieks, The' 10, 35, 36, 37, 38
'Brothers' 176

'Captain of the 1964 *Top of the Form* Team, The' 1, 22, 39, 40
'Caul' 22
'Century' 6
'Circe' 52, 113
'Clear Note, A' 10, 64, 153, 155
'Cliché Kid, The' 165
'Comprehensive' 11, 47, 156–7
'Confession' 22
'Correspondents' 10
'Crush' 22, 41

'Debt' 10, 164
'Delilah' 113
'Demeter' 54, 108, 116–17
'Deportation' 10, 86–90
'Devil's Wife, The' 113
'Dies Natalis' 48, 83, 126–7, 137, 159, 165, 179–80
'Doll' 9
'Dolphins, The' 10, 124–6, 127, 138, 174–6
'Dream' 8, 9
'Dreaming of Somewhere Else' 163

'Dummy, The' 9, 10, 102–3

'Education For Leisure' 9, 41, 134, 157–8, 182
'Epitaph' 6
'Eurydice' 51, 52, 114–15, 166–7
'Every Good Boy' 10

*Feminine Gospels* 3, 5, 184–5
*Fifth Last Song* 8–9
'First Love' 22
*Fleshweathercock* 5–6
'Foreign' 10, 42, 43, 161
'Frau Freud' 113
'Free Will' 9, 65, 155–6
'From' 6
'*from* Mrs Tiresias' 2, 47, 56, 71

'Girlfriends' 66, 71
'Girl Talking' 11, 47, 148–9
'Grammar of Light, The' 3, 170, 171–2, 178, 179, 181, 183

'Hard to Say' 154–5
'Havisham' 22, 25
'Head of English' 11, 12, 13, 156, 157
'Homesick' 138, 163, 179
'Hometown' 18, 162

'Ink on Paper' 150–2
'In Your Mind' 18, 94, 96, 138, 147
'I Remember Me' 60, 61, 62, 63, 64, 65, 69, 125–8
'It Has Come' 33
*I Wouldn't Thank You For A Valentine* 4

'Jealous as Hell' 65
'Jemima Riddle' 190–1

'Job Creation' 19

'Letters from Deadmen' 16
'Litany' 22, 23, 136–7
'Literature Act, The' 158
'Little Red-Cap' 48, 49, 72, 109–11, 114
'Lizzie, Six' 9, 157
'Losers' 19, 164
'Lovebirds' 65

'Making Money' 20, 96
*Mean Time* 2, 3, 5, 21–5, 69, 71, 99, 140, 180
'Mean Time' 22
'Medusa' 52
*Meeting Midnight* 188, 199
'M-M-Memory' 19, 94, 95, 139
'Model Village' 159–60
'Moments of Grace' 25, 179
'Money Talks' 10, 83, 165
'Mrs Aesop' 105
'Mrs Beast' 30n, 165
'Mrs Darwin' 2
'Mrs Icarus' 1, 2, 49, 53
'Mrs Midas' 53, 166
'Mrs Rip Van Winkle' 61, 113
'Mrs Sisyphus' 52, 53
'Mrs Skinner, North Street' 19, 61, 93–4

'Naming Parts' 33, 35, 41, 65
'Never Forever' 8
'Never go back' 22, 25, 165
'Nostalgia' 22, 23

'Old Atheist Places His Last Bet, An' 165
*Oldest Girl in the World, The* 188, 199
'Oppenheim's Cup and Saucer' 63, 71, 184

'Originally' 18, 91–2, 95, 137
'Oslo' 164
*Other Country, The* 5, 6, 9, 17–21, 56, 64, 66, 69, 71, 78, 83, 91, 92, 93, 94, 95, 96, 146, 158, 182

*Pamphlet, The* 58, 70
'Plainsong' 61, 140, 141, 166, 167
'Poem in Oils' 183
'Poet For Our Times' 2, 19, 39, 40, 96
'Poker in the Falklands with Henry & Jim' 10, 164
'Pollution' 6
'Postcards' 41
'Practising Being Dead' 42, 43
'Prayer' 3, 63, 140, 141, 170
'Professor of Philosophy Attempts Prayer, The' 145–6
'Provincial Party 1956, A' 10, 152
'Psychopath' 5, 10, 13, 33, 38, 40, 41, 64, 66, 132–4
'Pygmalion' 113

'Queen Herod' 33, 11–12, 166
'Queen Kong' 113
'Queens' 71

'Recognition' 10
'River' 18, 138, 158–9, 176–7

'Saying Something' 61, 65, 134, 153–4, 170
*Selling Manhattan* 4, 18, 9–17, 64, 66, 83, 91, 95, 103, 121, 160, 180
'Selling Manhattan' 10, 84–6
'Shooting Stars' 10
'Sit At Peace' 135–6
'Small Female Skull' 3, 22, 99–103
'Someone Else's Daughter' 165–6
'Somewhere Someone's Eyes' 162

'Stafford Afternoons' 22, 25
*Standing Female Nude* 4, 8, 9–17, 47, 56, 58, 62, 63, 64, 65, 69, 70, 121, 140, 148, 183
'Standing Female Nude' 13, 14, 15, 16, 37, 38, 39, 183–4
'Statement' 10
'Stealing' 10
*Stopping For Death* 4
'Strange Language in Night Fog' 180

'Talent' 168n
'Telephoning Home' 60, 61, 62, 63, 71
'Thetis' 53, 55, 111
'Thief, the Priest and the Golden Coin, The' 188–90
'This Shape' 59, 63, 65
'Three Paintings' 10
'Till Our face' 65, 153
'Too Bad' 18
'To the Unknown Lover' 71
'Translating the English 1989' 19, 20, 96, 160, 172–3
'Translation' 159, 166
'Turn To Me Now' 6
'Twenty-One Love Poems' 9
'Two Small Poems of Desire' 66, 67, 68, 69

'Warming Her Pearls' 1, 10, 33, 34, 35, 71
'War Photographer' 15, 150
'Waves' 8
'Way My Mother Speaks, The' 18, 146–7
'Weasel Words' 155, 173
'We Remember Your Childhood Well' 18, 160
'Wet' 8
'What Price?' 15

'Where We Came in' 65

'Whirlpool' 196–9

'Whoever She Was' 129–31, 132, 133

'Woman Seated in the Underground' 1941' 10, 127–8, 130, 132–4, 162–3

'Word, The' 193–6

'Words, Wide Night' 35, 146, 178, 181, 182–3

*World's Wife, The* 2, 3, 5, 6, 17, 33, 47, 48, 55, 56, 58, 71, 105–17, 165, 184

'Yes, Officer' 10

'You Jane' 10, 13, 64, 65, 131–2, 133

# General index

Adcock, Fleur 4
Adorno, Theodor 60, 61
Aesopus 106
Agard, John 4
Alsop, Rachel 123
Angelou, Maya 4
Archer, Jeffrey 173
Arendt, Hannah 103
Aristotle 103
Armitage, Simon 4
Artaud, Antonin 159
Auden, W.H. 2, 4, 155, 192

Bakhtin, M.M. 36, 42, 196
Barthes, Roland 41, 57, 68, 169, 170
Baudelaire, Charles 62
Bauman, Zygmunt 60
Beauvoir, Simone de 103
Bech, Henning 69
Beckett, Samuel 162
Bell, Steve 39
Benjamin, Jessica 89
Bertram, Vicki 81
Braque, Georges 14, 184
Breeze, Jean Binta 4
Breton, André 4, 62, 63, 64, 65, 72

Brittan, Simon 1, 2
Bronfen, Elisabeth 101
Browning, Robert 2, 4, 11, 13, 58, 129
Burns, Robert 59
Butler, Judith 105, 122–3, 135, 141

Calasso, Roberto 49, 53
Calvino, Italo 48
Carew, Thomas 72
Carter, Angela 6, 7, 73n
Childs, Peter 81
Cixous, Hélène 103, 104
cobbing, bob 4
Cockerill, Maurice 8
Coleridge, S.T. 180
Conquest, Robert 79
Cope, Wendy 1, 4, 72
Corcoran, Neil 81
Craig, Cairns 82
Crawford, Robert 29n
Croesus 106
Currie, Edwina 40

Dalí, Salvador 62
Dickens, Charles 20, 25, 73n

Didsbury, Peter 12
Donne, John 5, 6, 72
Derrida, Jacques 88, 97n, 122, 169
Dimarco, Danette 140n
Dunn, Douglas 79
Durcan, Paul 4

Easthope, Antony 200n
Enfield, Harry, 41
Ewart, Gavin 4
Eliot, T.S. 3, 4, 10, 11, 13, 33–45, 58,
    60, 62, 75n, 152

Farnthorpe, U.A. 4
Featherstone, Mike 74n
Fenton, James 79, 80
Fisher, Roy 4
Fitzsimons, Annette 123
Flies, Wilhelm 92
Foucault, Michel 97n, 122
Freud, Sigmund 16, 24, 62, 92, 94,
    117
Frost, Robert 180

Genette, Gérard 201n
Goethe, Johann Wolfgang von 57
Goodwin, Daisy 33
Gough, Kathleen 16
Graham, Henry 8
Graves, Robert 167n
Greer, Germaine 71
Gregson, Ian 13, 38
Grigson, Geoffrey 73n
Gunn, Thom 2

Halberstam, Judith 120n
Harris, Geoffrey 118
Harrison, Tony 12, 16, 79
Harwood, Lee 4
H.D. 75n, 114
Heaney, Seamus 4, 12, 79, 143, 179,
    180

Hegel, G.W. F. 103
Hein, Hilde 120n
Heller, Joseph 149
Henri, Adrian 3, 6, 7, 8, 30n, 72
Hill, Geoffrey 3
hooks, bell 69, 76n
Hopkins, G.M. 145, 180, 181, 194
Horner, Avril 3
Hughes, Judith 117n
Hughes, Ted 50, 114, 119n
Hume, David 151

Irigaray, Luce 16, 103, 104–5, 117

Jagger, Alison 102, 107, 117
Jakobson, Roman 41, 194

Kant, Immanuel 103
Kay, Jackie 4
Keats, John 11, 12
Kennedy, David 17, 20, 80, 142n
Kennedy, Ellen 103
Kenner, Hugh 33, 34, 35
Kinnahan, Linda 4, 37, 39, 40, 41,
    57, 105, 117–18n
Kipling, Rudyard 11, 12
Krafft-Ebing, Richard von 59
Kristeva, Julia 86, 90, 96n, 98n,
    123, 125

Lacan, Jacques 16, 165, 198
Larkin, Philip 2, 3, 4, 9, 15, 61, 63,
    70, 72, 168n
la Tour, Georges de 101
Leavis, F.R. 44, 49
Lennon, Kathleen 123
Leymarie, Jean 14
Lochhead, Liz 4, 28n, 82

Macmillan, Harold 12
Magritte, René 183

Marlatt, Daphne 56, 66
Maxwell, Glyn 29
McAllister, Andrew 75n
McEwan, Ian 58n
McGough, Roger 4
McGuckian, Medbh 82
McKinley, Don 8
Meredith, George 72
Merten, Kai 31n
Michelis, Angelica 5, 18, 57, 97n
Midgley, Mary 117n
Milton, John 53, 145
Müller-Zettelmann, Eva 200n
Murray, Les 174

Nietzsche, Friedrich 103
Nodelman, Perry 200n
Normal, Henri 4
Nutall, Jeff 8
Nye, Andrea 104

O'Brien, Sean 1, 39, 62, 136
O'Hara, Frank 9
Oppenheim, Meret 63, 184
Osborne, John 3
Ostriker, Alicia 108–9
O'Sullivan Maggie 4
Ovid 47–55

Parker, Andrew 142n
Pateman, Matthew 75n
Paterson, Don 164
Patten, Brian 63
Planudes, Maximus 106
Plath, Sylvia 4, 5, 6, 7, 58, 106–7,
    110, 111, 114, 115, 120n
Pope, Alexander 192
Pound, Ezra 13, 63
Prynne, J.H. 4
Pugh, Sheenagh 1

Raworth, Tom 4, 12

Rees-Jones, Deryn 8, 10, 13, 14, 16,
    37, 39, 41, 42, 43, 63, 83, 118n,
    119n, 181, 182
Reid, Mark 2, 3
Rich, Adrienne 8, 16, 17, 56
Roberts, Neil 3, 5, 18, 118n, 142n
Robinson, Alan 35, 41, 142n
Rodin, Auguste 100
Rosemont, Franklin 64, 72
Rousseau, Jean Jacques 103
Rowland, Antony 3, 4, 11, 119n,
    120n
Rumens, Carol 4

Saussure, Ferdinand de 169
Satyamerti, Carole 4
Schlaeger, Jürgen 200n
Searle, Ronald 73n
Sedgwick, Eve Kosofsky 142n
Selden, Raman 170
Shakespeare, William 6, 20, 50, 59,
    71
Sheppard, Robert 3, 4
Sidney, Philip 59
Sinfield, Alan 11, 12, 13
Smith, Adam 103
Smith, Stan 167n, 168n
Spenser, Edward 59
Stabler, Jane 30n, 31n
Swift, Jonathan 147
Swinburne, Algernon 59

Tennyson, Alfred Lord 75n
Thomas, Dylan 6
Thomas, Jane E. 41, 67, 117n, 118n

Wainwright, Jeffrey 2, 71
Walsh, Sam 8
Weedon, Chris 125
Weeks, Jeffrey 74n
Weitman, Sasha 58
Willans, Geoffrey 73n

Williams, Hugo 58
Williams, William Carlos 143
Winn, Kiernon 28n
Wither, George 59
Wittgenstein, Ludwig 167, 169, 172, 181, 183
Wollstonecraft, Mary 103
Woods, Michael 21

Woolf, Virginia 78, 105, 110, 117
Wordsworth, Dorothy 114
Wordsworth, William 20, 38, 68, 74n, 179
Wouters, Cas 76n
Wyatt, Thomas 59

Zephaniah, Benjamin 28n